# News and Power

# News and Power

*Rodney Tiffen*

Sydney
ALLEN & UNWIN
Wellington London Boston

© Rodney Tiffen 1989
This book is copyright under the Berne Convention. No
reproduction without permission. All rights reserved.

First published in 1989
Allen & Unwin Australia Pty Ltd
An Unwin Hyman company
8 Napier Street, North Sydney NSW 2059 Australia

Allen & Unwin New Zealand Limited
75 Ghuznee Street, Wellington, New Zealand

Unwin Hyman Limited
15–17 Broadwick Street, London W1V 1FP England

Unwin Hyman Inc.
8 Winchester Place, Winchester, Mass 01890 USA

National Library of Australia
Cataloguing-in-Publication entry:
Tiffen, Rodney.
    News and power.

    Bibliography.
    Includes index.
    ISBN 0 04 372043 9.

    1. Mass media – Political aspects. 2. Mass media policy.
    3. Mass media – Influence. 4. Press and politics. I.
    Title.

070.4′3

Library of Congress Catalog Number: 89-84069

Set by Graphicraft Typesetters Ltd., Hong Kong.
Printed by Chong Moh Offset Printing Pte Ltd, Singapore

# Contents

# Tables

# Acknowledgements

The early years of the research which culminated in this book were supported by a grant from the Australian Research Grants Scheme. Their support allowed me to employ two research assistants, first Francesca Beddie and later Susan Jackson. Both know only too well that even interesting research projects are full of tedium in their execution, and I am extremely grateful for their diligent, good-humoured and intelligent work. They helped me and this study immensely.

The ARGS grant also allowed me to conduct interviews with 223 journalists around Australia. Overwhelmingly, I found these interviews not only enlightening, but enjoyable, and I would like to thank collectively the interviewees (listed at the back of the book) for their time and cooperation.

Many colleagues, such as the ever-optimistic Murray Goot, encouraged me through this seemingly endless project. Ken Turner and Helen Nelson made all-too-incisive criticisms of individual chapters, which improved them greatly. My greatest academic debt is to Henry Mayer who, over the last thirteen years, has supported my work in so many ways. Most especially he has always unselfishly made the time to read and comment upon work in progress, even though I ungratefully adopt only half his suggestions and, by his alarming standards, never seem to have read anything.

Finally, I wish to thank my family: my parents who gave practical help as well as encouragement, Kathryn who applied both her psychological and literary skills with great forebearance, and lastly Paul and Ruth, without whom the whole thing would have been finished much sooner.

# Introduction

The allegedly so-called free and democratic press. What a press! It is owned for the most part by financial crooks and is edited for the most part by mental harlots. (Arthur Calwell, 1952)

Slimy white things that crawl out of sewers. (John Gorton on journalists, 1969)

I think it's now not possible for a government in Australia to be elected, or to remain in office, if opposed by the media complex. In general, and in this sense, it's the media that now determines who govern Australia. In this sense the media is the most powerful force in Australia today. (Dr Jim Cairns, 1975)

The greatest thing that could happen in the state and the nation is when we get rid of the media. Then we would live in peace and tranquility and no one would know anything. (Sir Joh Bjelke-Petersen, 1986)

There is something intoxicating about the media which excites wild generalisations and extreme opinions. Across the political spectrum from Joh Bjelke-Petersen to Jim Cairns and beyond, politicians come together in asserting the media's power and decrying its pernicious effects on our political life. Even the reputedly moderate Don Chipp once described some journalists in the Canberra press gallery as 'scum', 'raw sewage', and 'grubby.'[1] The details vary, but it is easy to find outspoken criticism among both business and trade unions, among diverse pressure groups, and in the Public Service and judiciary. Hostility to the media creates such unlikely bedfellows as Germaine Greer: 'Australia is a huge rest home where no unwelcome news is ever wafted on to the pages of the worst newspapers in the world'; and Sir Arthur Tange: 'The power of journalists to divert the executive from seriously addressing real national problems is great and destructive'.[2] Probably no other social institution elicits such ready

1

criticism, and few other topics proceed with such a disparity between the strength of opinion and the quality of evidence.

Some journalists and editors revel in the criticism: 'When all sides are criticising you, you know you are doing a good job'.[3] It is claimed that the spread of criticism is evidence of impartiality, or of the media's scrutiny discomforting decision-makers. This is a precarious and paradoxical defence: in no other profession would universal hostility be taken as evidence of high quality.

However it must be admitted that most media criticism is at least partly wrong-headed. Much is self-interested special pleading—for some critics, their group or cause never gets proper or fair attention, while for besieged public figures, it is a common ploy to allege that misreporting or media persecution is the sole basis of their unfair embarrassment. Similarly the media present an easy target for elitist criticism: people can demonstrate their own superiority by deploring its vulgarity while specialists display their own expertise by ridiculing the superficiality of news reporting.[4] Finally much criticism is mis-informed having little idea of the exigencies or conventions of news production, and so wrongly assigning intentions or significance when interpreting particular stories. An unfortunate consequence of the prevalence of unfair criticism is that many media practitioners have become adept at unthinkingly deflecting all criticism as ill-informed, ill-motivated or impractical.

Disputes about the political significance of the news media are prone to fall into a stereotyped and often sterile form. On one side are external critics who allege systematic bias, who see news content as the result of deliberate choices designed to achieve political effects. The media's defenders, especially its own workers, respond by point-ing out the biases of those making the charge of bias, and defend themselves as professionals seeking objectivity. The debate is reduced to one of bad faith versus good faith, deliberate bias versus mirror of reality.

Discussions about the effects of the media are equally polarised. Some picture the public like litmus paper turning pink or blue de-pending on the latest trends in the news. In the simple, 'hypodermic' view, the audience is jabbed with a message, and there is an immedi-ate, tangible effect on public attitudes. The other main view is the opposite: people have strong existing attitudes and selectively perceive what's presented to reinforce what they already believe. In addition, consuming TV news or skimming through a newspaper is typically a casual rather than intense experience—the information washes over a not very attentive audience with little lasting impact. The difference between the two views couldn't be greater: one is asserting enormous effect, the other almost none.

Concern with bias and with media effects forms the basis for most popular commentary on news and for much research and theorising. Both concerns arise naturally from the nature of the media: the distinctive feature of mass communication is that a small number of senders reaches a vast audience, so questions about effects are as old as the media themselves. Similarly the basic questions about news content involve accuracy or error, comprehensiveness or selectivity, so bias seems a logical concept through which to approach the adequacy of news performance.

However, as a central term of analysis, 'bias' has many unfortunate characteristics. It presumes authoritative knowledge from which the offending coverage is seen to depart; and so leaves in abeyance whether those facts are still contested, and whether they were apparent when the story was written. In other words, it takes no account of the ambiguities and barriers to knowledge that may have confronted the news producers at deadline. Like the concept of false consciousness, bias offers an almost irresistible temptation to substitute negative evaluation for substantive description.

Moreover, criticisms of media bias commonly insinuate explanatory propositions without explicitly asserting them. Bias often implies intention and sometimes has connotations of deliberate conspiracy, but typically there is no attempt to outline in detail or to test any tacit claims about how the biased stories happened. It is essentially a static approach. Prescriptions for reform are limited to replacing the 'bad guys' with some 'good guys'; to substitute good quality for poor. There is rarely an institutional analysis.

The problem is not simply that disagreements over bias and media effects on mass attitudes are endemic. This is true in many crucial areas of political analysis. But the disagreements rarely progress to more fruitful insights or findings. Framing questions about the political role of the news media solely in these terms constricts the inquiry, largely focusing on unproductive areas while omitting the most important political and theoretical questions. In any inquiry, but especially on a subject as controversial and confused as news and power, the first important step is to ask the right questions.

## Approach

This book's approach can be summarised in three propositions, which will then be elaborated in turn:

1  that news should be understood as the product of institutional demands and processes;
2  that the news media are a central political arena, and so news must also be understood in relation to the interests and opportunities that different political groups have to influence its content;

3   that the political impact of news should not be sought primarily in its effects on largely passive mass opinion, but rather as a dynamic element in the relations and actions of participants.

### Newsmaking

A genuinely explanatory approach to news content must give primary attention to understanding the processes by which it is constructed.[5] The emphasis on process contrasts with the views sometimes found in journalistic folklore, which picture news as a daily, chaotic scramble, a unique mixture of luck, missed connections and the actions of dominant individuals either in the news room or among news sources.[6] In this view, news practices remain inexplicable but unproblematic:

Cecily:   'What field of endeavour are you engaged in?'
Felix:    'I write the news for CBS.'
Cecily:   'Oh! fascinating!'
Gwendolyn:   'Where do you get your ideas from?'
Felix:    (looking at her as though she's a Martian) 'From the news.'
Gwendolyn:   'Oh yes, of course. Silly me . . .'[7]

A newsmaking approach should not underestimate the unique contingencies which may affect a particular story.[8] Nor does it deny the ulcers and uncertainties in producing each day's news. However the recurring dilemma for news organisations is the regular production of an irregular and unpredictable commodity. This organisational feat can only be sustained through institutionalised routines, predictable and productive means for gathering news, and shared conventions about newsworthiness and presentation.

So a newsmaking approach challenges any notion of news as a 'mirror of reality' or an unproblematic reflection of events, but equally it undermines a view of news as the direct and systematic expression of one person's or one interest's ideology. Unlike a conspiracy theory it emphasises the constraints and complexities of news organisations and the multiplicity of aims within them. Individuals will still aim to exert influence, but the approach directs attention to situations and processes rather than the qualities and biases of individuals performing set roles. Only by understanding the organisational context does it become possible to specify precisely how and when news may be manipulated, either internally via managerial intervention or journalistic prejudice, or externally by particular news sources. Understanding the institutional processes of news production 'is a prerequisite for understanding what the news means.'[9]

### News As Strategic Arena

The elaborate internal operations needed to gather and present the daily news do not occur in a vacuum. News organisations are often both vulnerable and constrained in their interactions with the environment from which they gather their news. Precisely because the media are the central forum of political communication they have become a key arena of political conflict. Access to news coverage is a crucial weapon in winning public support and the appearance of public support. Disclosure of information and 'image' considerations have become a more central part of the political process and one which is played more calculatingly and intensely. The second prerequisite for understanding what the news means is to relate it to the interests and strategies of those seeking to influence it.

*Impact*

The study of media effects has passed through three major stages,[10] which are all present in contemporary thinking. The first genre pictured unidirectional effects, based on the ideological homogeneity of news content, which inevitably carried society along. It began as a conservative critique where it was primarily a suspicion of the dangers of democracy, or the threats of propaganda and mass culture. Today it is mainly a left-wing view, found in works stressing the ideological hegemony of the media, or reaching conclusions like 'news legitimates the status quo'.[11] There are also right-wing versions stressing how the liberal or left-wing biases of media workers produce a growing crisis of legitimacy in modern government.[12]

All unidirectional approaches share common problems. By their nature they are strong on assertion and rhetoric, but weak on evidence. Probably it is inevitable that there will be a vagueness about specifying the 'status quo' or the 'system' and how the process of 'maintenance' occurs. But the imprecision on key terms diminishes the possibility of satisfactory evidence, in judgments about content or effects. It is equally plausible to contend that such views attribute 'too much power to journalists and too little common sense to the audience'.[13]

Apart from problems of evidence and procedure, the basic objection to the approach is, in Marxist terms, that it is idealist. It fails to take seriously the emergence of the mass media as a major social institution. Content is the sole dimension of analysis. Institutions and relationships, conflicts and processes, are dissolved into a disembodied ideology, always victorious and uncontested.

The second stage studying media effects concentrated on attitude change among individual audience members. The major emphasis was on the persistence of opinions ('the obstinate audience'). Early influential studies showed how few people changed their voting intentions in election campaigns. While the first genre tended to picture the media as omnipotent, the second emphasised their impotence. The first generated unverifiable generalisations; the second has emphasised survey research on individual differences among audience members almost to the exclusion of larger theoretical discussion.

Insofar as any theory of political processes informs this genre, it places the amorphous entity of public opinion at the centre:

> Publicity is a force uniquely indispensable to the American system in which 'public opinion' is called on daily to arbitrate between the two competing branches of government.[14]

Such statements are more mystical than analytical. The alleged process of public opinion's 'arbitration' is at least as mysterious as that by which the media were alleged to maintain the system. The 'public' is only tangibly and decisively involved in voting, and even then the mandate which the vote represents is often disputed.

The approach's popularity stems partly from its methodological convenience and respectability. However survey research on individual attitude change barely begins to capture the range of media effects on politics. Conceiving of social structures as the aggregates of atomised individuals, and ignoring the interactions between media and political institutions and practices, is a major intellectual abdication.[15]

The orientation adopted here falls within the third genre of an expanded view of media effects.[16] News content is seen as more protean than unidirectional views allow, and its political roles as more various and less predictable. But the second genre is politically myopic. The political impact of news must be sought in its effects on how politics is conducted, how news practices interact with political processes and outcomes, how the presence of the media affects the distribution and bases of power.

## News and Power

The pen is mightier than the sword.

Four hostile newspapers are more to be feared than a thousand bayonets. (Napoleon)

Opinion, Queen of the World, is not subject to the power of Kings; they are themselves its first slaves. (Rousseau)

Power without responsibility, the prerogative of the harlot throughout the ages. (Stanley Baldwin on the press)

(I know of nothing so powerful as *The Times*) unless it be the Mississippi. (Abraham Lincoln)

President Lyndon Johnson, at the height of the controversies over the Vietnam War, . . . said that the support of the *Washington Post*'s editorials was 'worth two division'.[17]

These quotations suggest how irresistible, but how difficult, it is to link news and power. Most propositions about the power of news lack any sense of proportion. Some assert the unqualified supremacy of the press or of opinion over all other political forces. Others are absurdly precise or incommensurable: how can one sensibly compare the power of a paper to a river, to army divisions or indeed to any other source of power? Despite the deliberate irony and hyperbole in some of the quotations, the difficulties they raise are real. It is common to omit the limits of media power or constraints upon its use. Nor is there any explicit idea of 'how the trick is actually done',[18] of how the power of news asserts itself, and no idea of how it might actually be investigated rather than simply asserted.

Power is the most central concept in political analysis, yet it is also one of the most confused and difficult.[19] In some cases, it is possible to observe the exercise of power directly: in obvious coercion through the use or threat of violence or economic sanctions, or where formal authority is exercised by a superior over a subordinate. However most of the time power is more complex and elusive. Power tends to encourage all-or-none assertions, yet in a complex society with inter-acting political factors absolute power rarely applies. The concept is most comfortably applied to situations analogous to battles, with both sides consciously aiming to subdue the other, and with definite show-downs and outcomes.

Discussions of power often wrongly conflate intentions and effects. The political significance of the news media is not confined to their potential as organs for propaganda. Most of the time most producers of news are not deliberate propagandists, but that does not mean the news media have no power, or are irrelevant to the exercise of power. News clearly is politically potent, yet it is a form of power typically very distant from the battle situation described above.

The centrality of the news media in political communication makes them a strategic arena in the struggle for power.[20] An 'arena' is not necessarily a neutral or inert venue in participants' battles. The advantages and disadvantages of newsworthiness and access are not bestowed equally. The factors that produce publicity are rarely within the total control of any one group. The publicising efforts of rival participants, the intrusion of unplanned newsworthy events, indepen-dent information-gathering by reporters all conspire to make the pro-cess of news coverage one of the less predictable elements in political equations. Similarly publicity cannot be simply equated with success. Its political impact is far from uniform—being apparently vital at some times and seemingly irrelevant or marginal at others.

A crucial but little explored impact of news on politics is its direct interplay with political processes—through which the content of news is influenced by the publicising strategies and actions of various participants and in turn feeds back into subsequent actions, and the ways in which the news media's role as an independent source of information disclosure and presentation is a factor in political initiative and momentum. All political actors are sensitive to what appears in the news. Given this universal concentration, the news media are often the venue through which battles are fought, both overtly and obliquely, and publicity is frequently the trigger for further moves and shifts in these battles.

## Research Design

Defining the theoretical approach and problem in the ways sketched above sets a demanding, perhaps impossible, research assignment. Two principles guided the present design. In an area marked by vivid examples, of both praiseworthy and egregious media behaviour, the first was to seek representative data. The other was to encompass all the 'moments' in the central transactions between news and politics: not to reify content without paying attention to the processes of its production; not to study media organisations without looking at how other groups seek to influence the news; not to isolate news production without acknowledging that the social significance of news lies in its content and effects; but not to look at effects in a way which caricatures the media as a cause without any constraints upon it.

The first main source of data is interviews with 223 journalists. The interviews were conducted chiefly with journalists in five principal roles: editors, federal and state political reporters, industrial and business or economics correspondents. A variety of others (e.g. press secretaries, investigative reporters, feature writers and some other specialists)[21] were included but not systematically. There were no conscious biases in selection, except toward more eminent or senior journalists. There were very few refusals, although exigencies of time and availability, sometimes possibly contrived, meant that several who preferably should have been interviewed were not. Interviews were conducted in the five mainland State capitals and Canberra, mainly between 1981 and 1983, and included journalists from all media and all major media organisations. The average length of interviews was about one and a quarter hours, but they ranged from half an hour to more than three hours. About 30 journalists were interviewed more than once. In about 90 per cent of interviews, I sought to take comprehensive notes, which were later analysed extensively.

The purpose of the interviews was to learn about the journalists' relevant experiences and their reflections upon them. To the extent that there was method in the meandering, it could be summarised in three principal aims:

1   for respondents to make comparisons within their own experience
    —between different periods, organisations and news rounds;
2   to recount and reflect upon events they had witnessed, and their
    impressions of particular people and episodes;
3   to gauge their attitudes to various issues involving the quality or
    principles of news coverage.

Because the interviews were open-ended their content varied depending on the individual's career and position and on their responsiveness
and concerns.

The interviews comprise a rich vein of data, but it is not the book's
aim to give a descriptive outline of the views or experiences of individual journalists. Rather the data are used as evidence and illustration
for the arguments advanced. Individual responses have been aggre-
gated and contrasted to test impressions and ideas. Sometimes individual quotations are given, mainly anonymously, except when identi-
fying an individual helps to understand what was said, or where an
observation deserves acknowledgement.

I was very happy with the cooperation and apparent openness of
most journalists. There were of course great individual differences in
style, and there are areas where journalistic values stress confidentiality (especially sources and leaks) and others where 'double-talk'
or inconsistency are common (e.g. about objectivity, or employers'
virtues).[22] Many were informed and sophisticated analysts of their
own profession and their insights helped shape my own perspectives.
Whatever its limits, it is better to have interview data than not have it.
It supplies a freshness, authenticity and perspective that is typically
lacking when news content alone is studied.

However interviewing journalists is no substitute for the study of
content. The second main source of data is news stories. The extent to
which 'news has become a newsworthy subject'[23] gives the researcher
many advantages compared with a decade or two ago. News accounts
were a useful source of information on many developments within the
media. Most importantly they were the primary data (supplemented
by interviews and both academic and journalistic studies) for the study
of particular cases in Chapters 4–7.

The method adopted might be coined the 'comparative case study'
approach. Case studies seek to envelop their subject by using all
available means of data-gathering (documents, observation, interviews, informants) and so construct a total picture. Their chief
advantage is thoroughness. Their key disadvantage is that the representativeness of the single case remains unknown, and so research
findings tend to be non-cumulative, and fail to encourage more general theory building. By building comparison into the design, these
disadvantages can be minimised. The purpose of the comparative

approach, focusing upon the unfolding of individual episodes, is to distinguish particular contingencies from more immutable features of the interaction between news coverage and the political processes being examined.

The approach was most pertinent in comparing contemporary Federal elections and twenty-three party leadership challenges between 1968 and 1985.[24] It also informs the approach to data in the chapters on overt and covert news manoeuvres, but less systematically as their profusion of examples cannot be so conveniently bounded. It should be remembered that often the data is inherently controversial, with conflicting claims and sometimes deliberate secrecy and deception. It is impossible to be sure of being comprehensive in the coverage of complex or extensive episodes. Moreover there are systematic biases and omissions in the data (such as the usual over-reliance on print rather than broadcasting materials, and within print on the quality press, and on Sydney and national publications). The bases and limits of knowledge are indicated as precisely as possible at pertinent points.

A final source of data, used principally in the early chapters to illustrate various characteristics of news, was a content analysis of news coverage in four newspapers and on Sydney television for a week in early May 1982.[25]

## Organisation of this book

The book falls into three parts. The first examines news production—the practices, conventions and constraints of media institutions. The second part examines the interests and strategies of those who seek to influence news content. The final third is concerned with the interactions between news and politics.

Each of the three chapters in Part I analyses one of the principal aspects of newsmaking: organisational production, news gathering and news values. Chapter 1 concentrates on organisational factors: the constraints of time, staffing and economic factors, the differences between different types of media and organisations, and the nature of power and conflict in news organisations. Chapter 2 examines the processes of acquiring newsworthy information in different news rounds, how factors of information availability and source structure affect the quality of news. Four rounds are specifically considered: federal politics, State politics, industrial reporting and economic and business reporting. The production and supply aspects of news considered in Chapters 1 and 2 need to be supplemented by a consideration of how news values determine the definition of news. Chapter 3 examines how perceived audience interest and competition determine the demand for information, and how news presentations are shaped by conventional formats and professional ideals.

The second part moves beyond the internal operation of news organisations to their interaction with the environment on which they report, specifically how various groups seek to use news coverage to advance their own interests. Chapter 4 is concerned with how this is done overtly, in public relations strategies, while Chapter 5 examines covert manoeuvres, the use of leaks and background briefings.

The final part of the book looks at the political impact of news. In each chapter the factors encouraging and inhibiting news attention, especially the publicity interests of participants, are examined, and then the impacts of news attention on the unfolding of political relationships and actions are traced. The most constant political players in the news are the political parties, and Chapters 6 and 7 examine the contrasting patterns of publicity interests and news impacts in inter-party and intra-party conflicts. The concluding chapter (Chapter 8), considers the processes involved in the construction of public political agendas.

# PART I
# The Production of News

# 1

# Organisational Imperatives

The central dilemma for news organisations is the regular production of an irregular and unpredictable commodity. The general aim of covering the news is open-ended and infinite. Both its definition and pursuit are full of uncertainties. Yet the creation of news occurs within rigid constraints on production and distribution, with severe economic penalties for lateness.

The two parameters which govern news routines are the 'deadline' and the 'news hole'. When the first American paper appeared, in Boston in 1690, it promised to appear 'once a month, (or, if any Glut of Occurrences happen, oftener)'.[1] However, neither the size nor the scheduling of news production is tied to the volume and vagaries of events. Whether it is a heavy or light news day, news is essentially produced according to set times (deadlines) and to a format of pre-determined size (the news hole).[2] News production demands bureaucracy, but is dealing with a product which is always threatening to defy it, and much of the flavour of news organisations derives from this tension.

The special characteristics of news organisations derive also from the unusual variety of goals which they house: 'no other type of organization has the news organization's dependence on advertising and sales revenue—plus their involvement in non-revenue activities'.[3] The basic animus of the organisation—news gathering and processing—is oblique to and remote from its supporting sources of revenue. Moreover, the plurality of goals and consequent goal bargaining occur in a situation of weak evaluative tools. Specific measures can rarely be tied with assurance to particular outcomes. Economic constraints are ever-present, but profit maximisation, even if completely dominant, is

15

not easily or rationally translated into specific news practices and editorial decisions.

Media technologies for production and distribution are increasingly sophisticated, but human activity is still the key resource in manufacturing news content. News must be re-created afresh every news period. It depends centrally on the deployment, capacity and coordination of journalistic activity. Like other bureaucracies, news organisations are a combination of hierarchy and division of labour. Their distinctive configuration has been aptly described as 'middle-heavy hierarchy'.[4] This reflects their divergent demands—on the one hand, centralised coordination to assure smooth routines and consistent presentation, on the other, widespread interaction with a diverse and unpredictable environment to generate news. Overall authority and decision-making are concentrated in a relatively small group of editorial executives, below which is a large and diversified middle stratum of reporters and processors.

Understanding how news is produced helps in interpreting its content, and so is a necessary starting point in our exploration of news and power. This chapter seeks to illuminate the problems and characteristics of news organisations. Some are common to all, but there is also great variety depending on the medium, the cycles of production, and the company's traditions and commercial position.

## Print

The traditional distinction in newspapers is between quality and popular. Quality papers are broadsheet size; have smaller, predominantly middle-class circulations; rely on classified advertising as a major source of revenue; have news priorities which emphasise international news, politics, business and major social institutions; present news more soberly and have a serious conception of their role, perhaps seeing themselves as a 'paper of record'. Popular papers are tabloid size; have large, mainly working-class, circulations; rely on circulation sales and feature advertising as major sources of revenue; have news priorities emphasising crime, sport, sex and human interest; have presentations featuring large dramatic headlines and pictures; see themselves primarily as commercial operations, or cite their large circulations as evidence of their virtue.

These are caricatures and most existing papers have elements of both. Like the United States of America, Australia's newspaper market comprises a series of 'city states' rather than a single national structure.[5] There are two national newspapers—*The Australian* and *The Australian Financial Review*. Both are politically important, but comprise minute proportions of any regional market. They are usually bought as a 'second' paper, rarely displacing that city's major morning paper. There is competition between local morning papers only in Sydney and Melbourne[6] and, until March 1988, between afternoon papers in Sydney. Elsewhere monopoly reigns.

The competing morning papers in Melbourne and Sydney display many of the traditional differences between quality and popular papers. The content analysis revealed the following contrasts:

**Table 1.1  Quality & popular newspapers: priorities and presentation**

|                                        | Age % | SMH % | Sun % | DT % |
|----------------------------------------|-------|-------|-------|------|
| Stories >20 paragraphs                 | 17    | 19    | 12    | 8    |
| Political/economic/social policy items | 60    | 53    | 40    | 37   |
| Headlines 5+ columns wide              | 13    | 18    | 22    | 21   |

*Notes*
1   The four newspapers are *The Age* and *The Sun News Pictorial* from Melbourne, and *The Sydney Morning Herald* and *The Daily Telegraph* from Sydney. All are morning papers. The sample on which these figures are based is described in Introduction, note 25.
2   The detailed categorisation of subjects in news stories can be seen in the coding handbook. For present purposes, such 'serious' topics as politics, social and policy areas, business and industrial news were grouped together, in contrast to all other items, such as crime, human interest, sport and entertainment.

The biggest differences in content are that the popular papers have more items on sport and very little on business or economics, and while politics is also one of their staples, they carry considerably less than do the qualities. While roughly half the items in all papers were straight news stories, there were clear differences in the number of feature or comment items (from 12 per cent in *The Age* to 1 per cent in *The Sun*), while the tabloid papers had higher proportions of non-news items such as cartoon strips and astrology columns.

Differences in content are paralleled by differences in organisation. Daily newspapers, especially quality ones, are the biggest bureaucracies among news organisations, with the most differentiated division of labour. *The Sydney Morning Herald* and *The Age* employ most 200 full-time staff journalists while most others employ 100 or less. The greater absolute number of journalists is accompanied by a similar or slightly higher proportion of news gatherers than processors, and a larger number of reporters on set rounds. There are more people assigned to producing features and commentary. These two papers have the equivalent of about five people doing leaders (editorials) while most popular papers have only one.

The political role played by different papers is not simply an index of their circulation. The greater journalistic resources of the quality papers makes them the most significant source of independent media disclosure. They carry an authority and political relevance the more popular media sometimes lack, partly because of their credibility, partly because they are overwhelmingly the news organs which political elites and participants consume most.[7]

### Changes: The Growing Gap

All newspapers have undergone substantial changes in the last 25 years. The changes have had diverse sources, but the greatest stimulus has undoubtedly been the increasing importance of television. However, quality and popular papers have responded differently so that, as several journalists observed, the gap between them has increased. Both have moved beyond straight news reporting, but, to put it over-simply, the qualities have moved more into analysis and the populars into entertainment.[8]

The main changes which recur in journalists' and editors' accounts include increasing specialisation, more 'writing' as opposed to simply reporting, and more news features, explanation and comment. The superiority of broadcasting news in speed and immediacy has 'pushed specialist journalists more and more into before-the-event, after-the-event and behind-the-event reporting':[9]

> It's a much freer paper. It was very regimented in those days. Then it was all recorded speech and action. Now it's more explanatory, analytical and in a way which we try to control, there is more comment. Comment and analysis are different things. I like subjective writing, but it must be clearly labelled. It's changed for several reasons. Radio and TV forced us to change. We are no longer the bearer of all important news. We are still the major breaker of news in the state. I'm surprised that it's still our role, which is marvellous. We've got the biggest and best reporting staff, so we still get major breaks. But radio and TV must get many items first and then we must show how and why. We must cover the war as well as the battle. . . . Rather than pride of place, we're now the ones at the back who cause trouble. When it is a big affair, we're called in because only we can handle it. (Don Riddell, editor, *The Advertiser*)

> People have seen it on TV. There is no point in us repeating the TV. They speak in headlines. We are now in the business of saying why it happened. The single most important word in newspapers today is why.

On the other hand, quality papers are now less formal papers of record. The notion of a passive, comprehensive repository of official proceedings is economically unfeasible in its demands on space (especially with the proliferation of such proceedings), and, in a more time-conscious age, readers are unlikely to consume the columns of print involved. It means that there is a marked decrease in the reporting of official institutions such as High Court judgments, Parliamentary committees and, most notably, Parliament itself.

Popular newspapers have become more calculating in their marketing and news priorities. Those in direct competition with quality papers have accentuated their distinctive appeals rather than competing on the common ground of political coverage. Although the total mix of news organisations has grown, competition is more segmented, and the story priorities and markets pursued are very different. In some ways news, especially political news, has become more irrelevant to the latter:

> The old [Packer] *Daily Telegraph* ran the news. It had an idea of its obligation to cover the waterfront for its readers. The concept of obligation has died altogether now.

> The markets are so different from *The Age* since we decided to go down market in the mid-1970s.

> The accountants have taken over—they are the real decision makers now. ... The attitude now is for getting the paper out at the least cost.

In 1972, two of the most important reporters in the Canberra press gallery were the Melbourne *Sun*'s Laurie Oakes and the *Daily Telegraph*'s Alan Reid. Now, regardless of personalities, it is almost structurally impossible for any political reporter on a popular tabloid to gain the prominence they had then. Ironically, the increased marketing orientation has sometimes been accompanied by a decreasing sureness of touch in news judgment:

> In the old days you'd get a story, phone through, it was straight on to the street. The editor knew a good story. These buggers don't. ... Today subs read it, editors read it, they chuck it around, then to the chief sub. They're playing around. A good page one story is held back, buggered up. ... Now they lack confidence. ... A story is not good unless it's been in other papers. They're more defensive, cautious.

## Weekly Publications

Naturally weekly publications have a different working rhythm and staffing pattern from dailies. Sunday newspapers, which in many states have higher circulations than the dailies, have a fairly small number of core staff (from a dozen to about 30) and a low number of specialist reporters—although like feature writers, their general reporters may have time to develop contacts and information on a story. They also tend to employ a higher proportion of casual contributors (especially in service areas, like gardening) and sub-editors:

> I've worked on Sunday papers a lot. I enjoy it. It takes a particular sort of journalist. ... It's different from a daily which is dealing with what happens immediately. On a Sunday, you can dig a lot deeper. You develop a wider sphere of contacts in the community. It can be much harder, during an election campaign for example. ... You get a sixth sense on knowing stories that won't be knocked off. ... Here you've got to do stories, which (a) will

still be true for Sunday, and (b) not get knocked off. . . . You like to give people more of a read on a Sunday morning compared with a daily. . . . People aren't rushing to work etc.

Apart from Sunday papers, there have been three national weekly news publications, which have at times played an important political role. *The Bulletin*, the oldest, is the only survivor. After languishing with circulations of 30 000 and less, it was rescued by the Packer company in the early 1970s, and now has a circulation which varies near 100 000.[10] The irreverent *Nation Review*[11] born in the late 1960s probably peaked with the election of the Whitlam Government, and finally collapsed in the late 1970s. *The National Times* was founded by the Fairfax company in 1971 and slowly gained circulation strength. Although its peak circulations exceeded 100 000, after periods of stagnation and decline, it was re-founded as the *Times on Sunday* in 1986, but was eventually closed by the newly privatised Fairfax company in March 1988.

There has also been a great expansion in the business periodical press. Apart from various investment and specialised industry magazines, there are two with more general relevance—Australian Consolidated Press's *Australian Business* and Fairfax's *Business Review Weekly*. They started six months apart, in late 1980 and early 1981, and competition between them is intense, although the most notable feature is how both have achieved substantial circulations.

The essential appeal of weekly and periodical news publications is that in an age of instant and continuous, but fragmentary and lowest common denominator news, they provide perspective, investigations, more comment and specialisation:

> The weekly element is nicely balanced between freshness and reflection.
>
> There is an association that develops with a magazine which is different from a paper. Stories live longer. You do them with some depth and thought and flair. You know when you've hit the spot.

As with current affairs programs, there is more discretion and less obligatory coverage in weekly publications, so there is more calculated decision-making about what to cover:

> A magazine does not have the same saturation coverage. We're at the top of the market and we expect quality. We look for self-starters, ideas, cross disciplines, people having more than one skill. They need then to have their own ideas. An editor can't have eleven scintillating ideas a week. . . . The failure rate on ideas is very high, well over 50%. . . . The reporters don't necessarily work to the same metre as the magazine. It depends on what they are assigned to. It may be three or four weeks for a big story. . . .
> You've got to plan ahead. I can't rely on the news rescuing me every week. You keep touching base on areas of interest to our readers. . . . There is nothing worse than a blank week. Everything goes blank at once.

Periodical publications are more obviously dependent on the active efforts of reporters to initiate and pursue stories, so the quality of the final product is more tied to the quality and enthusiasm of staff.[12] Their capacity to initiate stories, rather than simply 'follow the news', and their more actively interested readerships gives these publications a political relevance beyond their circulations.

### Australian Associated Press

News agencies play a strategic, but publicly almost invisible, role in the dissemination of news. They supply news organisations rather than the public directly. Their role is most simply illustrated by the American situation. There are over 1750 daily papers, most with circulations of less than 100 000 in small and medium-sized cities and towns. For these organisations to cover the world beyond their own locality—interstate, national and international news—they depend mainly on subscribing to agencies. There are also 4500 radio stations, most of which depend mainly on the agencies for their 'rip and read' hourly news services. Larger news organisations, such as *The New York Times* or CBS, use agencies as a supplement to their own resources, as insurance against missing stories, and as a basis on which their own reporters may build.[13]

AAP has up to 60 different services and every major news organisation subscribes to one or more. The services include its overseas news, its main domestic news service, special news services aimed at radio, a Federal Parliamentary report, a stock exchange service in conjunction with Reuters Economic Services, and a public relations wire for distributing press releases.

Although founded over 50 years ago, in 1935, the most notable aspect of AAP's history was its slow growth. The major hindrance was the relatively small media market in Australia, compounded by its oligopolistic ownership. The press proprietors, who were also AAP's owners, had their own news-sharing arrangements and had no interest in AAP developing an independent news-gathering capacity.

The crucial turning-point in AAP's development as a domestic news-gathering agency came in the mid-1970s. In the next decade, the number of journalists employed grew from about 30 to more than 130. Previously, independent news gathering had sometimes been discouraged. One journalist recalled being instructed to wait until a paper had written a story and then report that they had reported it. Now 'our biggest delight is when (the papers) are running in circles chasing our stories'.

Even now, AAP employs a modest number of journalists for an organisation that aspires to be a national agency. It still covers several areas by having reciprocal arrangements with local papers rather than an independent reporting capacity. Traditionally AAP had a reputation as a 'staging post' where journalists worked early in their careers before moving on to better things.[14] Agency work is seen as offering a good grounding, where journalists learn stories must be '(a) sourced, (b) balanced, (c) free of any taint of litigation, (d) fast'. The forces encouraging journalists to move on were that agency work sometimes involved 'sweat-shop' conditions, and the lack of any internal career structure. According to senior journalists with AAP, 'the flow of defections has been slashed', because of improved conditions and more opportunities inside the company.

The priorities of agency news are speed, brevity, 'hard news' (rather than features or analysis), strong, simple lead sentences, and precise attribution for all statements ('hard sourcing'). The American agencies, supplying clients of diverse political views, are often credited as crucial in the rise of objectivity as a principal criterion for news reporting.[15] Agencies' time and space constraints differ from newspapers. The time pressures are even greater, stressing immediate and continuous distribution, a 'deadline every minute' as the US folklore has it. The total space constraints are more relaxed, but to meet the processing preferences of their clients, there is a strong tendency toward brevity in individual stories.

The AAP self-image claims that it is 'fast, eminently dependable, comprehensive', that it is not constrained by editorial policy, but rather produces straight, balanced reporting where opinion and subjectivity are discouraged. Its journalists say they enjoy the competitiveness and immediacy ('really gets the adrenalin going'). Others disparage the homogenised reporting of news agencies—'nuts and bolts', 'like all products sold to large numbers it tends to be a bit bland. AAP is the Kraft cheddar cheese of journalism'. AAP's staffing pattern is more towards generalists than specialists. The agency stress is on immediate productivity, which discourages depth in compiling individual stories, and makes investigative work all but impossible.[16] A broad, basic coverage, reliable and without risks, is the primary demand from its clients.

## Television

Television is now entrenched as the medium from which most people say they get most of their news, and the one which they find most trustworthy,[17] and so also is increasingly the medium to which politicians attach most importance.

TV news has many distinctive features. The first is the brevity of the verbal information presented. The text of a half-hour news service would not fill the front page of a broadsheet newspaper.[18] In a commercial, half-hour news program, six to seven minutes are sub-

**Table 1.2  Types of newsfilm action**

|  | All news % | Domestic news % |
|---|---|---|
| No accompanying action film | 24 | 28 |
| Non-staged action, incidental or background to story event or scheduled performance | 33 | 38 |
| Staged performance, scheduled events | 31 | 30 |
| Spontaneous, non-staged event intrinsic to story | 11 | 5 |

*Notes*
Each item was coded for the piece of newsfilm which most closely approached spontaneous action. The category 'no accompanying film' includes brief items which showed only the announcer or reporter to camera, and interviews conducted by the reporter alone. 'Incidental film' includes film of participants arriving or leaving venues of meetings, court hearings, the aftermath of events or background illustrative film of e.g. a supermarket during an item on price rises. 'Staged performance' includes sporting events, public meetings, press conferences, etc., where the participants sought publicity or which were scheduled public events. The final category is the rarely captured ideal of unscheduled news action.

**Table 1.3  Newsfilm segment types**

|  | % |
|---|---|
| Announcer to camera | 30 |
| Action film with reporter or announcer voice-over | 30 |
| Reporter talking to camera | 12 |
| 1:1 reporter to interviewee | 9 |
| Collective interviews with interviewee | 5 |
| Graphics | 8 |
| Action with natural sound | 2 |
| Miscellaneous | 4 |

*Notes*
Each discrete segment of film in each story was coded.

tracted for ads and station promotions, plus a couple of minutes for weather, and perhaps five minutes for sport, leaving about eighteen minutes for general news. The production of TV news is dominated by a 'stop-watch culture'.[19] The content analysis found there were on average 14 to 15 items in a half-hour news service (including sport and weather), while the hour-long Channel 10 news averaged around 26 items. Most items (53 per cent) were between one and two minutes in length, with only 14 per cent of items running longer than 2½ minutes.

Visual quality is at the heart of the TV news enterprise. The construction of stories centres on the gathering and editing of suitable newsfilm. (See Tables 1.2 and 1.3.) The emphasis on presentation and the dominance of logistics has consequences for organisational structure and operation. Epstein has argued that it is uneconomic for TV stations to employ more camera crews than they need to fill the news time. Thus while the advertising slogan for NBC News claimed to be ringing the world, more than 80 per cent of its stories were produced by ten film crews.[20] Similarly, TV news relies on a small core of on-camera reporters, employed as generalists whose presentation and production skills are at least as important as their informational ones. One American TV correspondent estimated that TV journalism is 50 per cent logistics, 20 per cent knowledge of events and 30 per cent luck.[21] Consequently 'the television news organization is also a simpler and more flexible bureaucracy'.[22] Their work day centres more around the logistics of gaining and processing newsfilm, and more stories are centrally assigned than reporter-originated.

Because of the centrality of visual considerations a TV journalist's work day is differently structured from print reporters', and involves different skills:

> It may take me an hour to do a TV story. I may rewrite it a few times. I'm conscious that I've got to do it in two minutes. I talk to the camera man. I'm a strong believer in graphics, quotes and figures. That needs to be done in advance. . . . If you get a good, strong quote, put it up. The reporter works with the editor. You've got to allow one and a half hours every day to sit with the editor. You've got to explain. . . . There's a closer relationship with the editor and cameraman because with ENG [Electronic News Gathering] you can do it all in the studio. . . . A two man bureau means we are so busy. The technology is time-consuming. You've got to build the story on machines. . . . You do lose contacts.

> Thinking visually now comes naturally. The media is a combination of words and music. A story is so much more effectively told with a combination of words and pictures. They reinforce each other. You get one chance with the audience, to inform them. You must ensure that you don't waste a shot, a frame. I don't make any concessions. I don't pander. People are very quick to know when they are being spoken down to. The ideal story is a voice over with a shot of an interview, where the picture has to be utterly relevant. . . . I took a long time to come to grips with TV. . . . For two years I was a newspaper man appearing on TV, thinking of it as ephemeral background. Then I realised what I was missing out. (TV political reporters)

The audience intake pattern differs from print. The pace and emphasis is decided by the producer rather than the consumer. Because there is no possibility of skipping or re-reading items in TV news, the economic logic is to exclude stories of minority interest, whereas it may still be in a newspaper's interest to include them. Keeping complex stories easily comprehensible for an audience, who may be only half-attentive, but who have no second chance to view the item, is a primary concern for all TV journalists.

Intake is one of many aspects which contribute to a more pervasive concern with audience considerations. TV is the only news outlet where competition for audiences is so crucial and so volatile (see Chapter 3). TV and radio reporters get far more feedback than do print reporters, so audience response is a more tangible factor for them. Because such a large part of the TV reporters' job is to do with presentation and packaging, there are fewer countervailing pressures (such as relations with regular, confidential sources) toward other criteria for gauging story significance or organisational success.

## The Rise of Broadcasting

TV news was central to the audience, and so important to politicians, long before it had the newsgathering reach or sophistication to merit its political role. The history of radio and TV is one of their news practices lagging behind their political impact, constrained by both technological and professional limits.

Technological changes have allowed TV to become less bound to covering only local news with film. Before coaxial cables were laid (the first, between Melbourne and Sydney, was completed in 1962 and gradually extended elsewhere), film had to be transported interstate by plane, making deadlines very early. In consequence the first TV network to establish representation in Canberra, Channel 9, withdrew its staff in 1964 less than a year after their arrival.[23] It was not until the 1970s that full-time TV representation and studios were established in Parliament House. Improved transmission links within Australia have permitted more coordinated and regular networking between cities. Commercial TV news still has a strong local emphasis (in our survey 66 per cent of domestic news on the Sydney TV channels came from Sydney). But regular coverage from Canberra and of major interstate stories are now staples of TV news.

Later, the advent of satellites brought an explosion in access to overseas newsfilm (although it is still overwhelmingly from Britain and America). The survey week was exceptional, in that it was dominated by the Falklands war, but international items comprised more than one-fifth of all stories.

The introduction of colour TV in 1974 brought a new generation of equipment and allowed more presentation techniques in graphics and captions. Equally important was the transition from film to tape. ENG (Electronic News Gathering) allowed more flexible filming and processing. Tape is much easier to edit quickly and so individual stories are more elaborately constructed and internally differentiated. The content analysis showed a quarter of stories had 6–10 discrete visual segments, a figure certainly much higher than a decade earlier. Many commercial stations now have helicopters for helping to gather film. Nearly all are capable of doing 'live crosses' to outside locations during the news. Although also lending themselves to gimmickry, these changes have all contributed to the speed and flexibility of TV news, increasing its mobility and timeliness.

Despite its venerability, radio's more recent technological and professional developments have been equally dramatic: 'A major technical breakthrough for the radio news services came in the early 1960s, when the Australian Broadcasting Control Board gave permission to record interviews and statements obtained by telephone'.[24] Portable tape recorders became common only in the late 1960s, with one journalist suggesting their advent contributed to the downfall of John Gorton as Prime Minister, capturing directly for the first time a political leader's convolutions and over-hasty comments. 'Specialist radio journalists were not posted on a permanent basis in the (Canberra Press) Gallery until the late 1960s and early 1970s.'

Thus it is only within the last two decades that radio has assumed its current place within the news and current affairs mix. Now it offers immediacy and flexibility. Using the telephone and portable tape-recorder it is able to get 'actuality' and interviews from almost anywhere, cheaply and quickly. On a developing story it has greater timeliness. Radio excelled, for example, in covering the tragic bushfires of February 1983. On the other hand it suffers even more than TV from being only a headline service, and its reporters are sometimes disparaged by other journalists—'Radio is a disgrace. They shove a microphone in someone's face and say "tell us what you want to tell us".'

The generally high morale in commercial TV news in the early 1980s was not only due to technological improvements. (New technology in TV is typically a source of joy among the journalists, while in the press it is greeted with foreboding.) All networks gained a renewed grasp of the importance of news from around 1980 on. It was also an economically buoyant period for the stations with advertisers seemingly willing to sustain any rises in the rates they were charged. Evening news services were supplemented with extra programs and headline services. The changes were partly self-sustaining: innovation at one channel was a stimulus toward change at its competitors. Although previously TV stations had often treated news as an annoying statutory obligation, its commercial importance was increasingly recognised. News often begins the evening's viewing and theories of audience flow suggest that viewers tend to remain with the channel they are watching, unless they have a definite reason to change. As Phillip Adams' (pre-remote control) law of TV watching put it: the weight of the backside is greater than the force of the intellect. A news program also builds station recognition more than an anonymous imported series does.

TV reporters have also grown in both status and professionalism, having gained experience both in journalism and in TV techniques. TV journalists are very aware of the medium's impact, the importance attached to it by politicians, and the surveys showing its greater credibility to the public:

> In the last 10 years, TV news has got more impact, and become more professional. Now it is the form of news making which has the most public impact, and it is the most progressive and innovative. It has the advantages of all forms of news combined into one. . . . In the early years we fairly suffered the criticism of boys doing men's work. Now they have grown up. Australia now has a lot of high quality TV reporters. The early people were from papers and didn't know the medium.

This has meant a gradually more interpretative and presumptuous role replacing the previously passive orientation. *This Day Tonight* in the late 1960s, the first daily current affairs show, with its mixture of high ratings, cheekiness and a more cutting analytical edge was a major stimulus:[25]

> TV news was a cheap version of theatre newsreels. . . . We were always seen as the poor relation of [our newspaper owner]. In the late 1960s TV news was starting to move. Then a journalist recorded an interview, and did no interpretative material. . . . It was frustrating trying to convey what the issues were about, but you could only use interviews. . . . No interpretative journalism was allowed. . . . People were frightened of TV. We used to do 'vox pops' in the street, and people would always try to dodge.

Many TV editors and reporters thus had a tangible sense of improving capacity and quality within their own working experience, of increased modernisation and status:[26]

> Years ago we had music behind every story. We had a spaghetti board with titles of the story. It seems now kiddies' stuff.

> Morale in TV is quite high, ours is buoyant at the moment. Our management has an enlightened attitude to TV news. We have new equipment, a new news room etc. Morale in papers is not as high as it could be. . . . They may be envious of the importance of TV, the way we use helicopters etc for speed. Most of them would still see themselves as the senior service.

The paeans of praise from within the medium are hardly echoed by their colleagues outside. Except for some political reporters who recognise its importance, non-TV journalists overwhelmingly still hold derogatory views of TV news:

> TV reporting fills me with horror. (Editor)

> TV to me is the ultimate trivialisation of politics. It tends to need a moving picture and content is secondary. The Prime Minister could be gabbling a nursery rhyme. They only want 90 seconds.

Some questions asked by TV journalists are not befitting a journalist. They betray a very poor understanding. . . . The TV people would criticise us for being too long and boring. . . . It's astonishing to ever find radio and TV people breaking a story, except for the ABC.

In sum the reputed strengths and weaknesses of TV news are by now well-rehearsed:

The weaknesses are the obvious ones. We cannot ventilate issues thoroughly enough. We are too restrained by time to adequately explain. There is a tendency to lock into pictures which are not the story. Sometimes stories do not lend themselves to pictures and are ignored because you can't sell them to the audience. I've got no illusions about TV. It zeroes in, but it lacks the depth which is sometimes required.

The strength is the opposite. We can bring politics to a level at which most people can understand it. We can make people realise how important politics is . . . how government affects us all. (Ken Begg)

As the technical and logistical obstacles to TV news are progressively overcome, the accommodation of journalism's professional demands within an entertainment medium is the basic question which will determine the future development of TV news.

## Conclusion

Covering the news is an infinite, impossible task. News is therefore an exercise in imperfection, the product of a series of compromises. It is not surprising that errors and misjudgments occur. Stories compete for coverage. All are pursued and processed under the pressure of deadlines:

People outside don't understand the constraints. The press is not made up of plots. . . . A story got in too late, so it didn't make the paper, even though it was a better story than a lot that went in. Or suddenly someone produces a better story on the same topic. (Editor)

The constant production demands pervade all aspects of news work. News organisations probably have to make more decisions more quickly than any other large bureaucratic enterprise. The most recurrent concern the treatment of that day's news. The decision-making context has three basic features:

1  the immediate press of deadlines;
2  chronic overload; and
3  the high number of apparently idiosyncratic or exceptional cases, to which it is hard to apply general formulas.

The resulting style can be characterised as concrete decision-making, in contrast to the universalist decisional criteria of public bureaucracies. It is preoccupied with immediate practical problems, decisions aimed at concrete solutions rather than the construction or application of general principles. Such a decision-making pattern contrasts with an ideal-type bureaucracy, as represented, for example, by a university committee deciding policy. The committee deliberations involve a lack of urgency, a reluctance to take 'premature' action, and an attempt to cater for all contingencies (extending Parkinson, the more remote the contingency, the longer the discussion). Legislators and public administrators must be able to justify precisely all particular applications by reference to general criteria (even if loopholes are written in to give some administrative discretion). Deciding tomorrow's headline is a qualitatively different decisional process. Each case can be seen as involving a unique configuration of competing principles, which typically remain tacit rather than being explicitly debated. Consistency would be hard to achieve, but anyway, there is no institutionalised mechanism by which it is gauged or enforced. The decisions need no external justification beyond continued audience consumption. As a decision-making style it has a bias against coherence and against reflection, but so does the nature of the news enterprise.

The concrete decision-making style paradoxically makes news organisations both dynamic and resistant to reform. It breeds resistance to thinking about large-scale changes. The over-riding concern of most editors is with the day-to-day practicalities. Other concerns only emerge in the shadow of the paramount demands of production. News organisations are a classic case of being 'so busy manning the fire hose that [they] cannot devise a fire prevention program'.[27] Reforms and experimentation must be subordinated to the rigid production routines. The tightness of deadlines, the speed of decision-making, the need for coordination of effort and consistency of presentation all make any uncertainty over formats, procedures or judgments severely disabling.

Despite their resistance to one-off, large-scale change, news organisations are characterised by constant piecemeal change. The concrete decision-making style and the minimal external accountability leave the potential for long-term changes in reporting to emerge through attending to short-term exigencies. Somewhat in spite of themselves, news organisations are one of society's more open institutions. The nature of news, as we explore in the next chapter, forces them to be outward-looking institutions, responding to the social currents around them, and capable of learning from the events they are covering.

# 2
# Gathering News

How does news become known to reporters? This chapter focuses on the processes of gathering news and how they are intertwined with institutional structures and source interests. It will focus on how the infinite mandate to cover the news is institutionalised into a series of productive but necessarily limited routines of news gathering.

There is no guaranteed means of ensuring the detection of newsworthy developments, or gaining comprehensive and accurate accounts of them. The most important organisational device for ensuring the regular flow of newsworthy material, and the strategy which is most likely to produce accurate and penetrating reporting, is the deployment of journalists to particular 'rounds', (in American jargon, 'beats') where they are expected to be regularly productive and to cover all major developments. However, many organisations, especially weekly publications, commercial TV stations and popular afternoon papers, opt to have only a few specialist reporters, preferring the perceived economic and presentational advantages of generalists. Their editors argued that general reporters gave more flexibility and so were a more cost-efficient means of maximising regular productivity. There was also a widespread belief that generalist reporters communicate better because they have a stronger audience orientation and are more likely than specialists to be reflecting audience concerns.[1]

The most basic cost in news quality is that generalists are more likely to make errors. Specialists are better equipped to know where further information can be obtained, to detect discrepancies or suspicious developments, to be sensitive to the undercurrents and the hidden agenda as well as the highlights of developments. Their experience helps innoculate them against manipulation by sources.[2] Specialisation is also the pre-condition for an active rather than a passive orientation in reporting, for originating information that might otherwise not become public. Reliance on centrally deployed generalists means those organisations must depend upon four main channels in supplying news:

1 'tip-offs' from social agencies and the public about 'spot news' (accidents, fires etc);
2 the promotional activities of sources seeking publicity;
3 pre-scheduled public events (from sport through Parliament and court hearings to demonstrations); and
4 following up stories that have already appeared in other media, especially by gathering reactions through interviews.

In sum, reliance on generalist reporters forces the organisation to be more derivative.[3]

Even when the commitment is made to full-time coverage of an area, reporters' news gathering routines necessarily fall short of systematic surveillance. The chapter will proceed by examining first the institutional structures and accommodations which affect journalists' access to information on different rounds, and then the source structures and orientations, the interplay of publicity interests, which affect the amount of journalistic power in seeking disclosure and weighing sources' accounts. In examining news gathering, the chapter will focus particularly on four of the most politically consequential rounds—Federal politics, State politics, industrial relations, and business and economics.[4]

## Institutions and Disclosure

### Institutional Channels

The 'purest' form of information gathering, first-hand observation, is only rarely available or sufficient in politically relevant reporting. Following Roscho,[5] reporters are able to be direct observers if newsworthy occurrences are frequent; concentrated in known and open venues; have at least some degree of pre-scheduling; and are describable without the aid of technical expertise. Conversely, if newsworthy developments are dispersed over a large area; closed to outsiders; unpredictable in their timing; or require expertise for interpretation, there is necessarily recourse to second-hand surveillance.

The most common type of first-hand reporting is of pre-scheduled public events. News rounds differ in the number and importance of such set-piece performances. In sport and legal reporting they are central, and much reporting summarises outcomes or reviews performances. In sport there is increasing attention to developments outside the arena (tactics, training etc.), but in law there are strong constraints in probing into these:

> [Reporting the High Court consists of (1) covering what occurs in court and] (2) doing judgments. It's a matter of how much knowledge you build up and your own assessment of significance, tying it in with the rest of the world. It's a different style of reporting. . . . Leaks don't apply at all. There is no way you can break a story about a judgement. You would be kicked out.

Given the soberingly small proportion of news which is directly observed by reporters, the importance of developing routines of second-hand surveillance is clear. The surest and most prolific means is to 'plug' into information generated by other institutions. Journalists' considerations of source suitability 'have one over-riding aim: efficiency'.[6] Their news-gathering routines should offer the best news in greatest volume in the least time-consuming way, with some protection against the competitive danger of being 'scooped', and against the risks of unreliability and uncertainty in controversial areas. This all contrives towards reliance on the routine channels of official institutions.

This reliance is best illustrated by police rounds. 'If a reporter chose to look for crime news on his own initiative, he would have to simulate a policeman patrolling his beat.' The ratio of news gained to labour expended would be grossly impractical. Instead the reporter 'stations himself at police headquarters, thereby utilising an entire police force as his observer and news source'.[7] In consequence, journalists' access to newsworthy information 'is a consequence of the way institutions are organized':[8]

> It is useful then to think of the news as the outcome of two systems which produce accounts: a system of journalistic accounts and, underlying this, a system of bureaucratic accounts. . . . This can be termed the principle of bureaucratic affinity: only other bureaucracies can satisfy the input needs of a news bureaucracy. . . . It is quite understandable then why the beat round focusses on bureaucratic 'fountains of information'. . . . [Even the nature beat] depended on the Forestry service for its news. When it turned out that even rocks, trees, and squirrels are made available to the newspaper through official agencies, then it is no exaggeration to say that the world is bureaucratically organized for journalists.[9]

News mediates the wider socio-political environment to its audience, but in turn its content has been mediated by its reliance on how other institutions make information available. Despite journalists' adversarial aspirations, the preponderance of news stories flow through institutional channels and report the statements of certified office holders.[10]

*Institutional Accommodation*

Where there is continuing news coverage, concentrated upon a particular institution, the work of both sources and reporters is facilitated by institutional accommodation. A physical centre encourages a strong social base, where reporters from different organisations mix on a daily basis. It facilitates formal information dissemination, simplifying the PR efforts of sources and helping the regular productivity of reporters. The advantages for informal information dissemination are even more marked. The regular proximity of reporters to each other and to sources allows frequent contact in a less guarded and calculating atmosphere than in formal dealings.[11] This kind of contact allows reporters to see behind staged appearances, to make deeper assessments of the individuals involved, and to be more informed about the internal manoeuvering and the changing moods and perceptions of major newsmakers.

To illustrate further how the presence and strength of an institutional centre affects news gathering, we can compare two polar types of rounds. At one extreme there is a strong social base, frequent contact with other reporters and with regular sources, the institution has accommodated itself to the presence of the media with well-developed routines of information dissemination, and most of the stories involve similar skills and generate a cumulative store of relevant knowledge. At the other extreme, there is no social base to the round—reporters work out of their head office and see their competitors irregularly; routine information dissemination is haphazard or non-existent; newsworthy events are widely dispersed; there is little continuity of sources over different stories; and there is a variety of story types. The medical round, for example, falls closer to the second than the first end of the spectrum. Medical stories are very diverse: one article on the latest scientific breakthrough, the next on pressure group activities (about e.g. school tuckshops), followed by a heart-tugging feature on say a child's trip to the US for a special operation and finally an economic analysis of health insurance proposals. On these types of rounds, stories run by different news organisations are likely to show more variability because of the lack of strong common inputs. More importantly, whether a potentially newsworthy event falls within the press's purview is far more 'hit-and-miss', often dependent on sources' promotional efforts.

*Comparisons*

The greatest institutional accommodation of the media has occurred in Parliament. The Federal Parliamentary Press Gallery dwarfs any other concentration of journalists. Well in excess of 100 journalists inhabit Parliament House.[12] It houses the executive (Cabinet Ministers), the legislators, the political staffs and the press gallery all in the one building.[13] Information dissemination is prolific with official documents and press releases continually being deposited in the press gallery 'boxes'. Journalists spoke of 'the sheer efficiency of the building'. 'You can go through your whole working life without ever going out of the building.' Others estimated they spent 80–90 per cent of their working day there. Compared with other rounds, there is an avalanche of information. 'It's easy for journalists to live off the boxes' (that is, processing the information routinely distributed). In addition, there is a very active grapevine: 'You pick up so much gossip during the day'. The problem in Canberra is not scarcity of information but quality control. It is easy to get 'a story' but very difficult to get the 'real story'.

There is also a physical centre with a concentration of journalists in the State Parliaments and the industrial rounds. Accommodation in the Trades Halls is more basic than in Parliament. In Melbourne and Sydney, the two largest press rooms, the reporters share a common room—'a ghastly layout'; 'physically there's nothing to commend it'. Any tensions between reporters are easily antagonised. An important secondary site is the local pub where trade union officials tend to fraternise—in Melbourne, the John Curtin Hotel. A few self-consciously sought to avoid this pattern, one saying that while the pub was good for loosening tongues, it too often led to sloppiness and reliance on untested, second-hand information.

Compared with political and business reporting, formal information dissemination is primitive. Official public events—such as Arbitration Commission hearings—command heavy attention, but form a less important part of the round than Parliament does on political rounds. On industrial rounds, even more than elsewhere, reporters rely primarily on regular soundings with their contacts.

Business and economic reporting present a contrasting pattern. Although there is a strong competitive ethos among the senior writers—most are keen consumers of their colleagues' work—they are mainly based in their own head offices, and so personal contact with their competitors is less regular. There are press rooms in the stock exchanges, but most of the reporters who gather there are not the most senior. The core of both business and economic correspondence is the reporting and analysis of official statistics and statements, and, in business, of stock exchange activity and company reports and announcements. Economics writers focus upon '(1) statistics, (2) federal and state bureaucracies, (3) literature from academia, banks etc.'

Estimates of the proportion of information in their reports that became public through routine channels ranged from 60 per cent up to 90 per cent. The skills in such reporting include the capacity for accurate summarising of the essentials, the ability to penetrate any misleading gloss in the information released and in what has been omitted, and the ability to put details into a meaningful context. However, more obviously than most other areas, the quality of business reporting is primarily dependent on the quality of information which is routinely produced by the institutions involved. Systematically scanning business activity is difficult, because, compared with politics, 'the business stage is a lot more fragmented, and not subject to democratic critique. . . . Business leaks too, but less. In politics it is an essential phenomenon'.

Most correspondents felt that the formal disclosure provisions had improved greatly over the last two decades: the range and frequency of both official statistics and required disclosures by companies have grown considerably. Some pointed out that Australian companies were still forced to disclose less than in some other countries, and that there were still loopholes and anomalies. A few, reflecting their sources' attitudes rather than their own interests, thought that current requirements were already too onerous.

## Consequences

The institutional arrangements for the news media also feed into the nature of news gathering and the quality of news indirectly. Any strong concentration of individuals with common interests, dealing with fluid and uncertain situations, inevitably develops an active grapevine, where the latest gossip and conjecture are swapped, measured and frequently embroidered. In Federal Parliament, in particular, the confined space, 'everyone living in everyone's pockets' and all preoccupied with politics easily produces a 'hot-house atmosphere' which itself feeds into the political process.

Although reporters deny that they ever uncritically report rumour (with its connotations of unreliability)[14] they may use it as a tip to pursue:

> I use what other journalists tell me as a starting point, but sometimes if a journalist is faced with a deadline . . .

It is widely acknowledged that the collective mood influences judgments about individual qualities, and trends in relative influence:

> The grapevine is not orchestrated. It's more like a snowball. One story generates another and momentum builds up. It does have an influence on reporting. The Non-Members Bar is ripe ground for picking up stories passed on between reporters.

> We suffer somewhat from pissing in our own pocket.

Less obvious consequences of the concentration of journalists are equally important. The gallery has a strong life of its own which means journalists find their primary social support in the gallery rather than in their own organisations. They are 'a bunch of employees removed from their bosses'. Swapping between different organisations while continuing to report Federal politics is far more common than such swapping on other rounds. The strong social base makes possible a stronger collective dynamic, which produces more autonomy from both their employers and their sources.

The strong competitive and collegial ethos the gallery induces promotes a more active approach to finding out information. Nearly every member of the gallery confirmed that 'there is a massive sense of competition', based less on organisational considerations than a spirit of all against all.[15] It induces a more active and independent professional ethos. Gallery members firmly believe they work harder than other journalists: 'At home we worked a 40 hour week, here it never stops'. On average, this is probably true, although there are, of course, great individual differences. More than other areas there is a merging of work and social life, and work dominates—sometimes to the detriment of family and physical health. Gallery members also believe they have higher standards than other journalists:

> People here are much more into the profession. They talk about it all the time. You never get away from journalists. . . . They study the profession a lot more here.

> In Canberra everyone is tougher, more calculating, more professional.

Naturally these pretensions do not go unchallenged elsewhere. The Federal press gallery has many fierce critics: 'There is a large degree of conceit in the Canberra press gallery, especially the mega stars who think of themselves as more important than the politicians'.

The greater concentration of journalists, reporting through a variety of outlets, gives them greater collective clout with their sources. Greater size can help a gallery reach a 'critical mass' which gives it more impact, and makes it more likely politicians will respond to stories rather than ignore them. This has been one result of the more regular coverage of State politics by broadcasting organisations.

> TV reporting here has improved out of sight. . . . They rarely break new stories, but they help establish a political context. . . . They take up stories. . . . A press conference can now be quite a good grill session.

However, several reporters thought that the smaller size of State galleries, especially because senior correspondents have to cover nearly all aspects themselves, meant they were still 'more easily snowed' by the Government, and (mixing metaphors) it is easier for a State Government to 'pull down the shutters'.

## Source Structures and Relations

No matter how prolific the routine channels, they will never completely satisfy the needs of the news media. The competitive desire for
exclusive stories, the wish to penetrate the public facade—to be 'ahead
of the news' or to go behind it—all require more elaborate and
complex news gathering.[16] The scarcity of first-hand observation, the
delays and omissions in routine channels, and the desire for exclusive
information and penetrating analysis all lead to a strong emphasis on
personal sources. Their centrality means that the structure and orientation of potential sources is of crucial importance in affecting the
quality of reporters' surveillance. The main dimensions of source
structure on a news round are summarised by the answers to three
questions:

1  *Is there monopoly or diversity of potential news sources?* Some rounds,
   such as crime reporting, fall closer to the monopoly end while in
   others, such as industrial reporting, competition and conflict between sources are inherent. A Parliamentary round where the
   Cabinet usually includes the Prime Minister's main rivals within
   the party, and where there is a range of both inter-party and
   intra-party dynamics, has far greater potential diversity than the
   White House round in the USA, where all major sources owe their
   position to the one leader, who has much more control over when
   and where he chooses to be publicly exposed.[17]

2  *How strong are the publicity interests of the main sources?* While most
   groups are agreeable to achieving positive publicity,[18] the most
   important consideration is to trace whether and how an interest in
   achieving news coverage is built into sources' roles. This basically
   stems from having some dependence on large constituencies who
   are reached principally via the media, or from being subject to
   public policy in ways where positive publicity will be helpful in
   achieving the desired outcomes. Politics is the only sphere where
   publicity is the *sine qua non* of successful role performance. For
   pressure groups, trade unions, and some business companies, it
   may be beneficial but subsidiary in achieving their aims. For
   others, some businesses and some research scientists, not directly
   seeking public support, it is optional. For a few, such as organised
   crime figures or espionage agencies, nearly all public attention is
   undesirable.

3  *Are there predominantly regular or transitory relations between reporters
   and sources?* If journalists are to maintain a continuing relationship
   with sources there is incentive for them to maintain good will by
   reporting in ways that sources see as responsible: 'One of the
   safeguards in the system is that people you want to interview are

people you are likely to want to interview again' (TV news director).

On the other hand, with transitory sources who figure in accounts of spot news, or belong to groups only occasionally judged newsworthy, journalists do not have the same immediate incentive to maintain future relationships. Moreover, transitory sources typically lack an understanding of media conventions about when something will be directly attributed (and some journalists tend to be more careless of these with transitory sources). Nor do they have the same understanding of how the flux of conversation in an interview will be transformed into a headline and a story lead, how their statements will look in the cold light of print.

Together these three factors help determine the relative balance of power between journalists and sources and the quality of news in an area. Regular relations with sources produces more responsibility and constraints on both sides. Sources having a promotional orientation not only wish to achieve positive publicity but may be less able to evade critical probing. Publication of critical material is facilitated and can be rewarding when there is a diverse source structure:

> Everything you write will please someone and displease someone else. Everyone in politics has got an enemy. For every action, there is an equal and opposite reaction, and they've all got short memories.

A diverse source structure allows more cross-checking by reporters and so is also conducive to greater accuracy among sources:

> In the fifties the left-wing had X and the right-wing had Y. I'd ring one and get their line, then ring the other and get their line. You could lie one line on top of the other. The actual facts would be dead set; the interpretations would differ.

### Comparisons

The most diverse source structure, incorporating also regular relations with the media and strong promotional interests, occurs in Federal politics. The Gallery's most common sources are the other inmates of the building—MPs and political staffs including press secretaries—the people who are seen most easily and frequently. Sources vary with stories and periods. But in general, the most valued sources centre around the Prime Minister and Cabinet, because 'you must look at where power lies, and get sources there':

> Interviewing a Minister is always good value. The rule is always accept an opportunity to speak to a Minister. It can't be wrong if you do that.

Moreover, one said:

if I get information from a Minister I regard it as good enough to base a
story upon [sufficient in itself], although you often wish you hadn't.

The greatest constraint is that 'Ministers are hard to get to, because
they're so busy'. Backbench MPs 'often reveal what was going on in
the party room' but on policy matters they 'are out in the cold. They
rely on us for information'. 'The Opposition is easy to get to see'
because they are always keen to generate publicity, but Government
sources are generally more important. However, the Opposition is
often the focal point for information from (for example) disenchanted
Public Servants, and so are valuable for delivering tips and even fully
researched stories.

Because both the gallery and the potential reservoir of sources are so
large, individual compatibility and the development of trust are more
important than any forced relationships based on lack of alternatives.
There is such a maze of information emerging in fragmentary ways in
Canberra that one reporter said:

> half the trick to Canberra is knoving who's talking to whom. Public
> servants often talk more freely to lobbyists than to the press. . . . It's
> important to maintain your links around the gallery, to know what
> politicians leak to particular people.

Politically important groups outside Parliament House, such as the
public service and lobby groups, are covered less constantly. The
various lobby groups based in Canberra did not figure generally as
important sources:

> Sometimes they are good, but you must be wary because they are constantly
> selling a line.

> I don't spend a great deal of time with them, but they're important because
> they're a conduit out of Canberra.

Most political reporters agreed that the Public Service is not
covered as well as it should be, that bureaucratic politics are an important but under-reported area of power. One reason offered was that
Parliament House is so overwhelming, and it's 'awkward' to move
around the 'spread out' bureaucratic offices. Some journalists thought
that many public servants had no comprehension of the media. Despite the occasional furore about public service 'moles' leaking,
bureaucratic sources were valued most for their guidance:

> The best source of information in my view is a well-placed public servant.
> You often don't want secrets but good solid background information
> . . . clues and guidance.

> The value of personal contacts can't be over-estimated. . . . The average
> departmental guy knows his area very well. He feels journalists may misrep-
> resent his sacred ground. [There is little] manipulation. It's [usually] either
> frank or non-communicative behaviour.

State politics follows some similar patterns, although power and decision-making are more narrowly concentrated, reducing the diversity of valuable sources. The smaller gallery, the slower pace of State politics and the ability of both sources and reporters to disperse into their home lives, produce a less intense, less frenetic atmosphere. At the same time most State political reporters feel that their contact with politicians is closer than in Canberra: 'The politicians don't feel as threatened. There is more of a family atmosphere.' Others felt that this led to 'everything (being) spoonfed and clubby', so that 'the reporting here is fairly tame'.

Pressure groups and the public service are much less important than in Canberra. Pressure group activity is more sporadic and less professional than federally. The most common explanation offered for the small amount of contact with the public service was the lack of a 'tradition of public servants talking to the press at state level'. This is a vicious circle: because it's hard to get the bureaucrats to talk, reporters tend to contact them less, so the unfamiliarity reinforces their reticence. In addition, state public servants have traditionally been 'more conservative', 'less talented', and 'more involved in administration than policy'. Some state reporters regard them as an unnecessary second best:

> We don't need to talk to public servants because we can talk directly to ministers.

> In state political reporting, you don't need the public service, thank God.

Political as well as structural features explain the lesser contact— although the State bureaucracies are becoming more sophisticated, there was a distinct feeling in several States that access to public servants was declining rather than increasing:

> When I first started, public servants were important, but [the Premier] very consciously tried to silence them. . . . The public servants tell truths which are sometimes embarrassing. Now they won't talk at all. They are very reticent.

Compared with politics, publicity via news is a more incidental part of major figures achieving their aims in business and industrial rounds. Sources thus have more choice in whether and when to give access to journalists. Their primary aims lie elsewhere, and publicity may be but a secondary battleground in pursuing those aims. Although not a universal trend, some sources are willing to mislead journalists because their primary interests dominate to the extent that being caught in a lie may be less damaging than it would be for a politician:

> It's difficult because there is so much at stake, which means people are reluctant to talk to you at all, and those who do are not hesitant about

misleading you. They have got to satisfy their members, the Arbitration Commission and get results etc, all under press scrutiny. That means you must learn who can be trusted, who is knowledgeable etc. . . . You are forced to deal with a lot of people who are very reluctant to come clean with you. Some have astonishingly little compunction about outright lying. (Industrial reporter)

They are aware that when you catch them, they will get lumbered. But mostly getting caught in a lie is less embarrassing for them, than the information getting out at the time. (Business reporter)

Leaking in business is less frequent, 'less sophisticated and more inadvertent'. Moreover 'in business you can't (often) play two sides off against each other' as you can in politics. Publicity via the news media is irrelevant or even harmful to companies pursuing their interests. 'There is no conspiracy in business' but neither through the normal processes is there the same constancy of pressures toward disclosure. In general the most important sources are:

merchant banks, because they are busybodies by nature and clever people; the stockbroking area is a traditional one; [various regulatory agencies] and the federal bureaucracy. There's a lot of good stuff from advertising because marketing is so important. Lobby groups vary in how informed they are, and their closeness to their members.

The main characteristics of these sources are that their role involves collecting sound intelligence. They operate in the 'interfaces' between companies and their environments where information must emerge, and their own vested interests do not tend to produce distorted information.

The source structure of business reporting is overwhelmingly from within business. The main exception is government agencies, involved in monitoring and regulating business:

Proportionally, overall, government sources are not really highly important, but on a particular story, they may be crucial. A known and trusted public servant can make or break a particular story.

Trade unions and pressure groups outside business are rarely sources, primarily because they are seen as having little information of value— 'they rely on us for information'.

Before the 1970s, there was little penetrating reporting of business or publicity about companies' strategies and internal workings. Robert Gottliebsen recalled:

I was the first journalist to interview Ian McLennan, chairman of BHP. There was enormous preparation. The editor checked the questions from Sydney. . . . The first interview with BHP was like a summit. BHP was a shut shop.

Because business reporting has grown only in recent decades, and because individual companies and business executives are less regularly in the news, many journalists felt that business sources had a poor (although improving) understanding of the media:

> Business dealing with the media has shown some, but not great, improvement. They've still got no idea when they should and shouldn't release information. They don't appreciate our problems. . . . Companies vary a lot. Some have a phobia about the press. Some are only willing to talk when things are running well. Generally business people like to talk on background. They're prepared to tell you but not be identified. Politicians like to get their name in the paper. Businessmen only do sometimes.

In industrial relations reporting, the most prolific sources are trade union officials, although nearly all reporters stressed the necessity of having good contacts with both employers and unions. The proportions varied from some who said that they used employers and union officials equally often, to others for whom the ratio was about 2:1 unionists to employers. For those operating from the Trades Hall, there is certainly more casual contact with the union officials. Several stated their preference for dealing with individual companies rather than employers' associations, which vary in how informed they are and lack the authority to compel their member companies to follow particular policies. Because individual companies figure in industrial news only sporadically, the main union leaders are far more experienced in dealing with the media, and more likely to have regular relationships with individual journalists. With one or two exceptions, bureaucratic and legal sources were relatively unimportant.

More than the other rounds, the core of industrial relations reporting is conflict—involving immediate and frequent showdowns over tangible material stakes, with the two sides usually inhabiting different social worlds. Many compared it favourably with reporting political conflicts: 'it's about real actions, not just words'; and the conflicts are real rather than manufactured—'there is less bitchiness for the sake of making a political point just for the sake of winning'. The central conflict is compounded by the constant jostling for position within and between trade unions.

The consequences of the conflict for the ease and accuracy of reporting are mixed. The availability of competing versions constrains both sides to be more accurate, and it is possible to play each against the other to assemble a more comprehensive account. But it also means each individual account must be treated with caution: 'There are always two conflicting points of view. Your job is to decipher.' Less tangibly the round has a more combative ethos: reporters, especially in the pub, are likely to be told, with a minimum of euphemism, what was wrong with their story:

No journalist, except the most tame, can stay on good relations with all trade unionists all the time. . . . They approach you in the pub and say you bastard or come up with information etc. . . . There is a fair amount of vindictiveness. A lot of trade union officials are infected by the old slogans about the press. They don't know how to handle the media.

The prevalence of conflict is also manifested in the unique emphasis on balance as the guiding precept in reporting:

Industrial relations is an area of conflict. . . . To steer a middle ground can be a very nerve-wracking path. . . . If in any story or comment piece you were positive about one side over the other, that is certain death.

There's no problem in getting on with both employers and trade unionists. I'm not taking sides. I treat both equally.

Political reporters also mention balance, especially in election campaigns, but unlike industrial relations, many political reporters challenge the idea that balance is a worthwhile ideal, and it seems a less inhibiting factor in political reporting.

### Source Relations and Sycophancy

The importance of sources in gathering news poses dilemmas for reporters in maintaining close access and confidence of sources while also reporting their activities fully. Most have wrestled with dilemmas from balancing the conflicting considerations:

You are as good as your contacts, but you are also a creature of your contacts. There is always a price to pay for contacts.

The dangers in reporting politics are that you can become too close to your sources so that you are beholden to them. It can be a narrow road. All journalists say this. . . . How is a journalist ever going to get the best stories if you're going to be a prick with them. You've got to cultivate a relation that is very frank.

In journalists' comments, the greatest concern was expressed about self-censorship:

You use the pollies and they use you. You get big stories by who you work for, being good mates, and because they know you will print them straight and not dig around. You depend on that relationship for a lot of political stuff. The obvious corollary is that you don't do the dirt unless it is almost forced on you.

But the claim by one that 'you can only write 10 percent of what you know' seems more like a gambit of pub conversation than an accurate description. The evidence for self-censorship seems to relate mainly to publishing negative evaluations of principal figures or revelations about their personal foibles. It may well be true that there are differential standards of evidence required before major sources are publicly criticised, and an unwillingness to risk source displeasure on minor stories. But on important stories when the reporter actually has hard evidence rather than shrewd suspicions, there was little evidence of self-censorship in order to maintain access.

A more subtle aspect of source–journalist relations has more far-reaching consequences. Consider the potential role strains in journalists' relations with sources—dependence combined with a mandate to be 'watchdogs'. Kudos results from a steady stream of stories based upon access but cultivating such closeness is in tension with the need for an adversary scepticism.[19] Journalists' proximity to power and intimate knowledge of its exercise and yet their own relative impotence and marginal status may heighten the psychological importance of their acceptance by sources. Famous American columnists Joseph and Stewart Alsop expressed it transparently:

> A reporter can have no more satisfying moment than the moment when a man in a high position says, 'I don't really mind talking to you, because you know what I'm talking about.' That really happened to one of us once.[20]

When journalists develop close regular relations with sources, they become an important reference group, affecting their own perspectives and aspirations. Political reporters often seem to adopt the gladiatorial style of the politicians they report. Business reporters, perhaps reflecting their contact with businessmen, tend to be more ambitious than other reporters, are the most likely to express discontent with their income as journalists, and many leave especially to go into public relations:

> The best a journalist can hope for is [a fairly modest salary] with no perks. And the pyramid gets very narrow. There is a real problem with papers, with nowhere further up to go. Most papers have had a lot of finance editors, because the papers are not prepared to pay the fees they can get outside.

> It's a make-believe world, hob-nobbing with the rich as observers, which sometimes leads to envy, especially if you realise that [some are] not bright and you could do better.

On the other hand business writers are rarely involved in the Australian Journalists' Association, while many industrial reporters are very active in the union. Some were prominent, for example, in the major journalists' strike in May 1980 ('The deals that were done!'). They tend to be very aware of awards and conditions and to follow closely the rules laid down—but with less evidence of any relative deprivation flowing from the social milieu of their work.

It is not simply a matter of reference groups. Informed reporting requires 'role-taking' by reporters, learning to appreciate how the world looks to their sources, how they are likely to respond to developments, and to understand the nuances and implications of their comments, to become absorbed into their sources' world:[21]

> The result in extreme form is that reporters become spokesmen for their news sources rather than dispassionate observers. They become sloppy about recognising that alternative views may exist and about digging out and including alternative views in their stories.[22]

Such advocacy, which Sigal calls 'beat parochialism', is most likely when there are no countervailing influences. A speciality is most prone to advocacy when:

1 there is a monopoly of source type, and
2 little resistance from employers, competitors or audience to the legitimacy of their viewpoints.

The risk is smaller in political and industrial reporting since both have conflict between sources built in, and are written for an audience of mixed partisan views.

Advocacy is seen most obviously in industry newsletters and magazines, such as *Ad News*, where both audience and sources point in the same direction. It tends to be present also where the round constitutes one policy area within government, such as defence or primary industry, where there is little pressure for news reports to attend to competing public priorities but strong incentive to reflect the demands from within its own area. The ABC Rural Department's daily radio program, for example, was often referred to by others in the ABC as the Country Party Hour. Two prominent defence reporters described their own work in the following terms:

> (I am like a film buff who is committed to film, although) I don't mind what level. I understand competing demands and constraints.

> You get some national security information and you learn to live with it. The problem with being around a long time is that you get a lot of information that you don't use. You protect your own interests as a citizen ... [They are details which] wouldn't interest the public anyway. . . . It's an area where you need to have an adversary relation. They realise that. . . . I see part of my role as being an advocate for defence. I see weaknesses in the system, the whole machinery.

Of the four areas examined here, advocacy for their sources would seem most a danger in business and economic reporting. In economics, the single most influential source of information and interpretation is the Federal Treasury, which has its influence not only through specialist economic writers, but via the Federal Press Gallery. Treasury's influence is so central that one economics writer felt in the early 1980s, that '*the* economic reporting issue is "are we acting as a voluntary mouthpiece for Treasury?"' But, economics commentary has been a growth industry, and with its spread into banks and broking firms, Treasury's dominance has been somewhat eroded since. The politics of Treasury, varying with the attitudes of top personnel and their relations with the Government, have also been modified.

Business reporting—writing for a business audience while relying on business sources—is potentially prone to sycophancy, and there is considerable stroking of the business ego. However countervailing influences severely qualify sycophantic tendencies: there is a strong occupational credo that the reporter's role is 'to serve the public, not business'. The main general pressure which journalists mentioned as emanating from business was not against the disclosure of individual wrong-doing or poor performance, or to take sides in particular issues, but rather there were 'criticisms that you were trying to talk down the economy, and not boost business confidence'. Business leaders wanted the press to be on the side of optimism.[23] Almost without exception,[24] the journalists rejected this:

> It's not our role to talk the economy up or down. Any journalist who thinks that ought to get out. . . . If journalists try to lean in one direction, it becomes a controlled, directed press.

The common view that the 'best market is the best informed market' leaves great scope for embracing general business rhetoric while also airing critical perspectives and highlighting individual abuses.

## Organisational Attitudes

The news reporting of different areas is affected not only by institutional and source structures, but by organisational commitment. All four rounds considered here are among the most important reporting positions in news organisations, staffed by senior reporters, who stay in the role for long periods, and who, despite various frustrations, overwhelmingly find many intrinsic satisfactions working in the area. Reporters covering Federal politics and business and economics tend to have somewhat higher organisational status and autonomy than those doing State politics and industrial relations, although there are many variations.

The commitment to business and industrial reporting is much more variable than to politics. In the content analysis, the major difference between the quality papers and the TV news in the topics covered was the neglect of business and economics in the broadcasting media:[25]

> We don't go heavily into variations in the price of gold, the stock exchange etc., because there are a lot of pitfalls there. Our chances of doing it properly are remote. Is it usable information to our viewers? Those who are into that area know where they can get that information. That's not to say

that we ignore it. We do finance when it's important to our audience. (TV news director)

Industrial relations reporters were particularly disparaging about the ignorant and sensationalist coverage by news organisations which cover only major stories:

[Among news organisations which take industrial reporting seriously] the effort and the understanding and the accuracy are there. It varies with the individual and the bureau whether it's fair to good. Then you get down to the dangerously ill-informed realm which see industrial reporting as a source of beat ups. The reporting of industrial relations there is on a par with their reporting of everything else. If it's not on a government handout, it's awful. Commercial radio and TV, the *Daily Mirror*, are doomed to make horrible errors. If you look at *The Age* or *The Sydney Morning Herald* on major stories you find that it's all covered and no errors. That is not a fluke. . . . People who criticise industrial reporting often overlook the distinction between the two [groups].

Business and economic reporting have been the most dynamic areas in changing news practices. As economic management became a central and contentious political issue, and as the uncertainties and fluctuations of the business environment increased, economic and business correspondents became an elite within journalism. Compared to other areas, their morale and self-confidence are high.

Their growth was facilitated by several peculiarities. Unlike almost any other area within a newspaper, finance:

1 has its own regular section and so is not subject to competition with general news, and
2 is not required to attract a large audience, but to cater to its own constituency.

Writers have different attitudes as to how 'popular' they attempt to be, but political journalists would be unlikely to express themselves as this economic journalist did:

I write for a small audience first. Unless I gain the satisfaction of my peers of economists, you can just forget about it. If I wrote for one million people, and if my peers thought it was a load of rubbish, it wouldn't be worthwhile.

An historical peculiarity of Australian economic reporting has been 'the very self-confident mode of economic reporting which has been the speciality in Australia . . . based on the assertive pronouncement of trends and signs'. Far more than in other areas, economics writers openly proclaim their desire to have an impact on economic policy and debate. They are unafraid of opinionation and prescription:

Basically I write opinion. I analyse the news rather than write news.

> The motivation of economics journalists is to change the course of economic
> management. They write for the elite—for [the head of Treasury]....
> Economics writers have an incredible amount of licence.... I couldn't
> believe it when I got here.... I was the authority. That was accepted, from
> day one as a very junior journalist. Just say what I think.

The opinionated genre is self-perpetuating. It is buttressed by the
area's complexity and its scientific pretensions.

> There's licence because no one in the papers understands economics....
> The nature of journalism is such that it doesn't attract many numerate
> people —they're mainly artsy people. Editors know that economics
> is very important, but they're not interested in it.... You get someone
> you can trust, and give them free reign. The arrogance has built up in
> that environment. ...In editorial conference...they have furious
> arguments about an educational editorial. Everyone is an expert on
> education because everyone went to school. It's much easier to disagree
> with a political columnist. (In economics they just say you write it.)

Several journalists volunteered favourable comparisons of Australian business and economic reporting with US reporting, precisely
because of this assertive style: 'The New York Times and The Wall St
Journal produce twenty-word quotes from the captains of industry'.
Naturally the assertive tone and its temptations to lapse into the
parading of opinion also has its critics:

> Business reporting has got silly. Every Tom, Dick and Harry is writing
> articles. It's got absurd. They are most concerned with their own opinions.

> It has given too much power to some immature and inadequately trained
> people.

In nearly every one of these special characteristics of business
and economic reporting there is a strong contrast with industrial relations. Unlike business reporting, industrial news competes with general
news and its newsworthiness is more selective, stemming basically
from the possible effects on the public at large, usually the disruption
from strikes. While business and economic reporting has been transformed enormously in response to its changing environment, industrial relations reporting has lagged behind the changes in practice.
With the partial exception of the Fairfax quality papers, there is little
to indicate how, since the advent of the Hawke Government and its
accord with the ACTU, the industrial relations environment has been
transformed.

There is less interpretation and opinionation in industrial reporting.
Most, but far from all, industrial reporters are broadly in sympathy
with trade union aspirations and positions, yet this is rarely apparent
in news coverage. Indeed industrial coverage is a good antidote to
general claims that news coverage simply reflects either reporters'
attitudes or the attitudes of dominant sources. Moreover, the long-

term trends have been in 'contradictory' directions: employers have become more important sources in industrial reporting but serious industrial coverage has become less anti-union.

Industrial reporting attracts more criticism by other journalists than any other round:

> I help judge the Perkin award each year. Only once have I seen a good set of articles on industrial disputes. You never hear what is the essence of disputes. (Sir Theodore Bray)
>
> Industrial reporting is not done well anywhere. They give effects but not the causes.

Similarly, industrial reporters have more complaints about how stories are treated and how little is used, and (with important variations between organisations) are more critical of their own organisations' performance than reporters on the other rounds considered:

> Editors don't see the news value in industrial health and welfare matters. There are more man days lost in industrial accidents than disputes. Today there are a few more stories that indicate that. They feel that there's not news interest in those topics compared with a strike, which is emotive.
>
> The assumption is always that people on strike are in the wrong in [my paper]. Even to the extent where trade union leaders are described as idiots ... I don't think the facts of big strikes are fully or properly reported... The main weakness is that the human side of trade unions are not considered enough. Stories where the union helps an injured person etc. are seldom recorded...The press is sometimes the employers' voice ...You never hear about the good things trade unions do.

Behind the conflicts with news organisations and the widespread criticisms is the reality that industrial relations poses severe problems for news reporting (naturally accentuated if there is only a casual commitment to coverage). It is complex ('a labyrinth') and full of its own jargon:

> The national summit [in 1983] showed that a lot of employers didn't know what a centralised wage-fixing system was. I make a point of always putting in an explanation of what a term means e.g. productivity bargaining etc.

This complexity is of little interest to the public:

> One of the great weaknesses is being able to get enough space to tell the real story because of the complexity of claims and counter claims. If you are going to give the history of the claims it means you need half the paper and it only interests a limited number of readers. The fine details have got little to do with the general public.

Public statements during disputes involve the union's ambit claims (which anticipate bargaining and compromise, and so are more extreme than the expected outcome) and a good deal of bluff by both sides, including postures of intransigence and outrage. ('It takes a lot of time to get to know the participants, what they really mean when they say something.') This makes it difficult to report the real state of negotiations, and lends itself to 'beat ups' by news organisations:

> the deliberate misunderstanding of the ambit question in the Arbitration Commission always upset me. People would use stories about extravagant wage claims that were only extravagant because the system required them to be.

Perhaps, even more than in other areas, the accurate reporting of public claims and statements can be substantially misleading.

## Conclusion

Thomas Jefferson, in an uncharacteristically inane remark, once proclaimed:

> Were it left to me to decide whether we should have a government without newspapers, or newspapers without government, I should not hesitate for a moment to prefer the latter.

Without exploring further this government-less society, it is difficult to imagine the contents of its news. The routine productivity of news organisations is made possible by feeding upon the information which other institutions generate, of which the many layers of government—its struggles for political dominance and over policy direction; and its social agencies from the police to schools, from taxation to tourism—are the most prolific. Moreover, officially certified information is especially valued by news organisations, confronted by contention and ambiguity, in a world which grants them only sporadic and imperfect access.

News is the product of a series of transactions between media organisations and their environment. The quality of news is obviously dependent on organisational attributes. The constant pressures to productivity are conducive more to extensive scanning than intensive examination:

> The pressure is to be well-informed in many areas. In my position you must be a dabbler in everything.

> The big problem of gallery journalists, which people don't understand, is that one day you will write an article on the state of the economy, next day about the Sinai task force, next uranium, then pecuniary interests of Ministers. They've all got so many issues connected with them, and that's left out all the straight politics, like the Liberals and the Nationals in Queensland. The demands are enormous, and you must read most articles in most papers each day. You're working so quickly and taking snap decisions. . . . The big decisions are what you hit. You can't spend a lot of time getting on

top of a story if you don't write it. Instincts are very important, how you feel about people. Judgments. Again, you've got to do a bit of digging and probing or you won't get anything.

Less obviously, news quality also depends on the nature of the environment—whether it lends itself to easy surveillance, how reliably and conveniently different institutions within it make newsworthy information available, the publicity interests of principal sources and how their aims and conflicts interact to aid or inhibit disclosure:

1 News is a parasitic institution. It is dependent on the information-generating activities of other institutions. Where there is not a strong institutional focus with regular channels of disclosure, newsworthy events are more likely to pass undetected. The most informed and penetrating reporting occurs when concentrations of journalists and their sources allow continuing scrutiny, so that negative news becomes more difficult to conceal or contain.

2 Where there is a source monopoly, which reporters must use on a regular basis, and which has discretion about whether and how to get publicity, source power is greatest, and the dangers of self-censorship, sycophancy and skewed disclosure are likewise greatest. Where there are diverse sources with a strong interest in gaining publicity, which are regularly accountable to media scrutiny, journalists' power and news quality are greater. Conflict between sources of diverse viewpoints allows more cross-checking and facilitates the disclosure of critical information.

# 3
# News Values

Some events are judged newsworthy, others not. Princess Di's haircut can become front page news, mine passes unnoticed. Some people pursue publicity unsuccessfully; others can't avoid it even though they want to. Something is hot news today, but stale next week, and of little interest last week. Chapters 1 and 2 considered the production and supply of news. In building an explanatory frame, they are indispensable but incomplete. They illuminate the availability of information but not judgments about its suitability.[1] They provide no sense of what shapes demand, of what constitutes newsworthiness, or of the presentational formats in which news is conveyed. They give no clue that news values are embedded in the way information is gathered and processed:

> Attending a news conference inside a newspaper office, the outsider is at first startled that the entire business of the conference appears to consist of swapping headline-like sentences, each of a few words. . . . The details of the story are still uncertain, and the headline-like description summarises the major news 'angle' . . . . Thus members of a non-routine occupation which values individuality, personality and creativity are nevertheless programmed by organisational requirements to talk like precocious parrots swapping tomorrow's headlines.[2]

There are several dimensions of news values. The most basic is market demand: how perceptions of the audience and its interests affect news production. Feedback from the audience is at best sporadic and an indirect influence on news. The most continuing external reference point for news judgment is provided by competition, both direct commercial competition and in the general competitive ethos which pervades journalism. The final substantive section considers the formats and orientations basic to news processing. The chapter concludes with a consideration of the nature and role of news values.

## Audience

For most news organisations, even the ABC, a central measure of success is the securing of large audiences. All news organisations, but particularly popular newspapers, place great stress on communicating with, and reflecting, their community:

> I came to *The Sun* because I believe it's the best paper in Australia for communication. *The Sun* gets the story across better than any other paper . . . . *The Sun* is closer to a far wider range of people than *The Age*.
>
> I admittedly am biased, but *The News*, all things considered, is one of the best papers in the world. I don't mean it's *The New York Times* or *Le Monde*, but it very closely identifies with the community in which it works. It usually talks about what Adelaide is talking about, e.g. if there's a sensation in the football. [It takes issues up] very quickly. It's a very fast paper . . . . It looks good. Technically it's very good. There's usually skill and occasionally it's done with flair . . . . Popular taste exists and popular papers exist to sell.

In story selection and presentation there is constant effort to reflect and capture the public's concerns. Stories are presented in a way that maximises their apparent relevance to the audience ('How X will affect you'). Great energy and imagination are expended to find light, interesting stories which are thought to have wide appeal.[3] There can be no doubt that perceived audience interest is a central factor in organisational decisions, and that it constitutes a central element of the political economy of news. It is an element often omitted in critiques of the news which call simply for higher quality without reference to audience support for, or even tolerance of, such measures. It is also commonly omitted in left-wing accounts of media political economy, which tend to focus on ownership and control with little attention to audience demand.[4] At best it is dismissed by the assumption that current tastes are shaped by what the public has been fed, and will change when the media change.

In direct contrast, editors speak of public interest in stories in an unconstrained way, as an independent entity of which they have clear knowledge.[5] There is little acknowledgement of how public interest may be affected by the media, although some take the position that 'the public doesn't miss what it doesn't see'.[6] Especially in the popular press and television, editors picture themselves as responding to, rather than influencing, public responses; as passive and all but powerless in affecting audience concerns and perceptions.

It is easy to criticise both the theoretical and evidential bases of these views, but harder to substitute others. Journalists' knowledge of the audience comes from four main sources: changes in consumer behaviour; unsolicited feedback through letters and telephone calls; market research surveys; and informal feedback from 'near-audiences' of colleagues, sources, and others.

Changes in consumer behaviour are commercially crucial. News executives are greatly concerned about whether sales or ratings rise, or their competitive situation changes. Sometimes monitoring these fluctuations establishes a main selling point (e.g. Bingo, a dramatic story), but often it is difficult to relate format and content changes with any precision to trends in consumer behaviour.

Unprompted feedback comes from a minute proportion of the audience:[7]

> People are not generally very responsive to papers. If you got five phone calls about a story, you'd think you had touched a public nerve. (Business editor)

Although there was more feedback to TV, nearly all journalists felt the limited feedback that did come was a faulty indicator both of representativeness and validity:

> In news only one in 100 who wish to say something nice do so, while nine out of ten who want to complain do so.

> We don't get a lot compared to the size of the audience, but certainly some. It's more likely to be critical, and often from vested interests . . . . The allegations of bias usually show the bias of the sender.

Editors differed in describing their response to feedback:

> You're a fool if you isolate yourself and don't listen to criticism and then step back and assess it . . . . The audience has an inherent understanding of fair play which overrides personal biases. If we over-step that, they respond en masse.

> Sometimes we get ear-bashed over something, like a doctor listening to a hypochondriac. We must steel ourselves to treat them objectively . . . .

Certainly the general trend from this one tangible, spontaneous source of audience views is hardly a force to raise standards:

> It's funny sometimes. You get more feedback from e.g. a wrong word in the crossword than a brilliant feature.

> It's surprising what turns people on and off. Sometimes we hardly get any at all. We do something which appears of fringe interest e.g. the biggest cabbage and we get stacks from people saying I've grown a bigger one.

The third form of information about the audience, market research surveys, presently plays 'a marginal role in the news'.[8] Journalists usually disparage them, partly from a belief that such prosaic numbers could never match their peerless professional instincts. Editors are less dismissive. Their main use seems to be in selling market profiles to advertisers and for that reason surveys are becoming more common. However, they are not usually thought to be of direct help in editing:

> We've done very limited surveys. They're a very rough guide. I'm not fascinated by them. If you had asked Sydney people should we build an Opera House at Bennelong Point, who would have known?

> We do a bit of audience research. It's very complicated and expensive and not that revealing. We're about to do another one.

Having outlined the weaknesses of these three sources of evidence about the audience, it is timely to recall the apparent certainty of news executives and sometimes reporters about the audience. In fact, their presumptions about audience interests are often wrong, as Henningham has shown.[9] Despite the paucity of evidence, questions about the audience are not issues of live concern to journalists, and hardly seem to enter into decisions about stories:

> The 'problem' of the audience is not an urgent one for the communicator. You do not find people wandering around in a state of existential angst wondering whether they are 'communicating' or not. You do, on the other hand, find an intense obsession with the packaging of the broadcast, and comparative evaluation of others' goods . . . .

> Newsmen see themselves as in a position to take the role of the audience in respect of standards, taste and comprehension . . . .

> Ultimately the newsman is his own audience. When he talks of his professionalism, he is saying that he knows how to tell his story.[10]

The final source of knowledge about the audience is thus a combination of professional assumptions, of informal discussion with colleagues and, less importantly, others nearby, including friends and sources. In terms of representativeness this is the least satisfactory evidence. But it has compensations: it is plentiful and frequent; gathered not through special efforts from strangers, but as part of the daily routines; it comes from people well-known to the journalist and so their biases and importance can be more easily judged than can anonymous phone calls; it is directly pertinent to stories rather than a series of remote statistics or sales figures. It is little wonder then that most journalists seemed to endorse the view that 'feedback is mainly from players in the game'. For most purposes, the anonymous audience can be assumed to be an extension of the immediate audiences.

In sum there is a lack of satisfactory evidence about the audience but more elaborate and expensive measures are not likely to be particularly enlightening or contribute to improved quality. In some ways the quest for the audience is chimerical. There is necessarily an unequal involvement in news between producers and consumers. While the

production of news is constant, frenetic and involving for the participants, its consumption is often casual and unreflective. People may
not be giving the TV their full attention; whether and how they read
the paper may depend on the vagaries of each individual person's day.
The major preoccupations of producers may not even penetrate the
consumers' attention. They are often oblivious to the competitive
ploys being waged to woo their custom. To enshrine this lack of
opinion as the centrepiece of news communication will more often
produce disappointment than revelation.

The lack of clear evidence allows contradictory views of the public
to co-exist. Some are flattering to their audience, perhaps as a vehicle
for flattering their own performance: 'The public recognises sensationalism when they see it. They see who has integrity'. (TV news
director). Others spoke of the public with despair or disdain, or made
it a decidedly secondary aspect of their work:

> The greatest response was when I was covering football part-time. People
> take national affairs in their stride, but they get more upset about trivia
> ....People either don't read industrial stories or they have strong
> preconceptions.... [One particular story got a response.] That was
> trivialised enough for people to understand.

Whichever of these views is more accurate (remembering that different news organisations do have different audiences), those who adopt
the strongest audience orientations tend to agree with H.L. Mencken:
'Nobody ever went broke underestimating the great American public'.
Audience considerations are commonly seen as a force against more
serious or challenging journalism, even by those who embrace them:

> You have to take notice of feedback, but still pursue journalistic standards,
> even if it does offend some. There's a place for lightness. (TV news
> director)

> *The News* got down to the level of the man in the street under my
> editorship. While there was time for politics etc., you've got to get down to
> human interest, people. (former editor)

Vertical imagery dominates, and the constant danger is seen as getting
'above' the audience.[11]

Such audience concerns can be used to assert editorial authority.
News executives' presumed knowledge of the audience is a means of
controlling reporters, who possess more specialist knowledge of their
own area.[12] It can even lead to the belief that 'the best stories were
written when you didn't understand something'.[13]

In conclusion, incorporating audience considerations into decision-
making poses unresolved problems. It presents problems of implementation. A pre-occupation with changes in audience interests can
'de-stabilise' organisational formats and procedures:

If you panic each time the ratings go down, you will have a panic program. It's the same with callers. Some are round the twist, some are pertinent .... You've got to have the thickest skin, not let feedback rule your life, but look for warning signs. (TV news director)

It is not only a problem of marrying means and ends. There are questions about the priority of and relation between different ends. There is an uneasy tension between, on the one hand, democratic rhetoric, where the size of the audience is seen as a virtue in itself and as authenticating the work of the media, and, on the other, considerations of increasing news quality, of acting as a watchdog or promoting controversy, where the audience is often spoken of as a constraint. Many journalists have strong conceptions about the proper role of the news media, about normative ideals which should guide and constrain their activities, which may or may not align with audience appeals.

Many journalists resist the tendency for audience concerns to make news less serious and challenging, either by challenging the view of the audience on which it is premised, or by challenging the priority accorded the audience over other professional goals. Some even picture a direct opposition between audience and journalistic concerns:

> Current affairs has two choices—to titillate the mass audience or to present stories which challenge authority and generate friction. (ABC reporter)

Most journalists, especially in senior positions, would see audience considerations as more central and more benign. However many ambiguities and variations remain. The language of democratic rhetoric and mass appeal can easily slide into a celebration of conformity, where popularity becomes the measure of truth.

## Competition

The relative vacuum left by the paucity of audience feedback is more than filled by the immediate influences of competition. The constant reappearance of competitors' products provides a measure of performance which matches the frenetic rhythms of news production. Competition exists in an institutional sense, where two or more news organisations compete for shares of the one market. Beyond this a competitive ethos pervades journalism with many indirect influences on news practices.

### Institutional Competition

The most acute institutional competition is in TV news.[14] It is:

1  dynamic (TV ratings fluctuate far more than newspaper sales),
2  largely zero-sum (to the extent that one news service gains ratings, another usually loses), and

3   there are significant stakes involved, with immediate rewards and penalties in revenue and prestige.

As a result, although some avowed professional satisfaction was paramount, the role of ratings is central:

> You can't avoid being caught up in the ratings. The industry lives by it
> . . . . A lot of what you can do depends on journalistic success. If you get the ratings you can do more.

In the accounts of TV news directors, success in ratings is affected by several factors. Some are external to the news program itself, such as promotions: 'we've done promotions to get people to watch it. It made a change. It's important, but it's not the only thing', and, more importantly, the 'lead-in' and 'lead-out' programs, which contribute to the 'audience flow' for the news. Vincent Smith, for example, felt that a turning point for ATN7 news, which had been climbing in the ratings, was Ten's success with the 5.30 program *Perfect Match*, many of whose viewers subsequently stayed with Ten's news.

The internal factor most cited by TV news directors was the quality and popularity of the news announcer.[15] Some said that this could be worth ten ratings points:

> The announcer is vital. It doesn't matter how good the journalistic staff is, if the announcer is no good, you're stuffed. All the energy must be channeled through him.

Most emphasised that competition was less over producing 'scoops' and originating news, than in how it was presented:

> There's a surprising number of nights when [the commercial channels] run in tandem . . . . We're basically covering the same type of story. Occasionally one station gets a scoop on another on a big story, but not very often. Competition is on presentation.

Thus there is a constant preoccupation with the quality of production, of newsfilm and of 'pace':

> We evolved a slick presentation. Keep the stories short, aim for pace all the way through.
> Pictures do sell news. The best talking head in the world won't keep people long.

When talking of story selection, audience considerations were paramount:

> I think that TV like some papers often tries to be too clever. It needs to remember that it's going into sitting rooms and talking to quite ordinary people, that those ordinary people are interested in quite ordinary things. They want to know what's going on, but they have to be told in a way they can understand. They want to be amused, but they are a lot more selective

and easily offended than newspaper readers. A lot of old-fashioned news-paper and magazine ideas work—*Women's Weekly* ideas . . . All that can tend to make TV news so much pap. There's also got to be a hardness, a reality. It's got to be people news for people viewers . . . . 'Heartbeat and Tear-drops'. The stories that affect everyone are the ones to do.

We pitch it at the average TAB punter, at Mrs Moorabbin, not the snobs in Toorak. It's very much a blue collar service. There's a certain element of entertainment. Unabashedly we have a lot of human interest. We have the right mixture of local, national and overseas news plus sport, weather etc.

Last, but possibly not least, news directors were adamant that quality is central to ratings success. The viewer wanted reliability, credibility, consistency. Several commented on the futility of trying to chase ratings with 'stunts', or with many format or content changes:

[Our network] takes life very seriously. We're not into happy talk news . . . . The key to our success is consistency. TV news is nothing without two things—credibility and consistency . . . . Our job is to serve as the conduit through which information flows. There's audience acceptance if the conduit is always open.

Reliability—consistently select information people would choose themselves to know, plus information you feel they should know. I hold no truck with stunts to capture high ratings. It's ethically irresponsible, but it also has a derogatory effect on your standing.

## Competitive Ethos

Journalism's competitive ethos produces almost a war of all against all. It is institutionally irrelevant—Canberra press gallery journalists compete against each other, even though their publications sell in different cities. Sometimes it may even be institutionally perverse—ABC News competing against ABC Current Affairs, different Fairfax publications against each other. The competitive ethos sometimes extends to indi-vidualism and competition within organisations to see who gets the best story.[16] There is little collaborative or team journalism.

In an occupation with few clear criteria of success, competition provides a tangible measure of one's performance. With little feedback from the audience, and feedback from sources at best an ambiguous indicator, competitive success is a principal source of satisfaction. Being competitive almost becomes synonymous with pride in one's work:

The most enjoyable has got to be if you've got a break on the others—saying something that has not been said before, getting a good run and seeing the others responding to your story.

If you have any pride in your job and paper you must have [a strong sense of competition]. You don't like being beaten.

Even those who personally disavow strong competitive attitudes are not immune:

> I do competition more as a game than anything else . . . . I'm not personally very competitive. [After being on the round some time] I noticed I enjoyed breaking stories more and it used to get under my skin if I missed a story. But I tended not to gloat or let it get to me. That is self-defeating. As often as you get to gloat you end up with ashes in your mouth. There is a bit of one-upmanship on the round.

In the looser, non-institutional competition, there is no official, external scoreboard like TV ratings. This allows great scope for selective perception—apparently a psychologically benign system which allows a sense of winning to many more than it forces to feel the gall of defeat.[17]

The greatest competitive success is to break a major story which others then must follow up.[18] However this is relatively rare, and may often be due more to good fortune than great initiative:

> There's more merit in writing five news stories very well and getting all the facts, rather than one scoop, which may simply have come from a phone call from a source . . . . I'm not denying the adrenalin rush I got when I got the X story, because I know every other journalist would have wanted it. But I knew it was a matter of luck.

Most often competition is less on revealing whole new stories than on the further investigation and treatment of stories which are to some extent common to all.

Competition plays a critical role in news judgment. At any given moment the vague prescriptions of newsworthiness receive force and direction from what other news organisations are producing. Editors, reporters and sub-editors all tend to be keen consumers of other organisations' news,[19] and they provide a ready source of story ideas. ('I find the mentality in some afternoon papers of just following what's in the morning papers.' Afternoon paper reporter.) This mutual attention is the most immediate influence on news priorities:

> Competition is so deeply embedded in the ideology and occupational language of [British] journalism that 'news' comes to be seen as (a) what the competition is saying, and (b) what the competition is not saying, but would if it could.[20]

The ironic effect is that competition encourages conformity. One apt image likened Washington correspondents to a pack of beagles: 'The beagle is a highly competitive dog, but he is always ready to follow uncritically any other beagle who claims to have sniffed a rabbit.'[21] The forces for consensual judgment are heightened by the close proximity which competing reporters share on some rounds. Their subsequent 'shop talk'[22] helps form common news judgment.

This tendency is typically decried.[23] Although sometimes the news consensus that so develops may be out of touch with key aspects of the situation,[24] it can also help innoculate reporters against source manipulation, while collective problem-solving is often superior to individual efforts amid general ignorance and uncertainty.

The fate of a particular story is often tied to how it evolves competitively. It may fall at the first hurdle—if news executives are reluctant to take the risks of committing themselves without the support of others having done similar stories. While the occupational credo stresses scoops and exclusives, according to some reporters, the attendant risks make many news executives nervous. It is recognition in the priorities of other news organisations which most clearly authenticates a story's significance.

Competitive influences work somewhat erratically on the responses to others' exclusives. News organisations are reluctant to re-do 'stale' news unless there are fresh developments or details to report—even though their particular audience may not have seen the story. Competitive jealousies may dispose them to downplay the story's significance. In the information overload and segmented competition of reporting from Canberra, several correspondents thought that there was now less inclination to follow up others' stories. As a result, there is less collective pressure for further revelations on marginal stories.

However, competition can also enhance the development of a new story. Once it has become public with sufficient force and authority, competition is likely to keep it in the news, as different organisations pursue different aspects of it:

> Editors consider themselves obliged to run a story once it 'makes the news', regardless of their personal preferences.[25]

Competitive pressures help build a total momentum, which can produce sharp changes in news attention. The advent of a major new story, especially when it is broken by one of the 'opinion leaders', often changes news priorities. During the Vietnam War, following Harrison Salisbury's visit to Hanoi in Christmas 1966 and again following the revelations of the My Lai massacre, news attention suddenly became more sensitised to the issue of Vietnamese civilian casualties.[26] Such short-term changes in the focus of news interest tend to be self-sustaining. Somewhat like paradigm changes in science,[27] new definitions of importance and new approaches generate a rapid accumulation of fresh examples. Although such changes in news fashions may reflect a shallow thirst for novelty, the readiness of sources to fan new bandwagons, and unreflective conformity, they also demonstrate how competition makes news a more dynamic social force.

In conclusion, the most basic question is whether competition

improves or detracts from the quality of news. The vice most commonly attributed is that competitive pressures encourage sensationalism,
'beating up' the significance of a story. Competition is said to favour
the spectacular over the sound,[28] to emphasise scoops over careful
analysis. Besides a distorted sense of significance, competition is also
commonly given as a reason for errors made due to excessive haste
because of wanting to gain a competitive advantage.

In some ways, competition heightens the power of sources—
reporters may be less likely to seek alternative views when they are
receiving exclusive information.[29] On large competitive rounds with
concentrated sources of information, it allows, as Crouse said of
Nixon's press secretary, Ronald Ziegler, a 'divide and rule' strategy,
made possible because he knew 'one reporter will always cut another
reporter's throat for even the simplest scoop'.[30] Such attitudes clearly
inhibit the potential to pursue possible common interests, such as
reforming procedures of information distribution. One journalist
claimed that 'reporters compete where they should co-operate and
co-operate where they should compete'.

In situations of institutional competition it is often assumed that the
competition for larger audiences necessarily drives down the standard
of journalism.[31] Similarly, institutional competition may mean an economically more stringent situation, where financial priorities favour
promotion, and there is not the money available for such professional luxuries as foreign correspondents or investigative reporting.

However, while competition is seen as encouraging various sins,
ranging from the venial to the serious, in the view of most journalists
it has two cardinal virtues. The first is that lack of competition is
associated with complacency. Organisational convenience takes precedence over the challenge of gathering the news. There is no external
pressure to keep the organisation performing near its peak nor incentives to risk taking. The other is that a plurality of independent voices
makes suppression of information much more difficult. One reporter
described the reporting of Federal politics as 'the frenzied competition
of the ant heap. The whole thing militates against conspiracy'. Disclosure of information and diversity of views are both more likely to
result from a variety of companies pursuing their various interests,
rather than relying upon the *noblesse oblige* of a monopoly.[32]

## Formats

Formats are important in communication but are usually taken for
granted and so remain invisible. They are the structures into which
the content is organised. All types of institutionalised communication
develop formats which shape expectations for both senders and re-

ceivers and which define rules of relevance, procedure, style and standards.[33] Formats allow both audiences and producers to share expectations about message form and content.

Before they know the precise contents of news audiences know the likely overall pattern of presentation, and it is this on which their decision to consume is based: 'The basic fact about the relationship between the audience and the medium of broadcasting is that the former in a sense chooses the genre but not the content.'[34]

Format can thus refer to both the 'total mix' of a news program or publication and to the structuring of individual 'stories'. In the occupational ideology editors picture themselves as the hapless servants of the vagaries of news events. The insistence that they are simply reporting the news masks their active role in deciding news formats and the relative amounts and prominence of different types of news. Depending how questions are phrased, it is sometimes clear that such strategic concerns, although usually taken piecemeal, are part of an editor's role. The single main theme emerging (especially outside the quality press and the ABC) was the fear of being 'too heavy':

> I watch very closely the mix of the paper. At the moment I watch, not censor, the amount of gloom and doom. It's very easy today to get anyone to cry 'recession'. I'm not saying ignore it, but you could fill the paper with economic woes. It's twofold. You can't produce a readable paper and you've got a duty to take as positive a look at things as possible without avoiding the fact that there's big economic problems . . . . If you printed it all, you would produce something unreadable. (*HWT* editor)

> We are not out to re-educate people, but to provide a service. I don't see us as a serious paper. We can approach subjects in the way they deserve, but there is room for more fun in the paper . . . . Tabloids do better than all other papers. The quality of material is important. The balance of the paper is paramount. You must be able to entertain. It should not be all death and destruction. That is hardly the role of a daily paper. (News Ltd editor)

By its nature news is a miscellany of individual items, but the context provided by the total news priorities and presentation affects the individual impact of each item. A serious or heart-rending story in the midst of frivolous or sensationalist material is likely to have less effect.

Besides allowing audiences to know what to expect, formats play a crucial role in facilitating organisational production. In a collective enterprise as large and hurried as news production the shared expectations produced by formats are necessary to avoid chaos. In TV news:

> The use of filmic conventions and narrative forms enables reporters to ensure that their rendition of stories will not be mauled by editors. It facilitates the news organisation's ability to be flexible, to move reporters

from story to story during the day. It enables film crews to cover any assignment, to be generalists who can transform any idiosyncratic occurrence into a conventional news event.[35]

## The strength of formats helps journalists learn what is required.

[I began with AAP] Their style is relatively easy to learn. It's great training for a journalist: You can file quickly etc. Everything had to be straight, in the old news style, hard intro, everything is quoting their comments rather than making any of your own. After a while it gets stultifying.

Often there's a fairly rigid structure in which you write—the structures of the paper, the formulas of hard news etc. That's not to say they shouldn't be there [but sometimes I find them limiting].

Formats exist to discipline the routine performance. Often the work of genius will deliberately flout the conventions. Great novels, such as Joyce's *Ulysses*, appeal partly because they break our expectations of narrative form. Similarly within journalism, many have bridled at the constraints upon their expression imposed by 'objective' formats. The 'New Journalism' which flourished in the late 1960s achieved its effectiveness by, for example, putting the reporter at centre stage instead of as an unresponding observer, by stressing subjective reactions rather than a clinical detachment, and by describing the minutiae which revealed the personal meanings and dramas rather than staying only on the public surface.[36] Many works of insight and inspiration followed, but as an everyday product, the 'New Journalism' would be too reliant on individual inspiration and so more erratic in quality. Strong formats prevent individual variability interfering too much with organisational consistency.

Formats actively shape content. The very notion of 'story' affects the ordering and presentation of material:

The most basic format consideration, which is shared by all news media, is that news becomes suitable only when it is transformed into a story. The networks and the magazines set virtually the same requirements for the structure of a story. Every story must always include a lead, a narrative and a closer. Leads, which are also 'hookers' designed to attract audience attention, raise a moral issue, or question a common expectation (or stereotype). The narrative, whether film or the 'body' of the magazine story, documents or illustrates the lead . . . . Finally the closer assesses the significance of the original highlight, offers a momentary resolution to the issue, or debunks or reaffirms the expectation. This story format therefore creates or reinforces symbols, makes it possible for the news to become a morality play . . . . News which does not fit the story format, such as stories 'which do not make a point' or which lack an ending, can fall by the wayside.[37]

The story format favours resolution over doubt, the concrete over the abstract, the narrative recounting of recent, finite events over the analytical account of continuing conditions.

In addition to the narrative structure, the other main format considerations are those associated with objective presentation. While there is great disagreement among journalists over the meaning and desirability of objectivity, at the practical level there is more working agreement on the procedures and presentations through which individual opinionation is subordinated in news formats. Whether or not these conventions measure up to the ideals and pretensions behind them, they do provide a set of 'strategic rituals',[38] which provide both consistency of presentation and a set of defences against external criticism.

The conventions of 'straight news' or 'hard news' include the 'inverted pyramid' style of presentation, where the main point of the story is encapsulated in a 'strong lead'. A news story then begins not with a hypothesis or general proposition to be evaluated, and not with the personal reaction of the journalist, and not even with the chronological origins of the events—but rather with a crisp statement of the most significant or newsworthy fact. News processing continually seeks to crystallise an event from the flux of action or the flow of experience. One trivial example is that during an election day, broadcasting reports typically contrive to mention the election despite the absence of results or continuing campaigning by referring to how heavy the voting turnout has been (even though with Australia's compulsory voting system, the point is of minimal relevance).

The conventions of objective presentation are apparent also in the manner of presenting information and viewpoints in the body of the story. Precise attribution and the avoidance of apparent reporter subjectivity are the rule. In TV news formats, Epstein refers to the dialectical story model, where the story presentation quotes in turn the opposing sides while 'playing it down the middle'.[39] If the conflict is three-sided, the almost automatic stance is to elevate the middle position as moderate and sensible.

The distancing devices of 'objective' formats should not obscure the sharpness with which these formats delineate the most newsworthy point. It is the selection of these story 'frames' or orientations or 'angles' which is the essence of news judgment. Journalists do not generally gather information in an open-ended search, or think in more complete and sophisticated ways and then 'reduce' their material to a story. They approach the world as a subject for stories whose final format and most salient potential news points are frequently predetermined. Events are approached in terms of their 'highlights', and 'over the span of the selection and production processes, highlighting often proceeds in a spiralling manner.... News is thus often the highlights of the highlights.'[40] In its quest for immediate familiarity and relevance to the public this active winnowing is ripe for the reproduction of stereotypes:[41]

> The first assumption made by [TV] news executives and producers is that viewers' interest is most likely to be maintained through easily recognizable and palpable images ... Stories tend to fit into a limited repertory of images ... Of course, the repertory changes, but at any given time, images, especially emotional ones, which are presumed to have the broadest possible recognition, are used to illustrate news events.[42]

Pressures of time and space are commonly blamed for the short-comings of news. Reporters are often very busy for periods of the work day, but they often have 'spare time' as well. One compared reporting to war—long periods of boredom followed by short but crucial periods of frenetic activity. Such 'spare time' reflects:

1 a belief that principally news is something that happens, rather than that newsworthy information is always potentially present and waiting to be uncovered by inquiry; and
2 that journalists' information-seeking is circumscribed not only by deadlines but by story lines.

A surfeit of information is as great a problem as a scarcity. It may lead to complexity and conflicts, which cannot be easily and immediately used. Information-seeking is bounded by demand as well as supply, by subjective choice as well as objective constraints.

## Conclusion: The Nature of News Values

Journalists are in the grip of news values.[43] Individual journalists talk as if there were some force of newsworthiness, independent of them and over which they have no control, which constrains and guides their work.[44] They may feel completely sanguine about it or may lament how it is a force for trivia. Some may regret how 'petty and dirty [politics] can get ... but editors like that'. But most editors also feel subject to external constraint, although in their case its source and expression are less tangible—partly stemming from perceptions of audience interest, from competitive influences and most intangibly from conventions governing newsworthiness and professional practices.

The strength of news values transforms difficult decisions into routine choices, reduces an ambiguous and infinite mandate—covering the news—into a set of unproblematic routines, all but removing doubts and options:

News selection is usually fairly self-evident. (Editor)

I used to feel choices in how I did a story. Now it's an instinctive reaction. [In an] instant I feel that that is what the story is.

News values minimise the role of individual attitudes, so that news judgments transcend the preferences of the individuals producing it. Labour news, for example, does not result from the attitudes of the journalists covering it, but reflects primarily the perceived demand about what is newsworthy.[45] Observing the formats and procedures associated with objectivity helps to tame journalists' celebrated cynicism. Journalists are cynical but the news is gullible. I often heard reporters expressing cynicism at news events or in describing sources, but the resulting stories usually betrayed no trace of their attitudes. Indeed such cynicism may be partly a response to powerlessness, stemming partly from their inability to be more actively sceptical in their stories.

Despite the undoubted sense of direction and constraint, which news values give, attempts to enumerate them, although sometimes suggestive,[46] have never met the test of accurately describing the actual content of news or of differentiating news from non-news.[47] While we might compile a list of vaguely preferred story attributes— human interest, novelty, suspense, importance to the public, conflict—it is more important to understand the severe qualifications in any consideration of news values:

1 There is no elaborated universal formula. Journalists are often inarticulate about how they know what constitutes newsworthiness. The question may be dismissed by an answer like 'You get a nose for it'. (Judging by some of the noses, the process by which values are imbibed is a fairly fluid one.) Moreover, news decisions are relational rather than absolute. A story does not cross some imaginary threshold of news interest. Rather it 'competes' against the other stories available near deadline to fill the required news hole.

2 News values are not necessarily consistent. There are often tensions between the achievement of different values, between professional ideals and organisationally operative short-cuts. Conflicts arise between productivity and depth, between speed and reliability, between organisational estimates of a story's importance and its interest, between gaining exclusives and avoiding risks.

3 News values are not necessarily universally held or adhered to. Priorities and standards of performance vary with the organisation and the individual. 'The newsman has to meet few explicit standards of competence in performing his work'[48] and the external mechanisms for enforcing performance are at best erratic and limited.

4   News values are not necessarily realisable. Even if some internally
    consistent, universal ideal of newsworthiness did exist, and news
    workers all performed perfectly, there would still be supply factors
    influencing what events were detected and pursued. News values
    stress unpredictability but most news content consists of pre-
    scheduled or predictable events. TV news desires action film but
    the visuals of most TV news are often little more than visual
    'Muzak'.[49]

In approaching news values, it is also more fundamental to understand them as responses to the various cross-pressures in news production than to construct imaginary formulas of newsworthiness. As with
the evolution of values in other large organisations, means to ends
become ends in themselves. The obsession with speed and deadlines
elevates the importance of timeliness and novelty in news judgments.
The small proportion of news that becomes available outside routine
channels and through the enterprise of reporters is especially valued.
Similarly, because of competition the very fact of exclusiveness heightens the value of a story. The mandatory stories, common to all, are
less valued than those where the organisation has shown discretion
and enterprise, almost independently of content. Central figures are
believed to have the best information, so access to them may itself
become the basis for a story, whether or not they provide telling
insights. Presentation skills, valued for their help in communicating to
the audience, are appraised by fellow professionals almost independently of any actual impact on audience appreciation.

The content of news values is not subject to explicit codification. At
any one time, ideas about newsworthiness are a response to presumptions about current audience interest, to the mutual monitoring and
shoptalk that accompany the industry's competitive ethos, and to the
agendas of major sources. Reporting is shaped by understood formats
of presentation and organisational priorities and by a shared sense, no
matter how vague and shifting its foundations and how commonly
breached, of the rules of fair reporting, and the proper role of news.

The ambiguity and imprecision inherent in the nature of news
values is not organisationally disabling. Rather it may be functional
for an enterprise that has to face audiences with a range of beliefs, and
deal with sources of conflicting hues while maintaining its own
cohesiveness to meet production schedules:

> Conventions are useful for legitimating the selections made and for
> deflecting outside criticism. Their very imprecision makes them arcane—
> secrets, like social science jargon and 'legalese', understood only by
> members of the journalism priesthood.[50]

Similarly there is a useful mixture of, on the one hand, principles and
pretensions ('freedom of the press', 'a calling' etc.) and on the other,

the rhetoric of a commercial enterprise which cannot be expected to be altruistic or go beyond what its customers want. The first can be used against threats of external interference, and to boost self-importance, while the second, anti-messianic emphasis deflates criticisms of lack of performance.

The imprecision not only decreases external accountability, but increases internal cohesiveness. The precise content of news values at any one time can be implicitly negotiated and defined within each organisation.[51] In an industry with a high number of exceptional cases and rapidly changing topics of attention, the authority of editors, rather than rulebooks, is available to make concrete rulings. In an industry with a rapid turnover of material, and quick changes of news interest, there is no rigid barrier slowing down adaptability. There is little occasion for general doubts to grow. Rather, work is dominated by the immediate absorption in the particularities of new stories.

Ambiguous news values, and the responsiveness they entail, are also functional in relations with sources. They afford an independence from specific source criticisms, but also entail a degree of openness to sources' views and priorities, to give them an incentive for maintaining the relationship. Journalists' sensitivity to sources' public statements and to their private concerns and priorities helps to shape definitions of news importance. In many ways the media agenda is set by their sources' agendas: 'Journalists cope with the realities of power by incorporating it into news judgements.'[52] The sum of news practices and values form a pattern of responsiveness. As an institution news is particularly dependent upon and sensitive to external factors. Its central product is the deeds and words of others. Those others have their own interests to pursue and shaping news content may be one avenue toward their realisation.

# PART II
# The Politics of Information

# 4
# Overt Manoeuvres:
# Public Relations Politics

No-one can doubt the enormous importance political strategists place on media coverage. In issue attention, according to one lobbyist: 'an inch in the *Financial Review* might be worth a yard in *Hansard*, or a mile of submissions'.[1] And, in the projection of political leadership, according to one press secretary: '[Wran] never attended any function unless there was the possibility of getting [media coverage]. Wran equated media coverage with public knowledge of him'.[2]

News is, as we explored in the first part of this book, fashioned by the institutional demands of its production. But in addition it is the subject of determined and continuing efforts to influence its content by those who have the interest and capacity to do so. These efforts can be divided into overt manoeuvres, where the source is publicly known, and covert ones (explored in the next chapter) where the source remains concealed.

The resources devoted to influencing news content and to image engineering have grown exponentially. Public relations is one of the most spectacular growth industries in Australia. Remembering that it started from a small base, a very rough estimate would be that the numbers employed in the mid-1980s were at least ten times greater than those employed in the mid-1960s. Beyond the enormous, quantifiable growth in resources allocated and people employed, decision-makers and political operators seem more centrally and calculatingly concerned with the media and 'image' aspects of their own activities.[3]

The reasons behind the rise are both promotional and defensive. The primary impetus is the massive presence of the media, its centrality as a conduit to the public and the need to reach an institutional accommodation with it—better to have the journalist arriving at the front door than peeping through the key hole.[4] Organisations figuring in the news risk negative publicity which results not from actual weaknesses but from the haphazard release of information or an uncooperative demeanour. The demands and political importance of the media—the numbers of journalists wanting access, and the special needs of television—were growing at the same time as other demands on ministers and leaders were also increasing. The resultant rise in employment of press secretaries tends to be irreversible. In a competitive situation, the expansion of public relations strategies is self-sustaining. Just as after one second-hand car yard starts large-scale advertising, its competitors must do likewise, so political parties try to stop their opponents gaining a competitive edge. When PR fails, the proposed solution is never its abolition, but only its improvement and expansion.

In the more poetic versions, political PR is pictured as an irresistible 'black magic'[5] practised by a 'propaganda machine'. Such labels are a barrier to understanding: they substitute an image of impersonal force and unspecified product for a description of the flesh and blood activities involved. This chapter proceeds first by examining the strategies in political PR, especially by analysing how news production generates patterns of responsiveness which political leaders can exploit. Then it explores the limits and failures of news management, before concluding with a discussion of the political issues it raises.

## Managing the Media

The relationship between the news media and publicity strategists generates two different perspectives:

1 who and what the news media want to cover; and
2 who wants news coverage of what information.

The two rarely coincide in neat harmony, which leads to two apparently inconsistent propositions, both being true:

1 a low proportion of PR material given to news organisations appears in the news and even less appears exactly as its promoters wanted; but
2 a large proportion of news is predominantly or partially the product of PR efforts.[6]

It is a relation often marked by both mutual discontent and mutual dependence. Pedestrian accommodation is the norm on both sides, with occasional tactical flair by publicists and with general media cynicism occasionally roused into active investigation.

Neither press secretaries' nor journalists' comments give an adequate guide to the influence of PR manoeuvres on news. Both sides manifest discrepancies between general attitudes and particular behaviours. PR operates with a premium on secrecy about specifics, while at a general level there is both 'hype', over-selling its effects, and bland simplifications about better communication. A prerequisite to successful 'image-making' is to deny any is taking place. A politician may rejoice in a general image of niftiness but strenuously resent any accounts of his niftiness at work.

Similarly journalists offer general protestations of disdain:

> The art of public relations as it is practised at its highest and most cynical degree is the art of confusion and distraction. It is professional hypocrisy.[7]

One could not guess from the strength of these sentiments in a *Financial Review* editorial quite how much PR-originated material appears in that paper.[8] Nor, from journalists' interviews, could one guess that the dependence is so comfortable that as Graham Freudenberg found in the mid 1960s, 'It was increasingly difficult to get reported unless there was a press release'.[9] The critical variable is not the attitude of journalists towards publicity seekers, but the latter's ability to deliver news. One initially critical journalist then added 'Maybe I'm being too high-minded. It's grist to the mill and the mill needs grist.'

'The relationship between sources and journalists resembles a dance, for sources seek access to journalists and journalists seek access to sources. Although it takes two to tango . . . more often than not, sources do the leading.[10] Being the news generators, sources usually have more of the immediate initiative. Their initiative stems from their ability 'to create suitable news',[11] which in turn is largely a consequence of possessing other power, especially the ability to make decisions affecting the public in tangible ways. Thus, 'by virtue of their influence on events, whatever office-holders say may be significant, whether or not it is true'.[12] The news media's receptiveness gives major sources a publicity bonus—a latitude in their media relations which they can use, depending on individual skills and inclinations, to their own benefit.

Compiling a catalogue of the skills and stratagems involved in PR politics might be 'as hopeless as attempting an exhaustive list of the tricks that Houdini might try'.[13] but we can seek to specify those characteristics of news, its patterns of responsiveness and resistance, through which sources can influence its content:

1   that news is produced against rigid deadlines;
2   that it needs a fresh supply in every news cycle;
3   that stories 'compete' with each other for coverage and prominence;
4   that news is presented in brief formats, which 'lead' with the hardest news;

5  that stories with drama and colour will gain more prominence;
6  that performance attributes are important in broadcasting presentations;
7  that once reporters are committed to attending an event, coverage usually follows;
8  that there is scope for discretion in interpretations and news judgments, which can be influenced by media good will.

From the other side, the political interests and opportunities in affecting news are determined by the combination of three factors:

1  whether the source is relating to the media as patron or petitioner, whether it can command media interest by its capacity to deliver a major story, or whether it must court the media to promote information of marginal news value;
2  whether the sources are promoting and prolonging good news or seeking to contain and defuse bad news;
3  whether and how news attention is impinging on the political conflicts in which sources are engaged, and especially what sorts of publicity manoeuvres are being mounted by their opponents.

The strategies examined here are aimed at an audience whose relation to the events portrayed is basically marked by remoteness and passivity.[14] They are aimed at shaping impressions from fragments of information, rather than presenting a closely argued case, and at achieving the broadest possible public support rather than the active commitment of devoted cadres.

*Timing: Deadlines*

If the source is a petitioner promoting a marginal story, scheduling strategies should maximise organisational convenience. If patron, however, the opposite applies. Lateness reduces the chances for gathering reactions and gaining critical perspective:

> It's a very skilled thing when you drop something. If it is a page one story you hold it till 5 pm. If it is page six you do it before lunch.

Ironically the technological advances in TV news have in some ways made it more vulnerable to this type of manipulation. For a news-conscious politician, 'the introduction of the "live cross" trucks was a godsend',[15] allowing unparalleled and usually unchallenged access. Thus, in October 1987, amid controversy over his future, Sir Joh Bjelke-Petersen announced his intended retirement just as the TV news services were beginning—allowing them to cover it live, and allowing no time for critics to reply, or for preparing stories on the background to the decision.

The release of information can also be timed in relation to news schedules to minimise coverage. In December 1986, when one financial institution dropped Australia's credit rating from AAA to AA+, Treasurer Keating's staff dropped the news in press boxes at 2 am. Former NSW Premier Askin was a master of the art. Late one night he rushed a generous but complicated superannuation scheme for MPs through an approving Parliament:

> [Its handsome benefits were] expressed in such technical gobbledygook that it was impossible in the time available to decipher [their] full extent . . . [Journalists' reports] were scrappy.[16]

Askin's ultimate act of camouflage through timing was to release a series of tax increases late at night during the Press Gallery's Christmas Party.[17]

### Timing: Fresh Supply

The political leaders who are best at manipulating news are good at catering to its work-a-day demands. In every news cycle, the media is searching for fresh stories, new developments in 'running' stories, new variations on themes and issues in the news. The need for regular supply is caught in Sir Joh Bjelke-Petersen's flattering reference to 'feeding his chooks'.[18] One long, coherent exposition will only figure in the news once. Continuing favourable coverage requires learning to replenish the media's continuing turnover of material. Similarly, 'a stream of little facts [can] be used to obscure the absence of big facts',[19] and gives the political initiative:

> A fair criticism of the press gallery is that we're all working on a daily deadline, which often means we don't stand back and get a long-term view. Dale knew this. He was coming up with news angles, which meant that Wran was making the running.

Governments have become adept at wringing more public kudos from policies by prolonging the attention to good news. If they are introducing a clearly popular move, like tax cuts, there will be a long nurturing of expectations: hints that it may occur, an earnest profession of hope that it can be done, revelations that the government is seriously examining the possibility, a clear statement of intent, unspecific hints of its imminence, the actual announcement—to take effect at some future date—and finally, with appropriate fanfare, implementation.

Conversely, in containing bad news, curtailing its duration and hoping it will peak at an electorally irrelevant time are as important as affecting its content. The longer term scheduling of publicity for the most auspicious impact is harder, often impossible, to control. It involves for example achieving an effective blitz of positive publicity in the immediate lead-up to an election, or entering a controversy when the prospects for resolution are greatest.[20] The Greiner Government in 1988 brought to a new pitch conventional political wisdoms about taking the most unpopular measures early in its term. Many came together in its June mini-Budget:

> This mini-budget follows every cynical rule in the book: announce all your bad news in one hit, don't prolong the pain; announce all your price rises as soon as possible after the Premiers' Conference and Commonwealth mini-Budget so you can blame it all on the Feds; whack up charges immediately after an election so the voters have plenty of time to forget; and don't keep any of your promises to cut taxes until just before the next election, so voters have no time to forget.[21]

Two days after the mini-Budget, Greiner announced dramatic charges of misappropriating funds against former Labor Minister, Frank Walker. Perhaps coincidentally, these charges then split the headlines with the predictable negative reactions against the mini-Budget.

### Timing: Competition with Other Stories

News presentations involve a hierarchy of stories. The attention to any story depends partly on what others are available at the same time. Petitioning sources often choose to release stories on Sundays, which traditionally was the slowest news day of the week (although less so now because so many groups have adopted the strategy).

The same strategy can be used in reverse, to 'hide' negative stories alongside bigger stories. John Cain Senior, Victorian Premier in the early 1950s, used to joke that if he wanted to fiddle the Treasury books, he would simply chop down some trees in St Kilda Rd, and then *The Herald* would be too agitated to notice. In the 1960s, the ever-spiralling cost of the F111 aircraft was a continuing embarrassment to the Liberal Government. When they were proposing to make its ceiling price public, Howson suggested:

> We might do it on the eve of the election for the leadership [to replace Harold Holt], so that it might not achieve the prominence it otherwise would.[22]

Mungo MacCallum wryly commented upon the strategy at work when the Fraser Government announced the inauguration of the Defence Forces Academy, a proposal which had received considerable criticism, on a Friday night, after two other major stories, a Premiers' Conference and a Ministry reshuffle, had already occurred that day:

> When the jaded and indeed exhausted Canberra press gallery were pulling their wits together in the wake of the Premiers and the reshuffle, the Defence Minister, Jim Killen, whipped out the statement that [the Defence Academy] was all to go ahead. He could not have picked a better day. Not only were the media more or less wrapped up, but the Parliament—and in

particular those Government members who had argued against the academy—had scattered to the four corners of the globe.[23]

When, partly because of Foreign Minister Hayden's elevation to the Governor-Generalship, the Hawke Government had to undertake a Ministerial reshuffle, always a politically risky manoeuvre, it did so on the eve of the Budget, straight after the opening of the new Parliament House, and on the same day as Hayden officially resigned. The public impact was as muted as the Government could have hoped, nicely overshadowed by the other events.

Governments, with the news-generating advantages bestowed by incumbency, sometimes seek to 'bury' the Opposition's initiatives by creating more newsworthy events. When challenged on whether President Johnson was taking actions designed to overshadow Robert Kennedy's growing challenge, press secretary Bill Moyers quipped 'No we are not aiming to counteract Senator Kennedy, and yes we are sending Vice President Humphrey to the moon.'

Naturally politicians have only minimal control over the vagaries of events. NSW Minister Laurie Brereton recalled how as Chairman of the Public Accounts Committee, he sought, through 'a couple of background briefings [and] the correct timing', to achieve maximum publicity. The first edition of *The Sydney Morning Herald* had it on the front page, and Brereton went to sleep well satisfied, only to find in the morning an assassination attempt against the Pope had displaced his report.[24] Such unplanned intrusions can be welcome relief for politicians suffering negative coverage.

> A damaging news story was continuing to dog the [Wilson] Government day after day. 'Get it off the front page, Henry.' [The Prime Minister told his press secretary] 'I don't care how you do it, but get it off the front.' Later that day news of a grisly sex murder in Shepherds Bush broke. Sir Harold was back on the phone to his press secretary. 'Henry, you've gone too far this time.'[25]

Politicians have become more aware that the public relations battle is at least as much over the priorities as the content of news coverage. This seems partly to account for the decline in 'open slather, all-in' press conferences, even though any competent leader should be able to maintain control in such a one-sided encounter.[26] Although there is the risk of making gaffes, perhaps even more importantly, the leader cannot control the direction of questioning. Such open encounters do not lend themselves to dictating priorities.

### Formats: Capturing the Lead

A more elusive skill than the strategic considerations affecting timing and placement is a grasp of how to exploit news values and formats.

Political leaders must master the '40-second grab' for TV news and learn what information is likely to be included in a 10-paragraph compression of events. The brevity of news items, and so their severe selectivity, means that limiting information is as important as supplying it. The less information available, the more likely that the news will focus where the source wishes:

> Do not succumb to the temptation to feed the press more than you want it to digest . . . . In other words, don't trump your own ace.[27]

An ability for simplification, adapting the methods of exposition to the rhythms and demands of '40-second grabs' and crisp headlines are among the vital PR skills:

> In preparing urgency motions concern was always given to producing a simple line for the media to base their whole story on . . . .
> In all his speeches at these functions Wran determined what would be targeted for the media and would restrict his remarks to a 30 or 45 second 'grab'. Designed specifically for television . . . they were usually self-contained stories which the reporters had to 'top and tail'.[28]

Defensively, those in the news need to avoid negative comments or actions which will overshadow, or even substitute for, whatever else they are seeking to promote. In the 1988 Victorian election, Federal Opposition Leader Howard was constantly questioned about why Victorian Liberal leader Kennett seemed to be avoiding appearing with him. Exasperated, Howard finally threatened jokingly to kick some TV reporters out of his way. That became the sole coverage of his day's campaigning on most TV news services that night.

News presentations abhor the amorphous and the complex. Skilled PR strategists know that news headlines and 'lead' sentences will highlight the most dramatic or 'hardest' aspect of a story. A definite promise, a specific development or a direct allegation will always take precedence over, for example, a statement of principles. *The Financial Review* editorialised against the exploitation of this during health insurance changes announced by the Minister, Ralph Hunt:

> It was structured in a deliberately deceptive fashion aimed at exploiting the requirement of the media to acknowledge the authority of the Government spokesman on health to quote alleged savings . . .
> For purely public relations reasons—better still call it media manipulation—Mr Hunt incorporated the following sentence into his statement: 'Private health fund contribution rates are expected to . . . lead to a decrease of an average of 46 cents a week in medical insurance contributions.'
> Mr Hunt's media advisers knew that this particular sentence had to be given prominence in every radio and television broadcast of the proposed changes. The figure, quite capriciously and with deception aforethought, is plucked out of the air.[29]

Sources can also exploit the tendency in news reports to highlight the most dramatic possibilities raised. In Prime Minister Fraser's overseas tour of May 1982, the headlines were dominated by his plan that tariffs would be lowered if international agreement for steps toward freer trade were obtained. Nothing tangible eventuated, but the initiative served the Prime Minister's short-term publicity purposes admirably.[30] In news coverage of such cases, the drama of the dependent clause swamps the improbability of the conditional. The small print and the contingencies emerge later and with less prominence. Such differential newsworthiness is behind the common criticism that prosaic rebuttals receive less coverage than dramatic allegations.

Similarly, in grand announcements of a spectacular new project, news coverage is shaped by the attractiveness of the enterprise rather than the imminence of its implementation. After the bold initial announcement, projects often disappear, to be revived at some appropriate future occasion, or to peter out with little public attention. In terms of avoiding unfavourable news coverage, it is better to break promises by omission than commission.

### News Values: Injecting Colour and Drama

Coverage can be enhanced or reduced, and its focus shaped, not only by a story's substance, but by the incidentals which add or subtract news interest. The best way to add interest is to appear as if one is seeking to avoid coverage: Foreign Minister Bill Hayden took this to an extreme in his ostentatiously 'secret', 3 am flight to New Zealand to see Prime Minister David Lange in 1987, apparently about Libyan activity in the South Pacific. The surprise and the 'secrecy' added enormously to news interest.[31]

Making the leader available for interviews and 'actuality' gives a story a higher profile. John O'Hara recalled Menzies as early as the 1940s advising the NSW Minister in charge of price controls, 'You make the popular announcements and get the Under Secretary to make the unpopular ones'. The leader's involvement not only affects a story's immediate newsworthiness, but is an attempt to shape its interpretation. The one occasion when Minister Assisting the Treasurer, Hurford, was given the major public role in announcing a measure was when the Hawke Government reinforced the powers of the Prices Justification Tribunal. Keating's non-involvement was perhaps a cue to business and the media that the Government did not consider it an important move.

A feeling for colour and phrasing can set the desired tone. When, after prolonged speculation, Wran announced he was not going into Federal politics, he confided that he had decided the previous evening 'over half a bottle of Chardonnay'.[32] Every news report highlighted the phrase, which gave the impression of a completely relaxed decision, although one is left to ponder how history would have differed if he had drunk claret instead.

An unusual example of deliberately inhibiting news interest was adopted by Don Chipp as Minister for Customs in 1970. On an occasion when he decided to censor a film:

> In an extremely rare moment of inspiration I decided to take the press on. I wrote out a press release . . . [which] was accurate and explicit. It read: '*Like Night and Day* contains a scene which depicts a young woman performing cunnilingus on her sister while at the same time a man has intercourse with the young woman by entering her from behind.' I said . . . to the journalists from the gallery. 'Now let's see if you bastards have the guts to print that.' . . . [The result was] not a word of criticism for my act of censorship— because, in fact, by not quoting my press release they had all acted as censors themselves.[33]

### *Broadcasting: Strategic Performances*

The appearances of political leaders in the broadcasting media, in press conferences and interviews, can be called 'strategic performances'. Their purposes are extrinsic rather than intrinsic to the participants' interactions: the performance does not occur for the edification of the performers; or for the achievement of some common task. Rather the underlying aim is to achieve an effect on an audience. More primary than the content in such encounters are the personal impressions of the performers stemming from their interaction (remembering of course that the interviewers are performing too):

> In a television interview for most viewers the impression is everything. Within twenty-four hours, the actual words are largely forgotten but not what the person looked like.[34]

Moreover, as the situation is primarily one of personal interaction, if the interviewee can control the tone—speaking in a low-key, disarming voice, preserving the appearance of control and unconcern, it is possible to minimise damage even if the content is potentially damaging.[35] The trend produced a fashion among Australian politicians for responding to adverse developments by declaring how relaxed they were.

When the interviewee is evasive or seeking to avoid a response, the interviewer is far from helpless:

> You can probe because you just keep asking. The advantage of TV is that . . . if you keep shooting, they'll keep answering. It's not just a matter of what they say, but how they say it which is revealing.

But a skilled interviewee maintains a high degree of control. The flow of conversation in an interview is not analogous to a cross-examination in a courtroom.[36] There is no compulsion to answer the question in the interviewer's terms: interviewees can dispute the terms of the questions, or adopt various strategies of evasion and control, including, with varying success in practice, turning directly on the interviewer. Most issues contain sufficient complexity and detail for any embattled advocate to make points about conflicting principles, dubious evidence, procedural improprieties, their critics' ulterior motives and their disgraceful records—expanding any original uncertainties into a maze of confusion. Even faced with the most awkward accusations, a blancmange defence, offering no hard targets, refusing to be pinned down, may be difficult for even the most penetrating interviewers to penetrate:

> Interviewing Senator Stan Collard [about an overseas visit secretly sponsored by a corporation] must have been like trying to carry jelly in a string bag ... If their motives were that altruistic, persevered [Richard] Carleton, stuffing some of the biggest lumps back through the holes, why was it necessary that the identity of the other members of the consortium should remain secret. To this Senator Collard replied that it was better that those involved should be known to as few as possible and that perhaps they wanted to be like Caesar's wife ... A man who thinks that 'above suspicion' means the same thing as 'impossible to finger' is in his own way impregnable.[37]

## Hijacking Reporters

Once reporters are assigned to a story they are obliged to produce one. Sources know that once the commitment of time is made, coverage will follow. The most effective use of this strategy is the engineering of occasions with travel away from home base. The successful use of overseas trips often affords leaders far more scope to dominate the news than they enjoy at home.[38] Hijacking journalists in this way is inducive to favourable coverage—the journalists must justify their time and so may be inclined to inflate the importance of what occurs, gratitude at the excursion away from the daily routine may produce a receptive frame of mind; and being isolated, there is less chance of seeking alternative views. Moreover, 'both the Prime Minister and the senior correspondents share an interest in being on the front page'.

The most determined attempt to gain positive publicity is to stage one's own news events. Boorstin dubbed the orchestration of occasions which exist only for the publicity they generate, pseudo-events.[39] Slightly different is the attempt to crystallise and transform some positive development into a news occasion: an airline's inaugural flight; the opening of a new mine; a product or policy or even a 'campaign' launch, are most effective when they include a junket. In its full glory a junket involves free travel, an arranged itinerary with briefings and dossiers, plus receptions and generous hospitality. As one-time journalist Mark Twain quipped, 'you give me a good spread on the table, and I'll give you a good spread on the page':[40]

> Journalists often become advocates . . . They get duchessed, mining writers taken to Mt Isa etc, like political pilgrims to China. There are some blatant examples of mature journalists who ought to know better being duchessed and seduced by companies. It happens in mining because there is a sense of excitement and discovery. And heavy industry always looks more interesting. (Editor)

### Cultivating Media Discretion

Cultivating media good will is no substitute for the immediate news-influencing strategies above. But in areas where there is latitude, either in interpreting events or making news judgments, less direct influences may be important. The significance of developments is often open to surmise. There is no such thing as pure news judgment, unaffected by value-laden views of how the world works. Within the realm of normal news judgments, there is discretion for politically loaded decisions. How reporters and media managements exercise such discretion is subject to wooing by politicians. The wooing of reporters is usually through cooperation, briefings and perhaps the occasional exclusive. But occasionally patronage may be more substantial:

> "It's contract time," was all that was necessary for a television reporter to say in order to get two or three weeks of nice and exclusive stories from the Government. A run of good stories usually resulted in the reporter in question receiving a more lucrative contract.[41]

In seeking to influence media managements, all contemporary politicians would adopt the opposite approach from Arthur Calwell:

> My predecessor as Labor leader, Dr Evatt, always seemed to be on good terms with the newspapers, but I never thought it possible. So I worked on the principle that you must suspect the newspaper world and never let them mislead you or fool you . . . Evatt had gone ahead with his plans for a meeting with the newspaper proprietors. I agreed to attend, and Frank Packer, Rupert Henderson and Ezra Norton were all there. I was introduced to them, but I did not shake hands with any of them.[42]

Good relations with proprietors has allowed some successful political leaders to maintain only distant relations with journalists: 'You know I loathe the press' was Menzies' reply when, on first becoming Prime Minister, he was told about arrangements for press conferences. His views hadn't mellowed in his retirement, judging by his talk with David McNicholl about 'your stupid colleagues in the press, those rather vulgarian fellows who think they're Republicans'.[43] Sir Robert Askin taunted reporters:

> I get plenty of publicity anyway without having to hold press conferences. I don't know if I can trust you fellows. I talk to Sir Warwick and Rupert and Sir Frank. That's good enough.[44]

Restricting reporters' access or stonewalling defence strategies are more feasible if politicians are confident that media managements will observe partisanship through passivity—not initiating investigations of opponents' allegations, reporting only what is said rather than analysing evasions and silences. News Ltd's Paul Kelly observed that during 1975, Opposition Leader Fraser:

> maintained a close dialogue with the highest levels of the industry throughout the year and particularly during the constitutional crisis and election campaign. He acted with a confidence based on the knowledge that reporters could not hurt him.[45]

## Limits and Failures

> The ill success of either party [is due] to their glutting the market, and retailing too much of a bad commodity all at once. (Johnathan Swift, *The Art of Political Lying*, 1712)[46]

Despite the rhetoric of both practitioners and opponents, the most heartening feature of public relations politics is how often it fails. Despite claims to ever more sophisticated techniques, their effectiveness is limited by a range of countervailing factors. The precepts of successful public relations are more easily stated than achieved. For every convincing gesture of leadership there are countless examples of hollow hyperbole and cheap posturing, for every telling attack, many cases of ineffectual carping and mud-slinging. Moreover, the demands of the media are so constant and the standard repertoires of political PR so few, that, like the plot formulas of TV series, they become hackneyed and threadbare. The few original ideas spawn dozens of second-rate imitations, and quickly become banal clichés. Public relations tactics are a self-diminishing resource. Short-term success produces long-term cynicism.

The most important constraint is that image engineering can never occur without politics obtruding. The conflicts inherent in politics prevent one player from monopolising publicity. Fragile strategies can be easily punctured by opponents. Each side has an interest in undermining the other and, often, both are successful. The parade of claim and counter-claim, accusation and denial, soon acquires a tiresome predictability:

[In Opposition, Hawke] had a persistent desire to expose apparent discrepancies in Ministerial statements and was quick to label these 'lies'. Many Canberra reporters became quite cynical about this approach, reacting wearily when Hawke called yet another press conference to expose 'yet another Viner lie'.[47]

Conflict not only encourages the undermining of opponents, but its heat and urgency often produce temptations to oversell one's own side. The tendency to oversell specifics does more general damage—when the clock strikes thirteen, it puts in doubt all that has gone before.

The manner in which the interplay of competitive interests can confound publicity manoeuvres was well illustrated by the public embarrassments suffered by Nissan late in 1985. It tried to signal its discontent with aspects of the Australian Government's car plan and pressure the Government for change by including a hint that it might withdraw from production in Australia. The other companies, instead of also pressuring the Government, sought a competitive advantage by stressing their commitment to Australia, leaving Nissan isolated by its publicity feint, and having to do some embarrassed backtracking.

The constraints imposed by external conflict are accentuated by the difficulties of achieving internal unity. Internal division is a primary source of PR disasters. Although the Whitlam Government employed a multitude of press secretaries, its publicity strategies have become a negative model for all subsequent governments. The large numbers abetted rather than alleviated the problems:

> The Whitlam Government suffered from too many press secretaries. They couldn't coordinate. They were all fighting. Internecine fights. Quite extraordinary.

Both media and opponents are keen to pounce on internal inconsistencies. Again, to give but one example, when Fraser Government Ministers Street and Sinclair made contradictory statements on the relative danger of the Soviet threat, the discrepancy became front page news: 'Now there's a Soviet threat, now there's not'.[48] Only governments with an improbable degree of discipline and unity can completely avoid such embarrassments.

The quest for successful publicity strategies is further confounded by the different constituencies and conflicting demands which political participants must juggle. The multiplicity of games interfere with each other. Constituency demands, for example, often run counter to general image considerations. Perhaps this is most acute in trade unions, where leaders may need to demonstrate their ideological militance, or their ruthlessness in pursuing union interests, but in so doing make statements which are not helpful to the popular image of unions. In politics the party faithful are more determined to advance ideological principles, and less attuned to pragmatic strategies for minimising electoral risks and pressure group displeasure. In business, boasting about profits to attract investors may conflict with 'crying poor' when faced by demands from unions or governments; demonstrating 'hard headedness' to shareholders may seem callousness to the public.

Clarity in public relations strategies is impossible when there is no policy coherence. Publicity strategies are subordinate to political direction, so when governments are floundering on the policy front, their publicity skills invariably suffer also. Perhaps the most telling example in contemporary Australian politics was the decline of Prime Minister Gorton's once acclaimed media performances. As his political problems mounted, 'His once laconic, direct speech degenerated damagingly into long, convoluted utterances, incomprehensible and wandering'. Witness:

> The AMA agrees with us, or I believe will agree with us, that its policy, and it will be its policy, to inform patients who ask what the common fee is, and what their own fee is, so that a patient will know whether he is going to be operated on, if that's what it is, on the basis of the common fee or not.[49]

Image demands frequently conflict with other policy considerations.[50] Budgetary problems, bureaucratic capacity, conflicting interests, cannot be dissolved by symbolic incantations, although the visibility of their effects can sometimes be delayed. Moreover, there are increasing constraints on a government with the passage of time and the accumulation of promises and predictions. Expectations cannot be arbitrarily raised and lowered without some disillusion. The capacity for new tricks is limited by the cumulative record of the old ones. Even if each new piece of information is released with an optimistic gloss, it may not disguise the total pattern—'Yes, General, but aren't your victories getting closer to Saigon?'

Beyond all these political factors which obtrude into political publicity strategies, there is one confounding factor right at the centre— the public does not have a unified or consistent set of expectations of its politicians. Many manoeuvres flounder in the fickleness of the electorate. Different types of appeals gain and lose potency as the political ethos and the tides of news attention change. Moving to the (apparently) most popular stand on each issue may appear opportunistic and untrustworthy. Equally, showing firm resolve appears as lacking moderation and unconciliatory. Admiration of principle verges into distaste for rigidity, praise for pragmatism into criticism for expedience. The public mood shifts between the relative appeals of coherence and moderation in leaders as well as moving among the inconsistent expectations of government. Public relations will remain an inexact science partly because the market demand it is seeking to satisfy consists of shifting ambivalences.

Finally, and refreshingly, the capacity for simple human error intrudes. Beyond individual traits of skill and temperament, the tendency to commit gaffes increases the more that public facades diverge from private realities. The more that strategy becomes contorted, the more it involves treading a precarious path through inconsistent positions and artificial rationalisations, the greater the strain and the more likely that errors will occur.[51]

## Issues in Public Relations Politics

Ironically PR has a bad image.[52] Its general impacts on politics are widely deplored, and its growth poses some important democratic issues. Most obviously, access to PR is another unequally distributed political resource. The scale of the industry *vis-à-vis* the media themselves is one concern.[53] Another is that in political conflicts, the merits of different arguments are skewed in news coverage by differential possession of PR capacities. The rise of public relations politics has substantially increased the resource advantages of governments over oppositions, and still further blurred any lines between the administrative and political uses of the machinery of government. The discrepancies between government and opposition in numbers of press secretaries and other support staff, especially at State level, are now huge. Such differences are justified in terms of the differing functions of an executive government from an opposition party, yet the translation of responsibilities into an appropriate ratio of resources is an arbitrary exercise. Moreover, political debate on these issues is particularly marked by hypocrisy: each opposition rails against the iniquities of the government's bloated and misused propaganda machine, then promptly adopts similar practices after assuming power itself.

The question is especially pertinent as governments increasingly seek to wring the appearance of largesse from every activity. The public relations arms of the bureaucracy are increasingly geared to serving the incumbent's political advantage. Take for example, the Fraser Government's use of the Government Information Unit. After the much criticised growth in press secretaries under the Whitlam Government, Fraser did not reduce the total numbers employed but rather re-deployed them into a more coordinated system, made them less visible and gave them greater public service pretensions. The greatest news attention accrued to the GIU in April 1981 with a leak of Liberal Party documents detailing its participation in the 1980 election:

One of the documents was a memo from the unit's officer in Victoria, Mr Arnis Verbickis, which proposed tactics to be used when the Prime Minister, Mr Fraser appeared on Derryn Hinch's programme on 3AW....
'Paul Barber tends to feed questions and follow up points to Hinch. I would suggest that someone remains outside and talks and disturbs both Nankervis and Barber. I found this worked well with both Newman and Howard interviews.'[54]

Another leaked document (which passed with little attention) showed that 'the Government Information Unit suggested during [the 1980] election campaign that the Prime Minister, Mr Fraser, encourage rumors that Melbourne ethnic radio station 3EA would be closed down if it took a strong stand against the Government'.[55] Later leaks showed that a Tasmanian officer of the GIU assisted in the campaign of the Liberal Opposition in the Tasmanian election,[56] and that a Victorian officer was accused by people within the Liberal Party of being too close to critics of Premier Hamer and later assisting the Prime Minister against Peacock's challenge.[57] Harrassing interviewers, spreading false rumours, supporting State Opposition parties and scuttling internal party opponents are all novel departures for a supposedly Westminster-style information agency.

After the hypocrisies of the Fraser years, the Hawke Government easily slipped the unit—now re-named the Australian National Media Liaison Service (popularly known as aNiMaLS)—into an overtly partisan role. Under the Hawke Government it has functioned as a tax-payer funded 'hit squad' scanning and targetting Opposition statements for Government attack, and, quietly but skilfully, feeding material to the press gallery for this purpose.[58]

The size of government propaganda operations is no substitute for the PR skills of leaders, Ministers and their staffs in affecting major news coverage. Their greatest impact is probably with provincial media and suburban newspapers, and in areas where metropolitan media don't want to make the resource commitment to cover events independently.[59] However, the resource inequities and the political use of official informational activities do pose increasingly urgent policy problems, which no government is likely to address honestly.

Beyond the distribution of resources, the other democratic issues to do with PR politics all concern its content, especially the impact on the quality of public debate. The most basic criticism is that it represents the triumph of trivia, of style over substance. The distaste for its confected flummery stems partly from the view that serious pursuits like government should not be subjected to the same marketing techniques as deodorants or hamburgers; partly that it leads to the active avoidance of serious debate.

Such avoidance leads directly to another common criticism: that the engineering of images frequently involves achieving public exposure while reducing access and scrutiny. Sometimes dealing with a spokes-person takes the place of direct dealings with the principals, so that a leader's 'anger' or 'upbeat mood' are reported in the news, even though these emotions have been communicated only at second hand for a transparently political purpose. The news is giving its audience convenient fictions, rather than probing their resemblance to reality.

Many political leaders have concluded that 'where voters are concerned . . . one TV picture is worth 10 000 words'.[60] Broadcasting has many attractions for political leaders compared with print—firstly, it reaches a large audience; secondly, their own performance gives them somewhat greater influence over the finished product compared with the processing of an interview to print journalists; and thirdly, while broadcasting gives them access to the audience, it is less able to probe details—offering the adept interviewee more scope to control the transaction. Obviously television also poses dangers for politicians:

> It's dangerously superficial, . . . but I think TV has an X-ray quality. You can peer into men's souls, operating at a deeper level of consciousness.

> If the interviewee has not got the answer, the public will know. That is why TV is a most vital medium.

But it is increasingly the preferred medium for political leaders:

> While newspaper journalists found it difficult to get [Wran's press secretary, Brian] Dale to return telephone calls, television journalists found it hard to get him off the telephone.[61]

A short transaction, sufficient to be the focus for a two-minute TV story, allows political leaders both to appear on the most penetrating medium and, by limiting their remarks to the desired subject, focus news attention where they wish. The tendency reached its peak with Prime Minister Fraser's 'kerbside interviews' for TV and radio. Ken Begg described it thus:

> It's too one-sided. I felt like the Strasbourg duck after a while, microphones open and waiting to be fed. I objected to being used and manipulated in that fashion. The doorstops are conducted in such a way that it's very difficult to ask further questions or to seek elucidation because the Prime Minister is usually moving or surrounded by PR men. He says something and that's it. Like it or lump it. It suits the purpose of getting a thirty second grab for the cameras but not much more. [There's usually a maximum of two or three questions.] They're disjointed. People are tripping over one another. It's a rabble. I've lost count of the number of times I've been pushed into the rose garden.[62]

If the leader can achieve the desired exposure with such a minimum of cross-examination, there is no incentive but increased risk in allow-ing more access. Across the Western world, there has been a long-term trend towards governments seeking more control over public interrogations.[63] The quest for control and for PR effectiveness means leaders seek exposure without interrogation, minimising the potential for surprise and embarrassment, and restricting public attention to the priorities which the leader is pressing.

Wedded to the preference for broadcasting and controlled disclosure is the higher priority given to projecting leadership and to personal impressions than to policy exposition.[64] The best avenues of achieving a favourable public persona do not coincide with forums for public scrutiny. Leaders generally are keener to have an image-enhancing, cosy appearance on a 'chat' or variety show than to face a press conference.

The desire to avoid interrogation stems also from the fragile politics often surrounding the formulation of public stances. While being caught in a direct lie is injurious to the cause, public statements otherwise bear an oblique and shifting relation to truth. The battle of public interpretations is not analogous to a court of law. In court, two adversaries seek to relate the same evidence to a common body of law. In politics much of the struggle for political initiative is over which case is to be heard: will the public's/jury's agenda be dominated by, for example, the urgency of a particular reform or the need for tax cuts and fiscal restraint? Different values rather than a common law are invoked. Both sides seek to play to their own strengths and the other's weaknesses: to escalate and sustain some issues, while neutralising others. They are rarely addressing the same evidence.

As a consequence, political public statements are not characterised by logical completeness but rather by calculated vagueness. Rather than specifying pro and con positions, they are concerned with emphasis and omission. Unwelcome contingencies are avoided—'that's a hypothetical question'. Their success often depends on not being probed further, either for specific evidence or logical closure. The studied vagueness is often aimed at simultaneously mollifying different constituencies—maintaining alliances, reassuring the uninvolved while neutralising alternative appeals. In his 1981 policy speech, Premier Wran said: 'I have always been willing to criticise irresponsible strikes but more man days are lost through industrial accidents than strikes, and the government will set up a body to deal with the problem'.[65] The statement signalled that Wran was neither a servant nor an enemy of the trade unions. There was both critical distance and sympathy for the movement's legitimate role. The Premier chose to express this sympathy in the area where there could be least public antipathy. The success of the statement clearly hangs on its failure to specify which strikes he regarded as responsible and irresponsible. Similarly, but less successfully, after Opposition Leader Howard was engulfed in the controversy over Asian immigration which he had provoked, the Liberal Party's internal conflict was resolved by a policy that allowed it to maintain social cohesion by controlling numbers. Internal harmony required silence on whether or not the present position necessitated reducing the number of Asian immigrants.

The profusion of PR feints and strategies provokes another criticism—that in the increased 'noise' it is harder to discern the real 'signals'. The very profusion of news stories may even help political actors to hide their real reasons, as publicity feeds into the framing and justification of subsequent action. Politicians use it to reinforce and justify their intentions as, for example, Peter Howson's diary recorded:

> The Sydney Morning Herald today has a highly critical leading article on Dudley Erwin, and this will give me a tag on which to hang my general line of criticism.[66]

In situations of mutual bluff, its real effect is hard to determine:

> The premature release of information has stuffed a settlement once. We published a compromise. The employers withdrew their offer. Everyone abused us. I think they were looking for an excuse. (Industrial reporter)

The ritualised reporting of conflicts, of claim and counter-claim, produces postures based on participants using the news as a secondary avenue to pursue their primary aims elsewhere:

> I wonder, for example, if there'd be so many threats of disputes compared with actual disputes, if not for the publicity the trade union can gain with a threat, especially in crucial industries like fuel and transport. (Industrial reporter)

Although impossible to quantify, it is plausible that public words and actions used to bear a closer relation to each other; that today there are more verbal feints, aimed solely at affecting public impressions, and without substantial resulting action. Movement in media coverage may be oblique to action elsewhere, or even a substitute for it. Knowledge of news formats can be exploited to redistribute public attention, dramatising the apparent benefits of policies while diffusing the costs.

Finally, the intensity of the public relations enterprise makes it harder to maintain perspective because the over-reactions of the participants and strategists feed into framing the conventional wisdom. The coterie's evaluations of image considerations feed back into the image process, compounding the original success and failure of ploys and performances. A major image problem for a leader who is not succeeding is that there are many operators and experts saying the leader has an image problem. Whatever the original impact on an audience of strategic performances, they are multiplied by the subsequent analyses and prognostications built upon that performance:

One notices about the phenomenon of Mr Mick Young that it is the press who keep telling us how phenomenally successful he was in selling the Labor Party to the press in 1972. There's something strange and incestuous in all this: we are continually being told by the victims of Mr Young's wiles what a great guy he is.[67]

The importance of coterie communication in image engineering is like a hall of mirrors as the coterie are audience one minute, actors the next; targets of some messages, sources of others. The ironies and absurdities of the situation aside, coterie communication encourages self-reinforcing dynamics which compound and amplify the political importance of the original performances. Such cascading conventional wisdoms make public perspective even more difficult.

## Conclusion

The abundance of political lying is a sure sign of true English liberty. (Johnathan Swift)[68]

US President Calvin Coolidge once said 'they can't hang you for what you don't say'.[69] However, modern political leaders are more inclined to believe that their silence would vacate the news stage allowing their opponents to set the public agenda. The battle to influence news coverage is a central arena in most political conflicts.

Subsequently, public relations skills are a prerequisite to political success. Ability at handling the demands of the media is one of the skills of political leadership, like winning concessions in negotiations, administrative efficiency or organising numbers. PR capacities—the mastery of strategic performances, such as the 40-second TV grab, the framing and juggling of public formulas, tactics in focusing news attention—are not identical with these other abilities, but it is unlikely, at least in a Parliamentary system, that they can flourish in their absence. Being a 'pretty face' is no use unless the leader can also 'master a brief.' Being good TV 'talent' cannot take the place of sustaining an argument in the party room. PR strategies are an extension of other political skills, not a substitute for them.

The increase in the scale and intensity of modern public relations politics is an inevitable outcome of the democratic struggle for power in a society where the news media are the central forum of political communication. It is illusory to think that it can be abolished (such as Boorstin's suggestion that the news media refrain from covering 'pseudo-events') or to think that 'only the other side' practises it, or to wish they would play public relations games in a less professional way.

In considering how public relations manoeuvres have affected political practice, it is easy to stereotype the past as an age of innocence and honour. Politicians didn't need highly paid consultants to teach them hypocrisy and expedience. Dexterity at handling the media favours the glib over the thoughtful, but politics always has. Affecting the media coverage of developments is a new and different dimension from affecting the developments themselves; indeed the necessity for handling news coverage may be greatest when there is no scope for affecting actual developments. This favours the cynical over the earnest, but again politics always has.

The history of public relations growth is characterised by the twin themes of democratisation through increased supply of information but domestication of critical thrusts through controlled information release and limited access. The use of PR manoeuvres to pursue political aims both enhances and detracts from democratic debate and accountability. By promoting the need for sharp formulations, they detract from the canvassing of policies, 'demanding simplicity of drama while reality became more complex'.[70] The rise in information is inevitably accompanied by a rise in misinformation.

Deceptive practices are only effective so long as they go unchallenged by political opponents or the media. 'It used to amuse me how often press releases went in without change' (Press secretary). If so, the problem is not PR activity so much as news media passivity. There are several common frames for news coverage attacking PR politics: including the readiness to label a politician as a lightweight; indicating the disjunction between a general claim and the lack of supporting detail; talking of a credibility gap. On the rare occasions when PR is the explicit subject of media reporting, it is almost always unflattering—exposing the discrepancy between public performance and backstage behaviour, or mocking the pretensions and artifice with humorous features or 'diary' items.

However, one gets the impression that successful political leaders relate to the media as do parents to controlling an excitable two-year-old. They know that children get grumpy if not fed regularly, and that they are keener on sweets than savouries. They know that their attention span is short, and the constant appearance of novelty is necessary to maintain interest. They know that confrontations can be noisy, but are usually brief, are best solved by diversion rather than persuasion, and that memories are short and forgiving. They know that the shininess of new toys is more important than their durability, and that how something is done is more important than what it is. And of course the surest means of control is to make it look as if the child is getting its own way.

# 5

# Covert Manoeuvres: Leaks and Briefings

A central part of politics is shaping others' perceptions, directing the public focus, gaining currency for opportune issues and views. The last chapter examined how this is done through public relations strategies. This chapter turns to the more politically inflammable and convoluted means of pursuing publicity interests—the use of covert news manoeuvres where the source remains concealed. After considering some definitional ambiguities, we turn to the general factors which shape the incidence and impact of leaks. The core of the chapter is an elaboration of the political strategies behind covert manoeuvres, followed by some examples of misfiring leaks. The chapter concludes by considering how covert manoeuvres impinge on news quality.

## Definitions and Double Standards

Despite the prevalence of the term, the discussion of leaks is likely to remain a confused and contentious area, partly because it is caught up in the immediate publicity interests of the participants. The news media have a constant interest in stressing the significance and sensitivity of what they reveal, and the enterprise and difficulties involved in securing it. Thus they use the term 'leak' very liberally. However, the conflicting political interests surrounding any particular leak generate inconsistencies. Because leaking is seen as discreditable, there are shifting standards in how beneficiaries and victims of a particular leak portray it:

> Since Mr Fraser and Mr Howard admitted to leaking to journalists details of the Commonwealth's ultimate negotiating position with the Premiers, an attempt has been made in official circles to differentiate between a 'leak' and a 'background briefing'. The Prime Minister's staff strenuously deny

that what Mr Fraser and Mr Howard did was leak; they merely back-grounded. The implication is: a leak is a bad thing, a background briefing is either neutral or good.[1]

The same premise, that leaking is discreditable, or 'I brief but you leak',[2] leads not only to minimising what constitutes a leak from your own side, but inflating the label in attempts to further opponents' embarrassments:

> Fraser demonstrated his weakness for political overkill on the issue of the 'leaked' letter. This document was openly given to Lynch by Frank Crean after the senior Liberal requested to see it. Fraser's allegations about this perfectly normal transaction severely embarrassed Lynch, who apologised profusely to Crean about them.[3]

Similarly, while journalists often complained of press secretaries indulging in selective leaking, all to whom I spoke denied ever doing so:

> I played it very straight. No selective leaking. If a journalist developed a story, okay. Otherwise I gave [any information] to everyone.

These denials, frequently in the face of widespread allegations to the contrary, seem again to be premissed on the assumption that to leak is somehow wrong.[4]

The other definitional problem in discussing leaks stems from the vagueness of much journalistic jargon, which in this case leaves ambiguous the degrees of secrecy and confidentiality of the information published. There is a range between at one extreme what is institutionally released or promoted, including public events, and at the other, information which is institutionally designated as secret or which participants deliberately seek to conceal, either forever or for a certain period. In the middle is an enormous grey area which is neither officially disseminated nor self-consciously restricted. Many institutional proceedings are not usually publicised and may even have a general claim to confidentiality, but there is not normally great concern about them becoming public. In addition, politics inevitably generates conjecture, rumour and gossip, which are easily available to close observers.[5] The resulting stories are sometimes labelled leaks:

> What is a leak? For example, today I was talking to a senior bureaucrat who recently retired. Just chatting about why people leave and in the course of conversation he told me of someone else leaving. That's not a leak, just a titbit of information you pick up . . . . A lot of what's called leaks are [like that]. Journalists contribute [to the confusion] by beating it up, calling them leaks.

A leak can be broadly defined as the unauthorised release of confidential information. However this umbrella covers many variations—that release may come from a dissident but also from someone in authority seeking political advantage, that confidentiality ranges from the very sensitive to the innocuous, from what was intended to be forever secret to the about-to-be announced.

Background briefings can be distinguished from leaks in that they are semi-institutionalised; and usually given to a group rather than to an individual. The convention is that the information may be used but not attributed to the source.[6] Whereas in a leak the secrecy of the transaction is paramount, the identity of the briefer is normally an 'open secret', known to the coterie but only indirectly, at best, known to the public. Briefings are also given to individuals: the distinction from a leak here seems to be that they don't involve the planting of a single confidential datum but rather to giving the background or rationale behind a decision or action, and more problematically, that the briefer's motive is simply to inform rather than seek advantage. Perhaps 'pure' leaks should apply only to self-consciously secret information, but the label will always be used more widely for almost any information whose source remains covert.

## The Incidence and Impact of Leaks

Leaks and briefings are indispensible in contemporary politics. Many conflicts, such as intra-party battles, bureaucratic clashes and disputes between allied nations, cannot be publicly pursued without inhibitions of propriety or political safety. Some participants, such as public servants and Ministerial staff, have political interests in ongoing controversies, but lack the right to an independent public voice.[7] The publicity interests of all participants—what information and views they want in the public domain—at times exceed what it is politic for them to profess publicly. Briefings allow participants more freedom than in formal and public statements, freeing them at least partially from the demands of propriety and political caution. If we read a press report that Foreign Minister Hayden is privately more critical of US actions in Grenada than he has been in public, then we can surmise that Hayden is maintaining a diplomatic public stance, but also is quite happy in briefings to journalists and elsewhere for more critical views to be aired. Even the very vigour of public relations manoeuvres sets up countervailing tendencies for leaks to combat what is said, especially when there is a strong discrepancy between public posture and backstage behaviour. Covert information manoeuvres are integral, then, to shaping the ethos of policy-making, to the pursuit of some political conflicts, and to coping with the constancy of news media attention and the public relations thrusts of others.

Although many older journalists deny it ('leaks have not changed and never will'), the incidence of leaks is almost certainly much greater now than a few decades ago. The greater size and complexity of the polity, the increased strength of the media, plus technological changes ('It is possible that St. Xerox may be canonised by the believers of open government')[8] all make it extremely likely that leaks have become more prevalent.[9]

In the short-term the volume of leaks is most strongly affected by the intensity of conflicts, especially within parties and within the executive government. Bruce Juddery, who pioneered the reporting of the public service, used the geological image of techtronic plates rubbing together. Where there is friction or colliding forces, there will be leaks. If there is wrangling over bureaucratic empires or uncertainty over policy direction, covert manoeuvres increase. A spectacular example was the flow of leaks from the Department of Aboriginal Affairs in 1988, undermining the Minister, Gerry Hand. Similarly within parties, when the inter-party contests are less intense, and when the party leader's authority is lower, the number of leaks is likely to be higher. Possibly no leader suffered from leaks as badly as Opposition Leader Howard in the year following his accession to the leadership.[10]

The prevalence of leaks has not reduced their explosiveness. Three principal reasons explain their dramatic potential: firstly, because they involve concealment and deception they impinge directly on the integrity and conduct of relationships. Secondly, unauthorised disclosures raise questions of control, challenging images of authority and effectiveness. For these two reasons, covert news manoeuvres generate emotions and responses far in excess of what a purely intrumental reading of their content might suggest. Thirdly, by changing the timing and tone of how things become public, leaks often change their reception. They allow chances for counter-organisation and reaction, which can dramatically alter an unfolding chain of events.

## Trust and Deception

Interactions and confrontations between political participants are conducted both publicly and privately. Covert news manoeuvres generate curious interweavings, promoting spiralling reactions between both parties at both levels. The public account thought to be generated by one party has a parallel effect on the second party's future perceptions of their private dealings, modifying each participant's orientation to the other both publicly and privately.

A leaked news story is sometimes read as a public betrayal of private dealings. Its public nature can solidify personal antipathies and tensions into clear lines of conflict:

The turning point in the Fraser–Stone relationship came with the publication in mid-1981 of Stone's stinging criticism of Fraser in a letter . . . to the Prime Minister's Foreign Policy adviser Professor Owen Harries. Stone attacked Fraser's view that a major push was needed to develop the North–South dialogue on economic issues (describing them as half-baked proposals which lacked economic rationality and concluding . . . ) 'the Australian emperor is going to appear remarkably unclothed.' Fraser was deeply angered by the leaking of this letter and felt that Stone was both too indulgent and patronising.[11]

The leaked public account affects the private receptiveness of participants to the others' actions. Reading first publicly of the other's intentions before they have been communicated privately is taken as a sign that options are already closed, that the coming encounter should be anticipated not as a genuine interchange but as an occasion subordinated to the pursuit of a wider conflict. Cameron's receptiveness to any proposals from the Prime Minister were no doubt reduced because 'For three days Cameron had been reading in the newspapers that Whitlam intended to shift him from the labor portfolio'.[12] Similarly:

> The ACTU [claimed] in the National Labour Consultative Council that they'd been reading things in the paper all week, [but that the Government had not communicated directly with them].

The presence of leaked public information and the absence of direct private communication itself communicated that the Government's purposes involved scoring political points off the unions rather than negotiating with them or seeking some common path of mutual advantage.

Leaks are equally de-stabilising when the identity of the leaker remains unknown. The anonymity introduces uncertainties and suspicions into political figures' private dealings. Given the insecurities and egos of politicians living in a world of fluid fortunes, speculation about who leaked and why can easily become obsessive:

> *The Age* broke the news of Barwick's promotion to be Chief Justice. Only five ministers knew of this—PM, Holt, McEwen, Spooner and McMahon. Who gave the leak? McMahon told me it was McEwen. But was this to divert attention from himself?[13]

*Control and Effectiveness*

The personal dimension affecting responses to leaks is compounded by the perceived challenge to authority. No-one can doubt the extent to which uncontrolled leaks preoccupy political leaders. Politicians' responses to leaks are often shaped less by the substance of information, than by their loss of control over the immediate political process. Protestations about the damage from the revelation should be taken as a cry of political pain rather than a literal accounting of the leak's contents. Perhaps the clearest example was the harrassment of newsletter publisher Maxwell Newton by the Gorton Government, especially Deputy Prime Minister McEwen. It climaxed in a police raid on Newton's home and office, and the removal of all sorts of papers. The raid was to investigate Newton's publication of some innocuous diplomatic cables from the Paris Embassy and some leaks from the Primary Industry Department. Indeed the major question about the cables is why Newton chose to publish such boring material, except that it had been leaked. Moreover, Newton's newsletters had tiny circulations, probably not much greater than those authorised bureaucratically to read the material. However, because publication was perceived as a challenge to the Government's authority, the leaks generated a response out of all proportion to their apparent content and any possible impact.[14]

Politicians are inclined to view leaks against them as a hostile conspiracy, sometimes including the reporter among the conspirators. Sometimes such suspicions are well-based: in the late 1940s, the Netherlands Minister in Australia, Opposition Leader Menzies and Melbourne *Herald* controller, Sir Keith Murdoch, enjoyed close personal relations. When, during the Indonesian Revolution, first Menzies made a public charge that the Chifley Government had broken an agreement with the Netherlands, and then a week later a leaked document purporting to support the charge appeared in *The Herald*, it is understandable that the Government's suspicions were aroused.[15] Most often, however, politicians are prone to see more deliberate design behind leaks than actually exists.[16] Reporters commonly say they are less interested in the political impact than in getting a good story.

### Reception and Reaction

The control of information release is vital in shaping both the public impression of an event and the responses of the politically active. The two are related. Large parts of the coterie have their political antennae attuned in order to be on the winning side, to accommodate their positions to what is politically feasible, to deploy their ammunition to battles they can win. Different activities are elicited when the position seems fixed from when it is fluid. If a policy is clearly settled, allies, subordinates and pragmatic waverers fall into line. The public impression then is more likely to be of effectiveness and authority rather than confusion and challenge.

A dramatic example was the announcement in mid-1971 that President Nixon would visit China in early 1972. The preludes to this momentous announcement, reversing American policy of a generation as well as Nixon's previous public positions, were conducted with extraordinary secrecy. If preliminary negotiations had leaked, opposition to the move by the right-wing of the Republican Party and the 'China Lobby' would have been mobilised, and their criticisms would have flourished in the uncertainty. Instead the first public intimation was a dramatic *fait accompli*, a clean decision, effectively executed. 'Premature' publicity could have meant the difference between a public relations triumph and a political disaster.

The first and most obvious impact of leaks on the reception of political moves is that they undermine the hoped-for dramatic effect. Uncontrolled leaks have a detrimental impact on a government's public appearance, because they undermine attempts at coordinated public relations strategies, running the risk that good news announcements will be vitiated by damaging leaks.[17] Moreover, critical leaks from insiders have a greater effect on news coverage than the predictable attacks of opponents, because they are unexpected and because they have more newsworthy information to divulge. A government which cannot control leaks from its own ranks cannot control the news agenda. Thus many leaders have, more prosaically and less effectively, echoed Premier Wran's advice 'no matter how much blood is spilt on the Cabinet floor, we must all walk out arm in arm'.

If an intention becomes public before the actor's capacity to achieve it, a damaging period of wrangling or apparent ineffectiveness ensues. When it was leaked that in August 1972 many members of the McMahon Cabinet wanted to bring on an early election but the Prime Minister had refused, it added to that Government's image of division and indecision.[18] When it leaked that Prime Minister Whitlam wanted to move Crean from Treasury, the long public attention to his intention before his capacity to enact it, produced acute political embarrassments, adding greatly to Crean's humiliation.[19]

Some events are transformed when in the public gaze. If Attorney General Murphy had staged his dramatic 1973 visit to ASIO headquarters in Melbourne without public notice, the subsequent imbroglio might never have developed. However, its imminence was apparently leaked by both the Commonwealth Police and by ASIO— ASIO for self-defence, and the Commonwealth Police to boost themselves in relation to ASIO. The subsequent raid occurred in the full glare of TV cameras and waiting journalists, transforming it into a farce, and raising the political temperature in ways that were detrimental to all involved. In this highly charged atmosphere the original event became caught up in diverse political conflicts—ASIO vs Commonwealth Police, Liberal vs Labor, Whitlam vs Murphy. The profusion of leaks allowed the situation to develop in ways beyond the control of any, certainly damaging Murphy, the Labor Government, the Commonwealth Police and probably ASIO.[20]

The timing of disclosures affects not only the reception of events but their unfolding. Whitlam and Murphy were also involved in the most consequential leak in recent Australian politics—Laurie Oakes's reporting in *The Sun* of the imminent appointment of DLP Senator Gair as Australian Ambassador to Ireland, a move designed to create an extra Senate vacancy in Queensland in the upcoming half-Senate election and perhaps the chance then of an ALP majority. All non-Labor forces were predictably outraged, perhaps marginally more so than if the appointment had become known through a Prime Ministerial announcement. More importantly, it allowed the Queensland Premier to foil the Government's plan:

> Because of [the secrecy involved] Whitlam and Murphy made two astonishing omissions: they failed to get Gair's resignation in writing and they failed to foresee the way in which a determined opponent could counter them.[21]

Bjelke-Petersen was thus able to order the Governor to issue writs for five vacancies as normal, making the Gair vacancy to be filled as if it were a normal casual vacancy rather than having six elected at the imminent half-Senate election. As it transpired this became irrelevant when, in his indignation, Opposition Leader Snedden moved for a double dissolution through blocking Supply. But the Premier's outsmarting of the Prime Minister greatly aided his transformation into a political 'folk-hero'. It also contributed to the ALP's disastrous performance in Queensland, where it gained only four of ten Senate places. The reduced number permitted the Senate machinations of 1975.[22]

The political impact of a leak is determined by its context as much as its content. In January 1976 the newly elected Fraser Government probably wanted to refrain from any immediate strong public stand on the still recent Indonesian invasion of East Timor. A leak of cables from Ambassador Woolcott to the Whitlam Government, advising them in effect to go along with the Indonesians, was the catalyst for the new Prime Minister making his first public commitment against the invasion. This determined the politics of the issue for some months and even years ahead. Later there were other leaks concerning Australian attitudes to the upcoming annexation, perhaps in content more damaging than the first, but in a more settled policy situation, their impact was less.[23]

Impact is not synonymous with intensity of coverage. The most spectacular leak in recent Australian history, also by Laurie Oakes, was the presentation of the most salient aspects of the 1980 Budget two days before its official delivery. Oakes' report created an enormous flurry of activity and attention. Yet its effects, if any, and its aims, are very difficult to discern. Some speculated it was extremely embarrassing for the Government to have such a massive breach of security. Others thought it served the Government's purposes by deflecting attention away from the substance of the Budget to the drama of the leak. Whatever, its impact was less substantial than its leaking was spectacular.

### Aims and Strategies

Who leaks, when and why? This section explores the strategic purposes behind covert manoeuvres. The stress is therefore on the activities of news sources and on leaking as a politically purposive activity. It should also be emphasised that many leaks are due more to journalistic enterprise than to source initiative and that others have no political intent behind them.

It is impossible to determine the exact proportion of leaks which are due to journalistic enterprise against the number stemming from source initiatives. The reporting of Senator Gair's imminent Ambassadorial appointment, the most important leak over the last two decades, was due almost entirely to the determination and 'sleuthing' abilities of the reporter. Following an obscure tip to his *Sun* colleague, John Lombard, Oakes canvassed many possibilities before deducing and then testing the correct story. His investigation culminated in a phone call to the Gair family home in Brisbane. Oakes told Mrs Gair that he understood the Senator had been given an important government appointment and that congratulations were in order. 'Thank you,' she replied.[24]

There are always two parties to a leak, and the leaker has no direct control over how the story is used. Perhaps the outstanding example occurred during the Liberal leadership contest following Holt's death. Someone leaked to *Truth* the details of a court case about a Gorton family property several years before. The editor decided the story would create more interest after Gorton became Prime Minister. Because it was only published then, the story failed in the leaker's aim of sabotaging Gorton's leadership run.[25]

In discussions of the importance of confidential sources methodology sometimes merges into mystique: the Best Stories come from a Deep Throat who reveals The Secret, or The Key to what is happening. But journalists who are good at obtaining leaks rarely have one magical fount of information, but rather a range of good sources built up through past performance, extensive 'legwork' and their own knowledge of events. In journalists' accounts, the importance of

establishing relationships, the difficulties of enticing sources to talk
and the skill in asking the right questions are paramount in any discussion of leaks:[26]

> There is a lot of mystique about sources. A lot of the really good stories are
> gathered not by using clandestine sources but by close reading and under-
> standing of what's happened. Asking the right questions at the right time of
> the right person. Some of the best stories I've had were gathered by asking
> the right question. Often the politicians are prepared to answer, usually on
> background. Very rarely will they refuse to answer, and if they do, you can
> often deduce things from that, which means you can ask other people. A lot
> of it is less mystical than it appears. It's a lot of hard work.

Moreover sources may not actually deliver information, but a tip
that something is interesting or about to happen: 'You often get a tip
on a story from a source that may not be immediately involved'.
Others indulge in opaque games of 'I didn't really tell you'. Even if
specific information is not given, attitudes can be communicated:

> Howard believed Treasury, one way or another, would always get its view
> into the marketplace. The Treasurer once said of his Department: 'They
> grunt, groan, smile and mutter to great effect.'[27]

The willingness to divulge information is bound up as much with
personality as with strategic purposes. Many observers have stressed
that there are compulsive leakers, people who enjoy talking or respond
to the immediate social interactions without any ulterior motive. The
inadvertent or uncalculating leaker appears to have been a continuing
part of Australian politics.[28] Some leaks are more inadvertent than
others:

> Bill McMahon asked us to join him—awkward, because I thought Bill knew
> Bruce Grant. He told me afterwards that he hadn't recognized him. As
> usual Bill spoke rather openly, and then was rather annoyed when some of
> the things he mentioned tonight appeared in an article written by Bruce
> Grant in the *Age*. I told Bill afterwards that he's often spoken to Bruce on
> the telephone and shouldn't be surprised if Bruce expected to be known.[29]

Finally, it should be remembered that leaks can also occur because
of the actions or carelessness of some third party. Decisions or documents often have to pass through several hands—office workers, prin-
ters, and even cleaners and garbage men may come across interesting
material. One journalist claimed that the best leak he ever got literally
did fall off the back of a truck, taken by a friendly service station
attendant who thought he would be interested. One of the most
damaging leaks early in the Fraser Government was apparently
accidental. During his visit to China, Fraser floated a plan for an
anti-Soviet alliance of China, Japan, the USA and Australia. The idea
leaked when documents were carelessly left in a room of journalists.[30]

Former Prime Minister Whitlam made several criticisms of the Hawke Government at what he thought was a gathering of the party faithful. His remarks were publicised, however, because the audience included a Liberal MP who circulated his criticisms to the press gallery.[31]

The following discussion of aims below helps sensitise us to the possible strategies being employed.[32] But it is still impossible to authoritatively determine a leak's origins, especially from external evidence alone. Many leaks are still apparently inexplicable, and open to conflicting surmises about the political strategies involved.[33] Following the leak of the 1980 Budget, many, including *The Australian* editorial, blamed some vengeful public servant. Later others, such as Rupert Murdoch,[34] suggested a Cabinet Minister had leaked it. It is the very nature of leaks that such uncertainties will remain.

## Testing Reactions

The most obvious use of covert news manoeuvres among policy-makers is to allow them to gauge public response without publicly embracing a proposal, so that it is easy to retreat if the reaction is adverse. The manoeuvre inspires aerial imagery: to 'float a trial balloon', 'fly a kite', 'fly a flag'. Such non-committal feints are common to all governments:

> Before the 1980 Budget, proposals for cutting different areas of public spending were leaked to the press over the weeks. The idea was to soften up spending departments and to test public opinion about supposedly sacrosanct programmes like child benefits. If the outcry was too great the proposal would be quietly dropped.[35]

## Forcing Action

Leaking information is sometimes designed to highlight the urgency of a problem. By making previously unknown data public it is hoped to force remedial action. A classic example was the leaking in April 1986 of internal company data from Ciba-Geigy about the dangers of several chemicals then in use. This produced an immediate response from Health Minister Blewett, including proposals for uniform national pesticide laws.[36]

In situations of policy uncertainty, leaks may further the battle over priorities. Facing the twin problems of inflation and unemployment in 1974, the Whitlam Government budgetary direction was particularly uncertain with strong differences within the Government and the bureaucracy. As a result, there was prodigious leaking aimed at influencing what considerations should be paramount:

> Clyde Cameron carefully leaked unemployment figures in an attempt to discredit the Treasury. On the other side, some senior Treasury officers

reputedly held 'background briefings' for selected journalists [to put the fight inflation first priority].[37]

Covert planting of information in the news is a common way of forcing the hand of a reluctant decision-maker. When there are internal conflicts or the decision-making agenda is over-crowded, governments may find inertia an attractive option. Publicity, however, makes continued inaction more difficult. When the McMahon Government, for example, was edging slowly and far from steadily toward some action on Aboriginal Land Rights, the Minister Howson:

> Heard that Colin Tatz had announced on 'This Day Tonight' that he knew for a fact that Lord Vestey was prepared to hand over at least 1,500 square miles of Wave Hill to the Commonwealth. Tatz could only have got this information from Coombs, and I think it's been deliberately leaked . . . in order to make things difficult for us, especially as he knows that this matter is likely to be considered in Canberra within the next few days.[38]

A leak may be used to bring conflicts to a head, the external attention being used to break the internal deadlock. Such manoeuvres can even be used within the politics of the media themselves, as demonstrated in Evans' account of his enforced departure from *The Times:*

> [Searby] kept returning to the theme that unless I resigned immediately 'it' would leak. To which I replied: 'How can there be anything to leak when I haven't resigned?' . . . [Next day 'it' leaked, following a question to Murdoch.] The leak, having failed against me as a theoretical weapon the night before, had been turned into a reality with a planted question and a carefully devised answer. . . . It served me right in a way: when a year earlier Murdoch wanted to bring pressure on Denis Hamilton to stop arguing over the release of Gerald Long from Reuters he had said to me with a big grin: 'Leak it for me, will you, that Long is coming. That'll do the trick.' And it had.[39]

When a decision has been made privately but not yet announced, those fearful of a reversal may leak to make the tentative commitment irreversible. After the 1974 election, the Whitlam Government decided to fight inflation with a more contractionary attitude to public spending. This change of policy was first manifested at the 1974 Premiers' conference, but:

> the Premiers were not taken by surprise. On Monday 26 May *The Australian Financial Review* carried a page one story . . . detailing the decisions reached over the weekend and the new thrust of policy for the premiers' conference. Whitlam was furious and blamed John Stone for the leak.[40]

Even the threat of a leak may be sufficient to make a change of direction more politically difficult. Early in Kennedy's Presidency, the plan to invade Cuba at the Bay of Pigs was being considered. CIA director Allen Dulles warned of a 'disposal problem' if it were aborted: 'The determination to keep the scheme alive sprang in part . . . from the embarrassments of calling it off.'[41] As Halperin notes, such threats always come in the third person passive rather than the first person active—not 'I will leak', but 'it will leak'.[42]

## Mobilising Reaction

More often than not, covert news manoeuvres have a negative intent, to prevent something being done, or to attack an opponent. More common than leaks forcing action are leaks designed to mobilise reaction, through publicity to involve more participants so the proposal will be aborted or modified. Like early intelligence in war, leaks over proposed enemy plans allow the marshalling and concentration of counter forces. When the Whitlam Government sought to lower the reserve price for wool in May 1975:

> the cabinet decision was leaked to the press and reported in the Saturday papers, much to the concern of Labor members and of the wool industry itself . . . . By Monday it was clear the numbers [in Caucus] were there to change the cabinet decision.[43]

The leak's strategic importance is that it alerts forces not immediately involved in time to influence the outcome. It is doubly effective if potential opponents feel affronted by the secrecy of impending moves. Late in the career of Deputy Prime Minister McEwen, the chief proponent of high tariff protection through the 1960s, he sought to tame the powers of his main bureaucratic critics, the Tariff Board. McEwen intended to keep his submission from Cabinet until the last moment, and then overpower them with his determination. However, a leak on the front page of *The Australian* produced a hostile reaction which doomed McEwen's proposals. The hostility owed as much to McEwen's procedure, revealed and thwarted by the leak, as it did to the content of the proposals.[44]

Reaction is also most effectively mobilised when the proposed move contravenes stated policy or ideals. The tentative moves by Prime Minister Hawke to re-open consideration of mining some areas in Kakadu National Park, possibly but not necessarily including uranium at some future date, was effectively scuttled by a leak to *The National Times*. The leak portrayed the Prime Minister as seeking to overturn established policy, and despite ambiguity surrounding his real intentions, the immediate reaction stopped any revisionist moves.

For similar reasons, leaks are particularly effective at aborting conciliatory moves between public opponents, who cannot afford publicly to be seen as shifting ground unless they have a clear resolution to offer.[46] One journalist recalled a leak during the split between the South Australian Liberal Party and the Liberal Movement (see Chapter 7):

> Politicians play it very hard. In 1972 or 1973 I got a phone call, which said 'the Libs and Liberal Movement are about to amalgamate. Hall is calling a meeting today.' I said 'why are you telling me?' He said 'Because if you write it, it won't happen.' I called Hall. He said 'How do you know?'. I wrote it and the meeting collapsed.

In unfolding situations, first impressions frame later interpretations. Whoever makes their version current first will exert a disproportionate influence on later events. Telecom's effort in early 1988 to introduce timed local calls was effectively thwarted by early leaks portraying the negative effects of the policy, while Telecom management, caught off guard by the premature disclosure, was too slow in responding with its own case.[47]

Or another example:

> On the eve of the 1974 snap election, senior Labor ministers wanted to boost the Government's chances by persuading Hawke to contest a Melbourne seat . . . . But Clyde Cameron leaked the story that Hawke had been asked to run against Snedden in Bruce and effectively ended Hawke's chances. He would not challenge Snedden because the risk of loss was too great and he could not nominate for another seat without appearing to be running scared of Snedden.[48]

Some leaks seem designed to register dissent in some larger way, to express distance from the whole direction of policy rather than to affect details within it. In the early 1980s there were two significant leaks of documents produced by Treasury head, John Stone, severely criticising the Fraser Government. The first, cited earlier, was a letter to Fraser's Foreign Affairs adviser over the Prime Minister's embrace of North–South issues, while the second was a letter to Consolidated Press, outlining the relations between Treasury and the Government and deploring the direction of economic policy.[49] Both were written forcefully and colourfully. Both subsequently leaked. In terms of normal bureaucratic politics, the very existence of the letters was an indulgence and an indiscretion. Their publication would have reduced rather than increased any chance of Treasury modifying Government policy. They suggest a higher priority was placed on expressing disdain for the general direction of policy than on maintaining influence on immediate decisions.

## Discrediting Opponents

Praise is more likely to be bestowed publicly, while in criticism anonymity is more prudent. In describing problems and prospects on background it is not uncommon for the description to suggest quietly both one's own virtues and colleagues-cum-rivals' shortcomings. In early 1968, Air Minister Howson noted:

> [Don Chipp] is most unhappy to have learnt of the machinations of Malcolm Fraser, who has been going out of his way to set the press against both Navy and Air, and to a certain extent against Defence, and also against Bill Snedden, in order to increase the press estimate of Malcolm himself. Don has just had concrete evidence from certain press correspondents that this has been happening, and it confirms what both Don and I have felt over the last few weeks. This is one of the crosses, I told him, that we both have to bear, and this may worry us for some weeks to come. However as we are both aware of it we can take suitable action to deal with it in the forthcoming weeks.[50]

In Chipp's final months as a member of the Liberal Party, before leaving to found the Australian Democrats, he again found himself suffering from leaks he attributed to Fraser. A letter he sent to Fraser about his leadership style produced no direct response, but soon after there were press reports that his pre-selection would be challenged. Two sources, one in News Ltd, the other in the Liberal Party, told him the stories were inspired by the Prime Minister's office.[51]

In situations of internal rivalry leaks can be used to reinforce the desired images of opponents. Thus in 1982, the Hawke camp began the de-stabilisation leading to the July challenge by leaking polls, which reinforced the idea that Hayden was much less electorally popular than Hawke, while the Hayden camp leaked information relating to Hawke's non-performance in a party meeting.[52]

Leaks are particularly common after former allies fall out. The rupture generates a desire for revenge while the previously close association has provided the ammunition.[53] After Senator Withers was forced to resign in August 1978 following the McGregor Royal Commission into the electoral redistribution in Queensland, Withers' desire for vindication and need to vent his personal emotions produced one of the most notable briefing sessions recorded in Australian politics:

> In an extraordinarily frank briefing for journalists a day after his sacking, Senator Reginald Withers accused the Prime Minister of having attempted a cover-up over the Queensland redistribution controversy . . . .
> Those journalists who were there accepted that the briefing was on a background basis—that what was said was not to be attributed to Senator Withers . . . . Senator Withers was outwardly relaxed, but seemed to have a need to blurt out what he saw as the truth behind what had happened to him . . . .
> Senator Withers told the journalists: 'It was going to be buried.' The Senator also used the phrase 'swept under the carpet' several times. . . . Senator Withers described Mr Fraser as having 'a crash-through

mentality' and confided that when the Prime Minister was rolled in
Cabinet, 'he's like a wild bull elephant on heat.' . . .

By the end of the session which lasted about two and a half hours,
Senator Withers had—in the words of one of the journalists who saw and
heard it all—'spilled his guts'.

It is to be hoped it was therapeutic for him. It certainly was not for Mr
Fraser.[54]

Usually the attempt to attack partisan opponents is done publicly,
but occasionally leaks figure in discrediting inter-party opponents.
The attack will be more effective because it is seen as independent,
and the party avoids the risk of being accused of mud-slinging:

[Early in the 1983 campaign, the Liberals] believed it would be dangerous
to attack Hawke front-on because of his immense popularity. Instead they
opted to sow seeds of doubt about his abilities, first in the minds of
reporters they hoped might say these things for them.[55]

Before the 1987 Northern Territory election, in which 'Joh's
Nationals' were attempting to upset the Country–Liberal Party
Government, the Darwin political scene:

erupted with unsubstantiated rumours of a sex and drugs orgy involving
Government Ministers . . . .The National Party's media spokesman, Mr
John Anderson, who usually works for a Queensland Government minister,
admitted yesterday that he had phoned journalists about the story. But he
said he had merely rung around to find out if anyone else in the media had
heard it.[56]

### Playing Multiple Games with Multiple Audiences

The divergent demands and cross-pressures on politicians often give
rise to discrepant postures in public and private. Prominent politicians
sometimes seek to have their cake in public statements while also
eating it in background briefings:

Quite often a technique is devised in Canberra by Ministers in trouble.
They arrange for their press secretaries to suggest to the Press Gallery that
their Minister voted against an unpopular proposal in Cabinet and was
simply defending it in public because of the collective responsibilities of the
Westminster system.[57]

The need to simultaneously play multiple games is also generated in
conflicts between political allies. The usual pattern is for public praise
and private disparagement,[58] but sometimes political exigencies call
for the pattern to be reversed: leaders seek to publicly chastise or
distance themselves from an errant colleague, and the public account
is more politically important than the private transaction. During
Prime Minister Hawke's 1986 visit to China, after Treasurer Keating's
famous 'banana republic' warning about economic prospects and his

high profile stance on needed Government action, Hawke and his advisers thought the Prime Minister's leadership needed to be reasserted. This was pursued through a series of transparent background briefings to the travelling journalists. When Hawke actually telephoned Keating from China, the Treasurer said he was able to tick off all the points Hawke made by referring to the article in that morning's *Financial Review*. The 'private' call existed primarily to justify the public rebuke, already delivered by background briefings.[59]

Another moral about the relative importance of public and private 'realities' might be gleaned from the following:

> The Sydney *Daily Mirror* published on page two of its first edition a story about a Cabinet split over the Government's tax reform package. 'A bitter brawl broke out within Federal Cabinet today,' the *Mirror* story said. Foreign Minister Bill Hayden 'took a prominent role in today's Cabinet discussions' and 'there was considerable opposition inside Cabinet today' to cutting the top marginal tax rate but, the story said, 'in the end Cabinet had agreed in general terms to the thrust of the new compromise package'.

In fact the Cabinet meeting scheduled for 10 am was delayed until 3.30 pm, so the *Mirror*'s authoritative account preceded the actual meeting by several hours.[60]

Planting critical information in the public domain while giving private reassurances may allow a leaker to achieve public distancing while also escaping public retaliation from the leak victim. By 1981 the Wran Government's initial commitment to prison reform had cooled considerably as a stream of unfavourable publicity had grown in the tabloid press. After a meeting between the Premier and the head of Corrective Services, Dr Vinson, there were leaks in *The Daily Telegraph* that Wran had chastised Vinson, and expressed dissatisfaction with 'ultra-soft treatment of dangerous prisoners' and the escape rate:

> Naturally I hoped that the Premier would wish to kill a story that so inaccurately described the tenor and content of our meeting . . . I was told that the Premier, who was in Maitland campaigning for a by-election, considered that any statement from him would do more harm than good and cause further speculation . . . [Soon afterwards] the front page headlines of the *Truth* [read] 'Wran to sack gaol's boss'. On this occasion the Premier phoned personally to say there was not a word of truth in the story. Nevertheless he issued no *public* statement of denial.[61]

Similarly Chipp recalled an incident before the 1975 election:

> About five days before the election, [Fraser's] office leaked to . . . the *Daily Mirror* that I would not be in the new Ministry (despite public statements to the contrary). Tony Eggleton . . . phoned me on the day the story appeared and said, 'Don, Malcolm has personally asked me to telephone you and say there is absolutely no truth in the newspaper report.'[62]

As the leak prophesied, Chipp was dropped from the Ministry. The Premier's private assurances to Vinson did not alter the change of direction which elements in his Government had publicly signalled through the leaks. The moral in both cases would appear to be that only a public denial of a publicly appearing story has any political currency, no matter what may be said in private.

Another variation of the public/private interactions is the use of leaks as a public signal about the leaker's intentions in private dealings. By publicly making the stakes clear through leaks, a participant hopes to modify others' private actions. Chipp recalled an incident when he was Minister for Customs in the McMahon Government:

> I had refused to ban a certain book, *The Little Red Schoolbook*, which had offended the DLP and other pro-censorship groups. McMahon instructed me to change my decision, but I refused. He then said, 'Right, we will take it to Cabinet'. Over the weekend his office leaked stories to the Press that Cabinet would force me to back down. I retaliated by letting it be known to the Press that if Cabinet heavied me on this issue I would resign rather than retreat on a matter which I considered to be one of principle—namely political censorship. However it was half way through 1972, and being an astute politician McMahon knew he could not suffer a Minister's resignation in the middle of an election year. When Cabinet met, McMahon's first words were, 'We must support the Minister on this question.'[63]

### Shaping Interpretations of Public Events

It is misleading to counterpose public and private sources of information as completely separate. Rather, covert manoeuvres are commonly deployed to shape interpretations of public events, of success and failure, of intentions and portents. In complex or technical developments, briefings can highlight the 'essential meaning' of the details, to provide what journalists will welcome as a short-cut through the maze, but by doing so affording the briefer considerable scope for convenient selectivity. The meaning of opinion polls and some election results,[64] of economic reports and indicators,[65] of international agreements[66] often pass into the news after the filters of briefings.

Perhaps more intriguing is the use of covert means to influence the interpretation of public statements. When David Barnett resigned as Fraser's press secretary, he was interviewed by Laurie Oakes:

> Q:  The Prime Minister has suffered from a reputation for untruthfulness—if you like, in Winston Churchill's phrase, he is seen as a perpetrator of terminological inexactitudes .... Is that the real Malcolm Fraser?
>
> A:  Well, I thought that the real charge was of terminological exactitude. I thought that what Malcolm Fraser is mostly accused of amounts to using his words carefully and precisely, and not having them listened to.[67]

In August 1975 political speculation was dominated by whether the Opposition would block the Budget in the Senate. Fraser's public response in an ABC interview was 'We'll be following normal procedure in the Senate and with the knowledge we have at the moment, at this stage it would be our intention to allow it a passage through the Senate.' Read now, the caveats stand out starkly. The next day nearly every newspaper proclaimed that the Liberals would allow the Budget to pass, apparently oblivious to the qualifications. Was this an outbreak of collective incompetence or were there factors beyond the public words which explain their interpretation? Oakes has written:

> It was exactly the intention Fraser intended to convey. Before the program went to air members of Fraser's staff told political journalists that their boss would be announcing that the Budget would be allowed through, and that was the way it was reported. The Canberra Press Gallery had not yet learned to treat statements by Fraser like contracts with shonky hire purchase firms.[68]

In addition, Kelly noted that the interview was re-recorded after Fraser's refusal to elaborate or clarify the qualifications:

> His announcement was clearly pre-meditated and he read from notes during part of the interview, being very careful about the precise words used . . . . That night press secretary David Barnett indicated clearly to senior correspondents that Fraser's thinking was that the Budget should pass. . . . Most newspapers played up Fraser's comments after conferring with his office and the next day's headlines announced the election threat had been called off.[69]

Fraser's last election, in 1983, was also called early, and involved similar discrepancies between public statements and backstage briefings. Election speculation first reached a peak on 16 August 1982. Fraser stated publicly that he wanted the Government to run its full term, and denounced the speculation as 'totally and universally badly informed'. Despite this apparently unequivocal response:

> That evening Fraser's press secretary, Eddie Dean, rang senior newspaper reporters and cautioned them not to interpret these comments as ruling out a September election.[70]

The desire to supplement public utterances with background comment stems also from the perceived need to use the public stage to prosecute institutional conflicts, while in private sources canvass interpretations more freely. Many of the recurring conflicts in Australian political life involve predictable postures. Consequently, the stylised public language conceals the private expectations of the participants. Compare the dramatic divergence in the following two reports from *The Age*. The headline story began: 'Senior [Fraser] Government Ministers last night savaged the Arbitration Commission after its decision to grant a 4.5% national wage increase', while inside a News Analysis began:

> The Government is privately relaxed about the size of the indexation wage rise and positively pleased about some aspects of the Arbitration Commission judgement.
> The 4.5% rise is about what it expected.[71]

*Shaping Expectations*

Private briefings are deployed even more commonly to affect the interpretation of future public events by conditioning expectations. Covert manoeuvres can be used both as 'shock absorbers' for bad news and for sharpening expectation of good news. Gittins observed Treasurer Howard's responses to the rising inflation rate in 1980:

> Mr Howard faced the cameras with the air of a man who had grown used to success and had learnt to be modest about it.
> If anything, he said, the December quarter increase was 'a little lower than might have been expected.' He had predicted in his Budget speech that the figure would be 'relatively large', and this had in fact occurred.
> But had this victory turned his head? Never....
> 'Today's result gives no cause for complacency,' he protested...To understand the reason for Mr Howard's rather satisfied tone it has to be realized that a rise of up to 3.5% had been widely tipped. Late last year Government officials had been forecasting a rise of about 4%.

Gittins then showed how the previous three CPI figures had also been preceded by reports of expectations higher than the actual figure. Each time Howard was able to relate the actual figure to the 'expected' one:

> Looking back on this string of generally favourable reactions, it is rather puzzling that they accompanied an annual inflation rate which rose inexorably through last year from 7.8% to 10%.[72]

Sometimes it is essentially a matter of 'getting in first', of using a pre-emptive leak to influence the reception of some potentially adverse event.[73] The need to 'prepare the ground' with covert manoeuvres is especially great when there is to be a policy reversal. When the Australian Government was forced into an embarrassing somersault in its attitude to the Indonesian takeover of Dutch West New Guinea in 1962, External Affairs Minister Barwick reportedly briefed newspaper managements to defuse the impact of the public announcement.[74] By the time the Hawke Government finally announced in August 1988 that Hayden was to become Governor-General, the issue had been thoroughly canvassed after emerging first through some leaks. Although not an entirely successful episode in news management, what would have been a shock announcement was thoroughly expected when it was eventually made.

Similarly, when a government wishes to hold an early election, speculation about its likelihood may make the move seem almost natural when it occurs. In 1977, Prime Minister Fraser even gave such speculation, generated by his own office and colleagues, as one factor necessitating bringing the election forward.[75]

That hardly perennial of Australian politics, the Budget leak, is perhaps so prevalent because it can serve diverse purposes. Some are testing responses, others seeking to prolong kudos for benefits conferred,[76] still others an attempt by dissident Ministers or Departments to mobilise reaction against proposed cuts. One further use of covert manoeuvres before the public announcement is to condition expectations about the Budget's likely shape, about what parameters are desirable and feasible. Probably such expectations were best managed in the Keating Budgets of 1986 and 1987. Before the first the idea that a $4 billion deficit was the lowest achievable and would be acceptable to the money markets became extremely prevalent. When the Treasurer then announced a $3.5 billion deficit, it was, against the expectations he had so successfully engineered, hailed as a triumph. Having himself set the pass mark, he achieved honours.[77] Similarly in 1987, after assiduously spreading the impression that a balanced budget was not feasible, the Treasurer's proclamation of his achievement was again enhanced by the sense of expectations the Government had itself generated.

## Enhancing Media Relations

In addition to occupying a central role in adversary conceptions of the democratic importance of the news, leaks and briefings have a day-to-day importance for the media in terms of competitiveness. Successful publication of an accurate leak, especially if dramatic, is the most obvious way for news organisations to score competitive scoops. At the individual level, it is often taken as proof that the journalist is doing a good job and has strong inside knowledge. The advantages that having access to leaks gives to journalists implies that newsworthy information is a valuable commodity, offering opportunities for patronage and subsequent political benefits for those who can supply it. A final motivation for leaks then is not the achievement of any specific effect through publication, but in building debts and relationships with individual journalists.[78]

Once this logic is grasped, every government decision becomes a potential exercise of patronage, not to be announced but once, but an opportunity to bestow favours and in the process perhaps prolong and enhance coverage:

> Dale never gave it to one person all the time . . . . Here you all get official
> leaks. That is how Dale works. It didn't mean anything or hurt anybody.
> You fall into working on a daily news story. Your editor rings up and asks
> 'what have you got?' 'A leak on the Budget.' And your editor says 'that's
> good'. (NSW TV reporter)

Naturally such manoeuvres are most successful when least obvious,
when any patronage considerations emerge indirectly if at all. One
journalist recalled his relationship with Attorney-General Lionel
Murphy:

> Murphy seemed to have a good understanding of the voracious needs of the
> media. I once said to him that we were having a rather slow news day, and
> immediately he rustled in his papers and gave me a story about some sort
> of official investigation being undertaken into the mercury content of
> eggs . . . . We had a page one scoop about poisoned eggs. The day it was
> announced that he would be going to the High Court, I dropped down to
> say goodbye. The staff were packing up his office and Lionel said to Trevor
> Wright, one of his offsiders: 'See if you can find some Cabinet decisions for
> Richard.' It was a sort of farewell gesture which kept us going with stories
> for months.[79]

Compare that with the heavy-handed attempts of Minister Hurford's
attempt to get regular air-time on Jeremy Cordeaux's morning program on 5DN, where in writing he suggested that he could break
stories for a *quid pro quo* of a regular time slot. The letter leaked,
causing Hurford enormous embarrassment, including calls for his
resignation.[80]

### What Tangled Webs

Aims are not the same as effects. Leaks frequently misfire and prove
counter-productive to the leaker's aims, while their covert nature gives
rise to dangers for news organisations and reporters.

The basic reason why leaks misfire is that they are normally an
instrument of conflict, and the opposing side will be seeking counter-
moves:

> There is no perfect political move, no perfect strategist. Placing stories
> can backfire. There are always opponents who can come back with an
> unexpected reply. People make mistakes. The manipulative process is often
> very poor.

Leaks tend to produce resentment in those leaked about:

> Early in 1972, the Australian Government learned from British sources that
> James was about to be released. In an attempt to win publicity and praise,
> the office of the Foreign Minister, Nigel Bowen, leaked the news . . .
> Affronted, the Chinese Government changed its mind. James was not
> released until after the election . . . [after] nine more months in prison.[81]

Finally, the complexity of the political environment and the multiplicity of audiences means that individual aims cannot be neatly insulated. The Cameron 1974 strategy of leaking unemployment figures may have succeeded in securing it a higher priority in policy-making but simultaneously added to the general image of Government incoherence and of severe economic problems.

Four particularly counter-productive leaks, all involving the Fraser Government, illustrate the interplay of factors. The most spectacular followed the Premiers' Conference in early May 1981: 'The Premiers were [claiming] that they'd wrung the last cent out of the Government'. Fraser and Howard separately briefed reporters that if the Premiers had put up a stronger case then they could have been given another one per cent, roughly $70 million. Their aim apparently was to show the Federal Government's toughness and negotiating success. The reports based on the briefings were not reported prominently, but WA Premier Court seized on the claims and other Premiers quickly joined in. Events then moved quickly in the Canberra press gallery, culminating in a press conference at 8 pm with Howard being subjected to pointed questioning about why he had broken his oath of Cabinet secrecy in the briefing, why they had tried to make the Premiers look like fools, and why he, rather than Fraser, was making a public confession. Two hours later Fraser also faced a torrid press conference. For several days the Government received intense unfavourable coverage. Instead of appearing tough, they looked devious and out of control.

Another misfiring leak by Prime Minister Fraser occurred during the Commonwealth Heads of Government Conference at Lusaka in 1979. He and other Australians leaked details of a settlement ending the Rhodesian war and bringing an independent Zimbabwe into being, first to the Australian and then to the British press, before it had been formally agreed by the whole conference. The aim was probably to make it impossible for a reluctant Mrs Thatcher to waver, and to ensure that Fraser's own role was highlighted. The leak almost had the reverse effect. For several hours it appeared that the British, angered by the leak and fearful that the premature publicity would allow the Tory right wing time to mobilise, were going to refuse the agreement.[82]

The misfiring leak which had the biggest immediate impact on policy occurred in late 1976, with Prime Minister Fraser as its target rather than its instigator. A Cabinet committee had considered the desirability of devaluing the Australian dollar. Treasury opposed this strongly, fearing the inflationary consequences. Apparently in an attempt to 'lock the Government in' and force them to support the dollar, Treasury sources leaked that the Government was 'soft' on devaluation to *The Age*. Publication brought an immediate reaction from the Prime Minister but in the opposite direction. He announced a massive 17.5 per cent devaluation, 'much greater than even its advocates had been suggesting . . . Quickly the devaluation was wound back to 12.45% but this, if anything, caused even more confusion'.[83] Fraser also immediately ordered the splitting of the Treasury Department into two, with a separate Department of Finance. Many interpreted the move as revenge for the leak. Certainly a period of estrangement between Treasury and the Government ensued.

The final misfiring leak occurred because it verged into 'dirty tricks' and was exposed as such. Mullinsgate[84] originated in October 1979, when the Federal Secretariat of the Liberal Party received some documents from the ALP advertising agency, Mullins, Clarke and Ralph, about strategy in the next election. They retyped and collated four documents into one, put their own headings on them, and put on a new front page with the headings, 'ALP campaign strategy' and 'strictly confidential'. After some Liberal campaign plans were leaked to *The Australian Financial Review*, the Liberals decided to leak their newly manufactured document, passing it off as official ALP strategy rather than suggestions from the agency. It was leaked initially to *The Australian* and *The Sydney Morning Herald*, while Liberal Ministers, notably Viner, referred publicly to it as an official ALP document. Opposition Leader Hayden and his staff gradually realised where the documents had come from, and mounted an effective counter-attack. They first raised the question whether the Liberals had stolen it from the agency. The agency had been robbed in early November, and some cash taken, but so had several other offices nearby. Despite the ALP's initial suspicions, it seemed clear the theft was unrelated to the Liberal Party. But, as some commented, in clearing themselves of charges of theft, they effectively showed themselves guilty of deceit and forgery.[85]

Although the transactions surrounding covert news manoeuvres are mostly prosaic and transparent, the preceding example shows how their anonymous and partial nature allows more Machiavellian strategies.[86] One senior journalist said that a Prime Minister once leaked something to him simply so that he could rant at his Cabinet about leaks. Another recalled:

> I was told about a Cabinet decision that didn't happen. It was a straight-out lie, designed to embarrass me and it did . . . [although] it didn't cause the paper or the media generally much embarrassment because so few noticed.

The possibility of misinformation via covert manoeuvres poses special risks for news organisations. When covert sources are used, primary responsibility for the story's veracity passes from the source to the news organisation. If sources publicly say something foolish or problematic then any resulting odium normally attaches to them. But when the source remains private, the news organisation and reporter are held centrally responsible for the content. If details or nuances are slightly wrong it is easier for those offended by the story to discredit it, especially if it cannot be confirmed by the covert source.

The risks for reporters were graphically shown during the 1983 Royal Commission into the relationship between lobbyist, David Combe, and Soviet diplomat and KGB agent, Valerie Ivanov. *The Bulletin*'s Jacqueline Rees reported, after checking the story with Combe, that the Hawke Government had made offers about a deal: 'But Rees's story as it appeared was wrong in two details: she wrote of government overtures and offers to Combe and . . . "the government's preparedness to withdraw Justice Hope's warrant".'[87] Although some tentative and ambiguous discussions had occurred, this construction was misleadingly definite, and suggested that all the initiative was coming from the Government. The reaction at the Hope Royal Commission was immediate, and 'Rees was forced to resign by the publisher of *The Bulletin*, Trevor Kennedy. He told Rees the Prime Minister had complained.'[88]

Because of such risks, some news organisations have displayed ambivalent attitudes, or even refused to use 'off the record' unsourced information. The ABC news, for example, was very slow to accept 'leaks' as legitimate news:

The application by the ABC Canberra office of the traditional principle of no report without sourcing meant that developments inside the Government party room which led directly to the dismissal of Mr Gorton [as Prime Minister in 1971, see chapter 7] were not reported by ABC news. The absence of the Gorton story from major ABC news bulletins did not escape the viewers and there was a heavy volume of complaints to ABC management.[89]

It is apparent that the norms of confidentiality can cause tensions and uncertainties in news organisations:

In 1969, there was the Duntroon bastardisation story . . . . X told me to get the story. Duntroon said nothing. I finally got hold of a bloke who gave me everything. X was delighted, then said the editor wanted to see me. He asked me for my sources. There was a barney. I walked out. The story was not run. Next day I was asked to rewrite. I was summoned into the editor again. Again it was not run. The next day the same story was on page one of *The Australian*. I went in with a smug smile. I've never been asked for sources since.

This story has two noteworthy aspects: first the reporter's indignation over what he saw as a breach of professionalism, but also that the premium on confidentiality posed risks and questions of trust for the news organisation.

## Covert Manoeuvres and News Quality

Protecting confidential sources and honouring confidences is the ethical point most strongly and frequently volunteered by journalists:

> I've always tried to be straight with sources. I never reveal them.
>
> The golden rule is break a confidence and you're history.

The strength of these statements is testimony firstly to the drastic fate that some leakers have suffered after being exposed.[90] But it also suggests that we are dealing with one of those convenient ethical stances which carries pragmatic benefits. Some reporters went to great lengths to show their absolute reliability in maintaining confidences:

> A guy leaked me a story with one deliberate error so that they could attack my veracity. The strongest denouncer to me in the bar was the source. I didn't reveal anything. Later on he said to me 'I've seen your form now, anytime you want information...' (Industrial reporter)

The impetus toward confidential sources is the desire to go beyond the routines of public statements: 'I'm not a handout journalist, which means you have to develop contacts'. It stems from and reinforces an active, adversary approach to news gathering. The unauthorised publication of confidential or secret material is central to the professional self-image of many journalists. One editor listed as the first strength of his publication that sometimes it told people things which those in power didn't want them to know. The adversary self-image of news is found in such pronouncements as 'news is something that someone doesn't want you to publish; all the rest is advertising'. It strengthens the watchdog role of the media toward major power groups.

Moreover, if sources know they can talk without being directly quoted, more pertinent information becomes available to journalists. Less shackled by the constraints of party discipline, bureaucratic proprieties and the likelihood of suffering personal consequences for the airing of critical opinions or information, far more is given. It allows journalists to be more alert to the grapevines about shifting fortunes and imminent developments. There is a much better chance of informed, penetrating analysis, of understanding and anticipating developments, of going beyond public facades:

> One way in which sources are important is not in the news they give but the information about the way people and the parties are thinking. It is important to sit for an hour over a drink with a politician, and talk about politics and get a sense of direction. I get a lot for analytical pieces as a result of conversation, where thought is crystallised and you get a sense of what they are thinking.

The general prevalence of leaks is an incentive to all sources to be more forthcoming. Although any individual leak usually increases the stock of significant public knowledge only marginally, their prevalence 'pushes back' the bounds of what is routinely released.

> Stories tend to build on themselves. If you are trying to write something every day, you get contacts. You even start to create stories.

If sources see leaks as being inevitable, they are more likely to institute briefings or press releases, so that they may prevent more uncontrolled and damaging searches by journalists.[91] There is no doubt that the use of covert sources enlarges the public domain of knowledge. However its prevalence also has detrimental effects on news quality.

*Leaks Distort News Judgments*

Sometimes the spurious sense of drama generated by the leak twists judgments about the substance of the information. The equation of best news with private sources is partly rooted in the desire for a competitive edge. More substantially important information may be revealed through routine channels, but is competitively devalued:

> A good example of this occurred recently: one of my colleagues published a cable detailing criticisms of the Indian Government made by Australia's ambassador. The publication was very damaging to the ambassador concerned and nearly resulted in his being sent home. But...the same information had been published about six weeks previously—in the Department of Foreign Affairs monthly publication 'Backgrounder'. We had all received it and we had all ignored it. However, when one journalist was given essentially the same information with a 'confidential' classification on it, it became front page news.[92]

Secrecy produces an aura, suggesting something dramatic and glamorous. When *The Australian*, then exalting every action of Prime Minister Fraser as a political triumph, sought to highlight the success of his 1976 visit to China it reported that he had visited 'secret' areas of the country. When Professor Blainey was mounting his attack on the evils of Asian immigration, he asserted that there was a 'secret room' in the Immigration Department where such decisions were made.

Occasionally, governments can exploit this orientation in manipulating the news.[93] More commonly they are its victims. The most obvious construction to impose on leaked information is that of duplicity, that the private reality differs substantially from the public claims. In April 1975, a leak revealed that the Whitlam Government had sent somewhat different telegrams to the Hanoi and Saigon regimes, as Whitlam had already admitted in a general way in Parliament. *The Sydney Morning Herald* called it 'the greatest scandal in the

history of Federation' and in press reporting, the messages were transformed into the 'Prime Minister's secret messages'.[94]

Similarly when Brian Toohey obtained the confidential document
'Strategic Basis of Australian Defence', he was severely criticised by
Prime Minister Hawke and commentator David Bowman for selective
omissions. Perhaps in an attempt to dramatise a pedestrian document,
these led to a de-emphasising of Australia's continuing commitment to
the nuclear non-proliferation treaty that did not maintain 'the perspective of the original report'.[95]

### Leaks Permit Source Manipulation

The competitive rewards accompanying the publication of leaks makes
journalists more open to manipulation. They may be seduced by the
appearance of access and intimacy or the lure of an 'exclusive', and so
not fully explore others' perspectives. The wish to gain exclusives and
maintain favoured access can induce selectivity, limited search and the
possibility of manipulation:[96]

> For years the most inveterate leaker in the public service was a senior
> officer in the Tariff Board. They were being oppressed by McEwen . . . .
> He leaked to me, but he objected to me seeing the Trade Department to
> balance the stories. He wanted me to use his stuff uncritically . . . . It cost
> me a few other contacts—seeking both sides and not just following one.

The difficulties are compounded because journalists' partial knowledge of developments make it difficult to evaluate the fragments they
are given.[97] Some, however, regarded this as but one unfinished stage
in a total process:

> You are aware of being used and there have to be limits to that. Sometimes
> you don't know where the distortions are. You've got one part of a story.
> You must have as many sources as possible. On the way, there may be
> distortions, but the whole process means that the sum of knowledge is
> increased. One, I don't think it's the reporter's role to see themselves as a
> player. Two, journalistic competence means you must not be the passive
> instrument of other people.

### Leaks Permit Source Irresponsibility

Because the source remains covert, there is the possibility of them
adopting different faces in public and private unbeknown to the
public. The discrepancy does not always occasion outrage among
journalists, some of whom seem to make the quaint distinction that
for a politician to lie publicly is a political necessity, but to mislead
a journalist privately is a sin. However it can also embarrass the
journalist:

The background briefing becomes a substitute for the on-the-record press conferences where a Prime Minister or any other Minister must take public responsibility for what is said. It is a notorious fact in Canberra that background briefings are used to float ideas which are subsequently denied officially, leaving the journalist marooned and humiliated, unable to say where the information came from.[98]

### Covert Sources Camouflage Journalistic Incompetence

Like other types of secrecy, the prevalence of covert manoeuvres provides the possibility of abuse. Occasionally it may even provide the cover for invention. More commonly, it allows news reports to be framed with a hardness and certainty that is not quite justified, to blur the boundaries between knowledge and surmise. It also allowed journalists to magnify their sources, referring to them as plural when perhaps there was only one, exaggerating their closeness to key events:[99]

> When I was first in the Lobby I was amazed by the omniscience of my colleagues, and despaired of ever attaining it; but then I noticed that they were in the same places as me all day, and seemed to have few special sources of information; and the seditious thought began to dawn that these confident assertions, these detailed readings of the minds of Ministers, could not strictly be classed as more than inferences: inferences based on experience and evidence, but still not quite what they seemed.[100]

### Leaks Make Audience Evaluation of Information Difficult

'The basic criticism of source anonymity is therefore that the reader does not know what to believe. Stories may confuse and obfuscate more than they clarify.'[101] Sometimes there may be a misleading definiteness in reports. Just as often the use of covert sources means that news is more substantially based than the public realises. There was little in the news reports following the long post-resignation briefing given by Senator Withers (cited above) to suggest their basis. Anonymity often detracts from the impact of a report, making it easier for others to ignore.[102] At other times, anonymity makes it impossible to evaluate the shifting balance of opinion in situations of conflict or uncertain policy direction.[103]

### Journalistic Inhibitions Prevent the Examination of Covert Publicity Manoeuvres

Given that covert manoeuvres are so prevalent in politics they should be examined in the news as would any other attempt at political influence. However, when reporters get leaks, 'the motivation . . . is usually not mentioned, although that may be the most significant part of the story'.[104] The reluctance of reporters to examine the origins and patterns of covert manoeuvres in the news means that the news media are deliberately failing to explore one important part of the political landscape.

There is no finality about the value and influence of leaks. Contrast these views offered by two leading Australian journalists:

> Far from being the pinnacle of journalism, leaked material is mostly a perversion of what journalism is all about.[105]

> I still think that the leak is an important part of the democratic process.

Around covert manoeuvres in news gather a great variety of political purposes, some adding to the democratic process, others to political manipulation; some resulting from journalistic enterprise, others reflecting journalistic gullibility; some enhancing the public's right to know, others adding to their sense of confusion. Whatever the merits of any individual leaked story, the whole process will remain an inherent but explosive part of contemporary politics.

# PART III
# Political Impacts

# 6

# Inter-Party Politics and Election Campaigns

There is an unacknowledged irony in news coverage of election campaigns: the media maintain the pretence that they are reporting a campaign which exists independently of them, when in fact the primary purpose of those campaign activities is precisely to secure favourable news coverage. The largest audience for any campaign activity is the one that can be reached through the mass media, particularly television. It is not surprising, then, that campaign strategists devote much of their ingenuity and effort into achieving and affecting media coverage. News is not incidental or extraneous to the process of electioneering, but its central arena.[1] In no other area is the transforming influence of the media on political processes so immediately apparent.

The purpose of this chapter is to chart the dynamic interplay between news practices, parties' strategies and the changes in electioneering. The examination proceeds in four stages. First, the publicity interests generated by the nature of inter-party competition are considered; then the immediate influences on the reporting of campaigns— followed by how parties' campaigning strategies are developed in response to the first two areas. Finally, the impact of news on the election outcome and conduct is considered. The empirical material is drawn primarily from Federal elections since 1972, although there are also occasional references to State elections and contrasts with earlier Federal campaigns.

## The Logic of Inter-Party Politics

Inter-party politics is the only area of news coverage involving a zero-sum, winner take all conflict where the decisive basis for victory is public support. This generates publicity interests which have wide consequences for news coverage. Because public support is crucial, both sides are continually concerned with obtaining publicity. A two-sided party contest[2] is zero-sum: one side improves its electoral support only at the expense of the other. The nature of the game does not allow mutual advancement or accommodation and compromise. It is also a winner-take-all contest: only one side or the other forms the Government. The key to understanding parties' behaviour in elections is that there is an absolute chasm between winning and losing. There are no second prizes or second chances. Competitions of this kind— winner-take-all and zero-sum—are hardly conducive to a strong sense of fair play. Winning in whatever way is preferable to losing nobly.

The underlying logic of party competition, and its primacy in determining the party's fortunes, is the spur which ensures the eternal vigour of party conflict. Antagonistic interests exist irrespective of conflicting ideologies or substantive policy differences, or even the degree to which the parties reflect external social conflicts.[3]

The logic of inter-party conflict often leads to an exaggeration of policy differences. The extent to which the parties offer contrasting or similar prescriptions varies,[4] but the appearance of polarisation is constant. Their primary interest is not in canvassing the merits of alternative policies but in gaining partisan advantage. It is always in an opposition's interest to promote a simple equation: the blame for all existing problems is attributed to the government, and the solution lies simply in changing governments. Presidential candidate Nixon's statement in 1968, 'There is nothing wrong with this country that a good election wouldn't fix', is essentially echoed by most Opposition Leaders.[5] The situation does not encourage measured appraisals:

> The action we have taken is right to remove from Australia the worst government since the beginning of Australia. (Malcolm Fraser, on blocking supply, 1975)[6]

It is not in the parties', especially the Opposition's, interest to stress the constraints upon all governments. Party leaders often invoke the imagery of elections as 'crossroads', but not as alternative dead-ends, or the same road but with contrasting rhetorical accompaniments. What is bitterly attacked in opposition often, of course, remains unchanged or unsolved after gaining government.

Elections involve preferential rather than absolute judgments. Whether the public at any time has a high or low opinion of both major parties is irrelevant to the election outcome (especially in a system with compulsory voting). The combination of antagonistic interests and preferential judgments contribute to another guiding maxim of contemporary political practice: it is easier to sustain negative images of opponents than positive images of oneself. The result is the characteristic emphasis on mud-slinging, because attack is more potent than exposition. While the logic of the conflict is constant, its practice is dynamic, with each side reacting to the other's successes. The result has been a spiralling toughness and cynicism in the pursuit of party advantage. The inducements to restraint are few,[7] while the pressures toward ruthlessness are many:

> The chilling reality is that in three years the Whitlam Government sought supply six times and on only one occasion, autumn 1973, did the Opposition parties not speculate about blocking it. The lesson learnt by the Hayden-Hawke generation was that only a new ruthlessness within the ALP could combat the conservatives.[8]

*Incumbency*

Government is not only the prize, it is the key resource for future struggles. A party may win the election with promises that store up later problems—but once in government the party has substantial means to manage the timing and appearance of these embarrassments in the least damaging way.

Governments enact decisions and because action is more consequential than criticism they are inherently more newsworthy than Oppositions. Governments enjoy more initiative in their media relations: by their activity and show of concern they can help focus the news agenda into particular areas. Their capacity to do this is far from total, but neither is it insignificant. Opposition reaction is 'tacked on at the end' or even '[cut] because of time'.

Governments have further publicity advantages as the custodians of the administrative and ceremonial roles of the state. They may embody national unity on occasions of both national tragedy and triumph. The publicity given to Prime Ministers at sporting events, at national or artistic festivals, and a range of 'special events' (opening new buildings, etc.) is a commonplace. The distribution of government services can often be elevated into shows of beneficence.

Governments have an interest in generating occasions where the role of the Opposition is reduced to invisibility, and where partisan 'balance' is not a major consideration in reporting. In election campaigns and in the reporting of Parliament there is a general tendency toward symmetry in reporting claims and counter-claims. However on other occasions—such as the ceremonial and administrative events mentioned above, on Prime Ministerial travel abroad, or at a National Economic Summit—the Opposition's views are simply not sought, or they are reduced to a role of carping irrelevance.

Publicity through news is more vital but less easily attainable for oppositions than governments. Political journalists in all settings made comments like 'the Opposition is easy to see' and 'the Opposition is always very accessible'. Oppositions must change sufficient votes to win office, but in normal news processes they tend to be cast in a reactive and always critical role, reinforced by the common view that

governments lose elections more than oppositions win them and that
it is easier to tarnish the opponent's image than polish one's own.
Strategists from several oppositions affirmed the difficulty of 'grabbing
the offensive' and of generating positive publicity:

> It's very difficult in Opposition to get the news initiative. It's hard to avoid
> being reactive and it's hard to be positive . . . . The style we adopted was to
> lead with the positive. Announce what [our] Government would do and
> contain criticism of the Government within that . . . . You're trying to
> knock holes in the Government while appearing to be positive. Govern-
> ments have so many more opportunities.

The one advantage that an opposition has is that governments are
often held, indiscriminately, to be responsible for providing solutions
to any problem that arises. The processes by which credit and blame
are attributed has less to do with objective responsibility than with
subjective expectations, and with the perception that the solution can
be provided by the other party. While economic problems persist,
however, government longevity is never assured:

> Politics is on a merry go round all over the world . . . . The catalyst in the
> speed-up of political processes is the economy, but no one knows how to
> bring it under control. And that brings a new explosive, unpredictable
> element. It's the old wet gelignite under the house . . . . If you can't stabilize
> the economy, the whole of the political power base is destabilized and
> shifting. 25% of the electorate are potential swinging voters. (Peter Bowers)

## Election Campaigns as News

The interaction of three factors is pivotal to understanding news
during election campaigns:

1  The sheer intensity of campaign coverage. The herd journalism
   produced by the huge entourages following the party leaders[9]
   combined with the frenetic efforts of the politicians and campaigners produces a pressure-cooker atmosphere.
2  The profusion of public performances and the scarcity of other
   sources of news. Campaigns consist overwhelmingly of public performances and statements, while access to more private information is more limited than normally.
3  The framework for most news coverage is the campaign as contest.
   The competitive nature of elections makes this an inevitable orientation, but its attractions for news organisations are so great, that
   the campaign as policy forum becomes neglected or stereotyped.

In some ways election campaigns are easy for news organisations to
cover: a regular supply of developments is assured, and in a superficial

way at least, they allow more planning than many types of news events:

> Elections are easy to cover: one guy with the PM, another with the Opposition Leader, one waiting in the wings. (TV news director)

The reporters are caught up in the frenetic atmosphere of the campaigners.

> Election campaigns are real killers. You go from 6 am to midnight seven days a week for three weeks. I got sick at the end of it because of the fatigue.

> The campaign was so much fun. It was a rage from the start to the end. [It was good for our programs] because the candidates were gearing themselves to produce audio and visual material . . . . Each day you would get actuality . . . often superb actuality. And you would talk to people.

> I've enjoyed all the campaigns, the atmosphere and the excitement . . . the way they try to secure themselves against extinction, the ruthlessness.

However, campaigns also present news organisations with potential dilemmas, because substantial coverage is almost obligatory but a lot of election news is dull in terms of normal news values. News organisations, especially in Federal elections, are obliged to make a strong commitment to covering the campaign—because of public expectations about their importance, because other news organisations will be doing so, because of the wish to maintain their professional reputation, and because of the expensive staffing and travel arrangements made in advance. These almost dictate that correspondents' copy will be used irrespective of its intrinsic newsworthiness.

But in many ways the nature of election campaigns defeats the quest for the types of stories news organisations usually prize. Herd journalism produces conformity between competing organisations to the detriment of genuine scoops. News values emphasise dramatic events or consequential actions whose relevance to the public is obvious, but campaigns consist almost entirely of rhetoric, of dubious future importance. Moreover, considerations of balance further inhibit news selection: 'We try to ensure roughly the same amounts of time. It goes contrary to judging everything on news values.'

Party discipline and unity are typically paramount in the interests of the party more effectively waging the inter-party struggle, so the potential for damaging revelations or back-stabbing is at a minimum. Thus there is little scope for leaks, but rather a surfeit of carefully rehearsed public performances.

*The Campaign as Contest*

Covering the campaign as a contest has several advantages for news organisations. In the highly wrought atmosphere of an election, covering a contest is less dangerous and controversial. It neutralises some of the risks of appearing partisan, and the charge of imposing their own priorities and preferences. Not only is it the path of political safety, it is also more attuned to media ideas about audience interests. Policy expositions and debates are seen as boring, abstract, complex and static, while a contest is tangible, personal, fluid and simple.

The most obvious consequence of covering the campaign as a contest is the search for scoreboards, especially the use of public opinion polls. Until the 1969 election there was only one major polling organisation. But since 1972, there have been at least four organisations taking national polls during elections,[10] and they have played an increasingly prominent role in each campaign since. The polls appeal to the media because they appear as an authoritative guide to the intangible key to the contest, the electorate; because they are seen as independent of the parties, and a departure from the staple fare of party leader formats and partisan predictability.

Apart from scoreboards, another feature of many contests is an umpire. There are no sufficiently disinterested and authoritative referees in politics, or even agreed-on rules for them to enforce. But partial substitutes can be found in pressure groups which are independent of parties, which can make some claim either to represent the public interest, and/or to be expert in a particular area. The Australian Taxpayers' Association, and its spokesman, Eric Risstrom, became established as the epitome of such a group for a period in the early 1980s. Two other types of 'arbiter' sometimes produce heavy coverage. One is a group which is normally quiet, but makes an unexpected entry. The other is a defection by a group from the party it is expected to support, either to the opposition or to neutrality. In 1983, the normally reticent and presumably pro-Liberal Australian Bankers' Association criticised a statement by Prime Minister Fraser (see below), and attracted considerable publicity.

The campaign as contest provides not only a primary basis for news judgments, but for journalists' interpretative comments, growing out of their immediate experiences and observation of the parties in action. Most would feel it is beyond their professional role to comment on the rightness of policies, but legitimate, even mandatory, to observe whether a party's morale is high, whether their campaign is proceeding smoothly, and the tactical aspects of the day's events.

The campaign as contest serves as a filter for most reporting of the campaign as a policy forum. The reporting of policy stands as moves in the electoral game is certainly more realistic than a portrayal of them as based entirely on principle and rationality. However, it does have the consequence that the substance of policy is always secondary to the political interpretation of it. Pejorative interpretative epithets— such as 'extreme' or 'controversial'—which precede, or even substitute for, the description of the content of proposals, circumscribe the parameters of debate.

## Covering Media Manoeuvres

The nature of election campaigns as news occasions is as a series of public events and statements, as rhetorical jousts between the contenders. In the past, the news mainly reported events such as public meetings and rallies, at which the media were spectators. Such events, though, have been declining in importance in relation to events, which are either solely media occasions or orchestrated primarily for the news coverage they will gain.

Press conferences, photo opportunities, ceremonial events, TV talk shows and talk-back radio have increasingly become the staple of election campaigns. This is only rational, as the vast audience potentially reached is more important than any small-scale or local campaigning activity. There is nothing inherently wrong or false about parties staging events primarily for media coverage. However, the media's general shyness about acknowledging their purpose can lead to inane reporting. For example, Prime Minister Fraser's penchant for 'meet-the-people' street walks only made sense as a campaigning activity because of the TV coverage it was intended to receive. In 1980, Opposition Leader Hayden's carefully planned Sunday visit to the Navy base HMAS Cerebus was covered by all four major channels, most of whom said it was not an occasion for politics. Such media self-denial, in omitting any mention of the media strategy such events serve, leads to superficial, sometimes even distorted, reporting, and allows the leaders to stage them uninhibited:

> On Monday, a point that came up in group after group was that John Howard had not stayed up on Sunday night to watch Pat Cash win Wimbledon .... Bob Hawke, of course, not only stayed up but made sure everybody knew about it with the television cameras and radio reporters recording the Prime Minister's comments in a Bendigo motel room: 'Bewdy! Oh Patrick; fantastic; straight sets; isn't it marvellous.'[11]

## Gaffes

The restrictions on the media which force them to concentrate on the public stage during elections does not imply that campaigns are more comfortable for the leaders, or that their coverage is more predictable. The leaders are under constant scrutiny where their every mistake or discomfort is magnified by the herd of reporters and commentators. The instant reporting, reaction and analysis amid the highly charged uncertainty which elections induce in participants, means that issues or statements can assume a sudden intensity, quite unrelated to their past or future significance.

In recent Australian elections, intense and unexpected momentum in news coverage has been associated with 'gaffes'. Perhaps the trend began in 1966 when lack of cohesion among the principal Labor spokesmen and confusions over the timing and details of its policy on withdrawal from Vietnam provided ammunition for the Liberals.[12] But the importance of gaffes became particularly pronounced in the next two elections as Whitlam practised the politics of ridicule against Gorton and McMahon. The propensity of these two Liberal leaders to mis-statements and their lack of mastery of detail made this a rich vein for Whitlam to exploit. For example in 1972, McMahon as well as making the slip 'we will honour all the problems we have made', advised people they should read a Foreign Affairs report on China which was classified secret, and seemed to advocate price controls soon after he had denounced them, creating a stir among other Ministers.[13] McMahon's most important gaffe in the 1972 campaign came in the recording of a TV interview, when he expressed disappointment in the performance of his Ministers. This provoked an immediate furore, and Whitlam seized upon it as an admission of weak leadership.[14]

The escalation of gaffes was probably most politically consequential in the 1974 election, possibly even costing Opposition Leader Snedden victory. Snedden had committed himself to daily press conferences, and under close and pointed questioning his equivocations over specifics were highlighted. Most damaging were the contradictions between his views and Country Party leader Anthony's, especially on oil pricing. These greatly weakened the thrust of Snedden's campaign, and privately he blamed Anthony for costing him the election.[15] The damage that journalists' questioning had done to Snedden was a major reason why Fraser refused to be drawn on specifics during the 1975 campaign.

In the 1977 election, the floundering over economic policy was reversed, as ALP leaders stumbled over the details of their policies. The most embarrassing incident involved front-bench spokesman Hurford, campaigning in northern Queensland and being questioned on the radio program, *AM*. Hurford was awkwardly reluctant to answer a direct question on ALP economic policy, because he was clearly unsure what Whitlam and Hayden may have been saying. By the 1980 and 1983 elections, the search for and escalation of 'gaffes' by ALP spokesmen had developed as a core element of Liberal Party strategy:

Each day at the Liberal Party campaign headquarters . . . a massive monitoring of the media was conducted. Every radio and television programme in each capital city was taped and transcribed and then pored over by officials hoping to find gold.[16]

'Gold' was any inconsistencies, admissions of weakness, or evidence of Labor's 'hidden' costs or secret plans. In the closely fought campaign of 1980, the strategy had great success with the attack on Labor's wealth tax proposals. The escalation of this issue certainly changed the initiative and tone of the last week and a half of the campaign, and some have claimed it was the reason Labor lost the election. In 1983, both sides had adopted the tactic of seeking to escalate the other's apparent gaffes to an even greater degree. The Liberals made several attempts, for example, to attack statements by the ALP shadow Treasurer, Keating, that Labor could not guarantee its proposals would work, but they had only momentary and marginal impact.[17]

Instead, the single biggest gaffe of the campaign came from an attempted counter-attack which misfired.[18] Prime Minister Fraser claimed that under a Labor Government people's savings would be safer under their beds. This became a very damaging incident, in that:

1 Hawke laughingly dismissed the charge with the joke that they couldn't put their savings under the bed, because that's where the Commies were—this confident riposte of effective ridicule was shown on every TV channel;
2 it produced almost universally unfavourable headlines;
3 it prompted critical interventions by the Australian Bankers' Association and others—an intervention which must have had the Liberal pioneers of 1949 turning in their graves;
4 it put the Government on the defensive for some days, with other Liberals awkwardly distancing themselves from the Prime Minister;
5 it made it more difficult for Fraser to sustain other charges, as he was now characterised as desperate and willing to say anything.[19]

In short it was the archetypal gaffe.

In the 1987 campaign Opposition Leader Howard made a calculated gamble: to unveil his radical plan for tax cuts matched by government spending cuts during the campaign, so that its appeals would be fresh in the public mind on election day. The risk was that the proposal would be subjected to immediate scrutiny and criticism, so that any flaws or uncertainties could detract from its impact. This eventuated, first and most damagingly when it was revealed that double counting, which the Liberals had to admit, had damaged their calculations by a considerable amount; and second, with some uncertainties—for example, Senator Baume's remarks, seized upon by the government as a gaffe, revealed ambiguities about the phasing-in periods for spending cuts versus tax cuts, with implications for the deficit.

Why do so many gaffes occur during election campaigns? Many stem from a lack of clarity on policy, either by an individual leader or through disarray among colleagues, that is only revealed by the rigours of the campaign. Others come from the temptation to strain for maximum advantage, both praising one's own side and, more often, in extravagant attacks on opponents.[20] A major source of gaffes seems to be talk-back radio[21]—statements are isolated from the flow of conversation by the monitoring of the opposing party and seized upon as the target for counter-attack. Other gaffes occur because in the flood of words, politicians 'drop their guard and tell the truth inadvertently'; among the propaganda lines, there are, what Summers called, 'outbreaks of honesty'. The key factor, however, is not so much the greater propensity of politicians to make gaffes (although that is certainly there) but the extra scrutiny and intensity to which they are subjected, partly by the media, but more importantly by the other party, in the well-grounded belief that it is more effective to embarrass than to debate one's opponents.

## Campaign News—Leaks

Significant leaks are relatively rare during election campaigns, although when they do occur, the intensity of media attention can escalate their impact greatly. The political parties do a large amount of background briefings, giving partisan assessments on the progress of the campaign and previews of policy statements before their formal release in order to prolong and enhance their news value. But these are essentially predictable extensions of the publicly conducted campaign.

Common sources of leaks, such as intra-party manoeuvring and bureaucratic struggles over policy-making, are in temporary suspension. The leaks that do occur during campaigns are typically extensions of the inter-party contest, and usually come to the media via the other party. The party hopes to damage their opponent, using a leak to generate drama, to inject the appearance of the unexpected into the predictability of usual campaign formats. Often they have a contrived nature: in 1980 ALP shadow Minister Young announced one day that he had a leak, and then revealed its content the next day—generating two sets of stories for the one fairly mundane revelation.[22]

When bureaucratic leaks do occur in a campaign, it is usually via the opposition party and in the context of a declining government facing imminent defeat. The ALP had two leaked documents which they fed to the media during the 1983 campaign. They generated contrasting amounts of news attention. The major leak, which received wide attention, was a story by Max Walsh in *The Bulletin*, detailing how the Treasury, with the Treasurer's knowledge, excised passages from an OECD report.[23] In contrast:

> [when *The Age* ran a] much simpler story to get across: Howard had changed the tax laws to help some Liberals avoid liability and the Taxation Commis-

sioner had protested. But for some reason the story did not take off. In that week (the third of the campaign) issues fragmented and scattered like confetti.[24]

The most spectacular government-orchestrated leak for partisan advantage during a campaign occurred before the 1977 election. The Liberal Government leaked parts of the report of the Royal Commission into Human Relationships—originally commissioned under the Whitlam Government. The leak and its follow-ups dominated the headlines for a couple of days. It probably had the following aims: to create a diversion, so that the news would be dominated by an issue safe for the Liberals, and so make it more difficult for Labor attacks on other issues to gain momentum; to create the aura of a threat to social values and a reminder of the anarchy of change associated with the Whitlam years; to put Labor spokesmen on the defensive and encourage a situation where, in commenting on the report, they were more likely to say something controversial. It was a highly cynical and effective leak.[25]

## Campaigning Strategies

Campaign strategy and news media developments are in a dynamic relation to each other—the news media constitute the central part of the environment to which the campaigners must relate, while the campaigners produce the material and occasions which the news media report. But more of the initiative in the relationship rests with the campaigners because their clarity of purpose and concentration of effort far exceeds the media's.

### Centralisation and Presidentialism

Parliamentary democracy is based on the representation of local constituencies. Such a notion does not sit snugly with the dominance of political communication by the mass media, and their pre-occupation with party leaders. The increased size of communication units necessarily leads to changes in the relative importance of different political groups and institutions. In elections, constituency influences—the role of the individual candidate, local party organisation and public meetings and local campaigning—have become less important as campaigning has necessarily become more centrally organised, capital intensive and leader-centered. Throughout the 1950s both political activity and press coverage were much more concerned with public meetings. Today their role is negligible.

The media, especially television, cover an election principally by covering the leaders. In the 1979 UK election, for example, the two leaders, Callaghan and Thatcher, commanded almost 65 per cent of their parties' coverage—the second most cited spokesman for each party received just under 10 per cent.[26] Parties have little choice in this—even, for example, in the Victorian 1979 election when both leaders, Hamer and Wilkes, were rating poorly in the polls, campaign coverage still centered on them.[27] Leaders are therefore seen as the key to success—increasing both their leverage (when successful) and their vulnerability (when not clearly successful). The increased reach afforded by technological improvements has now allowed the focus on leaders to be realised nationally. Wherever the leaders are they will be on TV news around the country every night.

### The Professionalisation of Political Marketing

The clearest illustration of the campaigners' professionalism and the media's 'amateurism' is in the use of polling. While polls have become a larger part of campaign reporting, they have become integral to campaign planning. The news media display polls—a source for an exclusive headline and a simple scoreboard story.[28] The campaigners use polls—a tool to reveal the electorate's dynamics of mood and perceptions and so to guide campaign strategies.

Polling is the basis for planning which themes to pursue, which policies to highlight and which to downplay. Frequently the influence of polls on the presentation of policies slides into influence upon content as well. Pollsters are, therefore, close to, or even sometimes part of, the core leadership group that runs a party's campaign. The ALP's regular pollster, Rod Cameron of Australian Nationwide Opinion Polls (ANOP), had more influence on recent campaigns than the party's deputy leader, Lionel Bowen, let alone backbench MPs, let alone rank-and-file membership.[29] The logic of the polls is always a counsel of conformity—to endorse only what is instantly acceptable and unproblematic.

The professional political marketers have drawn two conclusions which have far-reaching consequences for modern campaigning. The first is that the swinging voters, who decide election outcomes, are the most ignorant and best swayed by simple appeals. The second is that TV news is the most vital communications channel—that the battle to woo swinging voters is first and foremost, although not solely, a battle to have the more potent presence in TV news.

The image of the swinging voters which has become the guiding rationale on campaign tactics for both sides is hardly likely to lift the standard of debate:

> The people who determine elections in this country are the least interested and the least informed about politics. You're talking about people who vote on whims.
>
> The next election will be decided solely on the votes of the 15% of

'swingers' who show any willingness to change . . . . They are basically ignorant and indifferent about politics. They vote on instinct for superficial, ill-informed and generally selfish reasons.[30]

The influence of polling on the parties' electioneering has steadily increased. Their impact was felt firstly in the presentation of policies and the choice of which issues and themes to emphasise, especially in advertising. These easily merged into the formation of policy, and in recent elections the day-to-day adjustment of tactics has been increasingly affected by pollsters' evaluations:

> Both parties recognised with wry amusement when lines from the swinging voter research were being fed to the party leaders. When Hawke said repeatedly that all the Liberals promised was 'more of the same', or that Fraser's 'seven years' was long enough, he was repeating lines which came up repeatedly in group discussions with swinging voters. When Fraser said 'I want to thank Tamie . . .' he was doing so with the knowledge that Tamie Fraser was immensely popular with voters and helped soften Fraser's own image.[31]

Throughout the elections of the 1980s, there has been a steady increase in the immediacy of the pollsters' influence and in the dynamism of campaign tactics. The increasing sophistication of their analytical techniques, especially the marriage of more qualitative probing in small groups with their quantitative mapping of the electorate, and the speed of such analysis allows immediate feedback, and so quick political responses to exploit or counter developing themes, to gauge what appeals are working, and pinpoint the main worries and threats.

Perhaps the most surprising aspect of TV's influence on election campaigning was how slow the parties were to develop expertise at its exploitation. As late as 1969, thirteen years after the advent of TV, for example:

> The television version of [the Liberals' policy speech] took the form of a closed studio presentation, with Gorton extolling the Government's virtues to his Cabinet colleagues and their wives. McEwen, stiff and sour, registered approval only when Gorton went down the line for high protection. McMahon was apparently asleep. It looked rather like an old-fashioned family will reading, and not a very happy family.[32]

With some variations and reverses brought about by individual differences in competence among leaders and their staffs,[33] the general pattern has been for increasing sophistication in the use of TV during campaigns. The major lesson learnt is the importance of providing visual interest and dramatic vignettes. Success at these cannot fully replace substantive exposition, but it is an enterprise only slightly related to policy presentation:

> Richard Farmer . . . is Labor's electronic images puppeteer . . . . Farmer's

task basically is to get images on the television news each night which emphasise the strengths and reinforce the positives of the Prime Minister and the Government . . . . Hawke basically has one major engagement per day . . . . We have the environmentally sensitive Prime Minister visiting Daintree, the caring Hawke at a hospital, the cultural Hawke who understands the arts, the sporting Hawke who is mates with famous sportsmen . . . The contrast with the Howard campaign is stunning. Mr Howard has a program packed with engagements. There are constant last-minute changes and cancellations. It's a nightmare for the TV crews. With so many events the Howard camp has little control over the pictures that appear on that night's television news bulletins.[34]

## The Decline of Programmatic Campaigning

As campaigning has become more professional, there has been a more ruthless evaluation of the factors that contribute to or detract from the likelihood of victory. This has had important consequences for election campaigns as a policy forum, as an occasion for the construction of, and choice between, policy programs for the incoming government. In a programmatic campaign (itself, admittedly an ideal type, rarely approached in reality) parties lay out policies which they are seriously committed to implementing, do this with specific details, and take some cognisance of problems, costs and alternatives. In Australian politics Whitlam's campaigns as Opposition Leader in 1969 and 1972 were the peak of effective programmatic campaigning. Three trends are associated with its decline since: the dominance of attack over exposition, with a consequent tailoring of programs to avoid offering targets for opponents; secondly, a lesser tendency to present the party as proposing one set of policy choices, but rather to present it as embodying shared aspirations; and, finally, a declining sense of post-election mandate.

Political rationality-cum-expedience has clearly decreed that there are more costs than benefits in being specific. There are few rewards for superior policy detail. The most popular media formats give it little opportunity to emerge:

[In the 1979 UK election] at times ITN packed points from six speeches into 50 seconds. The median length of speech extracts on the [BBC] Nine O'Clock News was about 45 seconds, and on [ITV] News at Ten, 25 seconds.[35]

On the other hand, the extra detail may provide a target for opponents to attack, and increase the likelihood of a gaffe:

The radicalness of Fraser's program received almost no media attention, simply because he refused to be drawn on it . . . . The role of the Canberra press gallery in the 1974 campaign had already passed into legend . . .
[They] had been a vital factor in creating the image of incompetence and

disunity that cost the Liberals so much in a close election. Fraser was determined not to make the same mistake.[36]

Fraser's success in winning with a minimum of detail in 1975 was not lost on the Labor Party. Hayden, despite his natural penchant for detail, in 1980 aimed the campaign toward short, simple media presentations. By 1983, 'the ALP only provided consolidated costings of its programme and refused throughout the campaign to give an item-by-item breakdown'.[37]

Policy construction and presentation, especially on the Labor side, are geared firstly to defence, to offer no target that makes them vulnerable to distorted attacks and scare tactics. Hayden's period was marked by 'political aggression and electoral caution.... Cynicism joined caution as the byword of the Hayden Labor Party.'[38] The crucial experience shaping Hayden's subsequent approach was the campaign mounted by the Liberals and the Murdoch press in the last week of the 1980 campaign against Labor's alleged wealth tax proposals.[39] It led to Hayden's determination to expunge all mention of a wealth tax from the platform at its 1982 conference:

> The argument is not about substance at all. It is about presentation. It is aimed at maximising our capacity to attack effectively our opponents and not be put on the defensive.[40]

One of the successes for Hawke and the ALP in the 1983 election was that they were judged to have run 'an excellent defensive campaign systematically denying Fraser the peg on which to hang the big scare'.[41]

The dominant trends appear contradictory: a degree of policy convergence but, if anything, an increase in polemical invective. But a logical unity underlies the apparent paradox, best illustrated by Keating's performances immediately following the 1985 Budget. In a joint TV interview, he asserted that John Howard would love to have his name on this Budget, that is, it was a Budget Liberals would approve of. The next day in Parliament he began by shouting that the Liberals were 'Cheats! Cheats! Cheats!' and that they had always been 'Cheats! Cheats! Cheats!', that is, inherently unworthy. Antagonistic interests generated by the party contest generate ferocity between the parties quite independently of the ideological distance or nearness between them. The opponents are not merely the purveyors of inferior policies, but the epitome of scandal, dishonesty and disaster.

A partial exception to the tendency of parties to 'tack together' in policy substance[42] was Howard's attempt to present a stark alternative in 1987, with radical proposals for tax cuts matched by cuts in government spending. However, here too, the winnowing of his original proposals demonstrated the laws of modern electoral evolution: avoid unpleasant subjects (instead of proposals for changing the tax mix, only talk of reducing the total tax burden); stress central themes and avoid specific targets (talk about financing tax cuts through cutting Government spending, but refrain from specifying where the cuts will be made); and avoid all sense of a trade-off between costs and benefits.[43]

This leads directly to another aspect of the decline of programmatic campaigning: where possible appeals are not framed to stake out a detailed policy position among options. Talk of winning and losing groups, or of conflicting ideals and interests, are avoided. Rather, the aim is to associate the party with a set of almost unarguable themes. Party competition is not only, perhaps not even primarily, a matter of staking out distinctive positions on central issues. Stokes makes a crucial distinction between positional issues (which involve choosing between a set of alternative government actions) and valence issues (simply associating a party with some condition, positively or negatively valued, for example, prosperity or corruption).[44] Thus in the 1952 US elections, the Republicans campaigned against the 'mess in Washington'. This did not mean that the Democrats were pro-mess. Rather, the Republicans were assigning the Democratic Administration responsibility for a condition, which, if established, all would be against. The role of the media may be crucial on valence issues because giving credence to a general claim or failing to do so is necessarily to favour one side or the other.

Modern electoral campaigning favours the emphasis of valence over positional issues in party propaganda. Presentations are increasingly cloaked in appealing imagery:

> An observer who noticed only the visual symbols of the 1980 campaign would have concluded that there had been a generous rush of patriotism to the heads of Australian politicians.[45]

The political attractions of campaigning on consensual issues are well captured by Bob Hawke in a planning memo before the 1983 election. Perceiving that Fraser's divisive style had produced a desire for healing, for a sense of common purpose, he urged on the party a strategy emphasising reconciliation:

> Whereas the individual elements of our policy can, and will, be subject to the dessicated costing calculations of our opponents, and may give rise to some areas of electoral backlash, the concept of the reconciliation strategy has these advantages: a. It is right. b. It represents what the electorate wants. c. In itself, it is cost-free.[46]

The battle in such themes is whether they can be made credible, whether the definition of issues and priorities gains public currency. Such rhetoric is almost immune from frontal attack—no jarring, confusing details, and what political party would choose to be against consensus? Success is not based upon superior policy detail, although the leaders must be able to maintain their brief with some semblance of consistency and mastery. Indeed the 1983 campaign even made vagueness into a virtue by stressing process, the consultations into which the Government would enter after the election.

Ironically, the rise of issues of economic management may also have contributed to the decline of programmatic campaigning. Mostly the argument is not about goals but their attainment. In such cases, perceptions and expectations become the central battlefield, with government optimism being almost obligatory. In 1977 and 1980 the Liberals campaigned on the expectation of imminent improvement. In 1977, there was the promise of a cut in interest rates, which did not eventuate.[47] In 1980 the Liberals stressed the coming mining boom and the prospect of a return to prosperity through national development. In 1987, the Hawke Government 'juggled two messages, "the worst is over" and "there is still a long haul" without being entirely clear . . . about what it is saying'.[48]

The pernicious effect of economic issues on programmatic campaigning by governments was also shown graphically in the 1974 election:

> Whitlam told his colleagues that the election was being held at a more favourable time than any likely to occur in the next eighteen months. It was a knowledge he could hardly share with the public.[49]

Not only did he fail to share it, he gave the opposite impression:

> We listened to Whitlam tell a radio talkback audience that, as far as inflation was concerned, 'we've turned the corner' and 'we're licking it'.[50]

Like Whitlam, leaders since have opted for shuffling expectations and managing perceptions rather than debating what the realistic choices and limits might be.

It is not surprising, given the behaviour before election day, that the sense of a binding mandate afterwards has also declined. Although few politicians have had a perfect record in keeping promises,[51] the turning point here was particularly stark. From both principle and political convenience, Whitlam elevated the idea of the mandate more insistently than anyone before: 'The platform is the Old Testament. The policy speech is the New Testament', said Kim Beazley at an early Cabinet meeting.[52] The jump to what some described as Fraser's 'doctrine of the disposable promise' was sharp—the reversal of the promise to support full wage indexation, the abolition of Medibank, the cancellation of the Australian Assistance Plan, the decision not to abolish the Prices Justification Tribunal and abandonment of the plan to give the Northern Territory statehood.[53] The result was not so much electoral retribution for the Fraser Government as a change in expectations. As broken promises have become more commonplace, their political cost seems to have lessened. Managing the timing and cover story ('the changed circumstances') for their breaking has become a well-practised art. It is now the norm for each incoming government to claim that its predecessors concealed the extent of the disaster they had produced, and its discovery now made implementation of the new government's policies impossible.[54]

## The Impacts of News

The news media are the central arena of election campaigning. This sets up their potential to have an active impact on election results, either intentionally or unintentionally. Before addressing how this might occur, however, there is a prior question: do campaigns matter at all? Ben Chifley claimed that—'the poll that counts is the one six months before the election'. Many others have also thought that 'Election campaigns are a waste of time and money. They only appeal to the faithful.' Certainly much of the frenetic activity of politicians immediately before an election serves more to assuage their own anxieties than to change the outcome. Moreover, campaigns clearly vary in their importance. Nothing the ALP (or the media) could have done in the 1966 or 1975 campaigns, their two worst post-war defeats, would have changed the result.[55] Parties' behaviour during campaigns is usually a continuation or accentuation of their previous performance, rather than a complete change of character. And, of course, no one can ever know how different results would be if a different campaign strategy had been adopted.

However, in the last twenty years, seven of the nine Federal elections (1969–87) would have been decided differently with uniform swings of less than two and a half percentage points. In seven of the last eight elections, the Morgan Gallup Poll recorded fluctuations of two percentage points or more during the campaign.[56] Given this closeness between the parties, neither can afford to assume that election campaigns are irrelevant.

### Momentum

In what ways then might news coverage have an impact? The media's most important impact on the immediate development of campaigns is in the cumulative building of a sense of momentum. Most of the time this favours the party expected to win. The campaign as contest coverage is to some extent self-fulfilling. The interpretative comments of reporters on tactics and morale feed into the general picture reinforcing their images as winners and losers. It is likely to generate unfavourable news for the losers: public pleas from colleagues to change tactics or complaints about poor 'communication'. Semi-consciously reporters sometimes behave less decorously toward likely losers, and are more willing to be aggressive and persistent. Their questions often focus on politically fruitless topics: what will be the leader's future following his defeat? How can the leader really believe victory is possible in the face of such overwhelming evidence? New policy thrusts in the campaign are more likely to be seen as desperation, and in fact through desperation, the losing side is more likely to make a gaffe or rash move:

> There has been enough evidence over the last 15 years in politics that when you are down you are down. No matter how hard you try you can't make it right.
>
> It's hard to think of any Opposition that has campaigned well when they knew they would lose.

Only one tendency of news coverage clearly runs counter to the momentum gained by front-runners: the party with a substantial lead wants a low-key campaign, on the grounds that unless some untoward development happens to change votes, it will win. A 'front-runner' election strategy then seeks to avoid close questioning and so minimise the possibility of gaffes and issues flaring with sudden intensity, and also to ignore the Opposition so that its charges and claims do not receive more prominence. The (far from insuperable) dangers are that the front-runner will appear evasive or arrogant, or that the Opposition will 'steal a march' in the absence of government initiatives.

Insofar as the news media have a vested interest it is that they dislike 'quiet' elections.[57] The media's wish for variation and freshness make them eager for departures from the expected, and so ready to emphasise any evidence of a surge by the losing contender. The potential conflicts were exemplified in the 1984 campaign, when the ALP wanted a quiet campaign, partly because it was so far ahead in the polls and partly because dullness was its message—that this was a cautious, pragmatic government, interested in economic recovery, consultation and consensus. However, over such a long campaign (seven weeks) this clashed with the media's wish for interesting developments. For whatever reason, instead of the anticipated swing toward the Government there was a chastening swing away from it, and a very close result.

It is much more possible for a State government to reduce the intensity of media reporting. Indeed the mastery of defensive electioneering techniques at State level includes timing elections so the campaign may be overshadowed by other diversions. In 1988, Victorian Premier Cain called an election so that the campaign coincided with the VFL Grand Final, the Royal Melbourne Show, and the school holidays. In 1986, Tasmanian Premier Gray and West Australian

Premier Burke both called elections for the first feasible date in February, so that the early parts of the campaigns were lost in the end of the summer holidays—giving new meaning to Churchill's slogan 'we will fight them on the beaches'.

Whether ahead or behind, both sides face the uncertainties of a sudden unexpected intensity attaching to a gaffe or embarrassment. If suddenly a story unfavourable to one side 'takes off', the unwanted momentum can become a crisis for the side adversely affected. Spectacular examples include the sudden focusing upon the business affairs of Treasurer Lynch in the 1977 campaign, which Prime Minister Fraser neutralised by requiring Lynch to stand down pending an investigation, and the ALP's inability to counter the Liberals' escalation of the wealth tax issue in 1980. The cumulative impact of the hordes of news organisations magnifies any passing hiccups into full-blown belches. A poor performance by a leader (for example, apparently losing in a debate) is reported, repeated and interpreted in a score of outlets, solidifying the passing flux of the performance into an immediate conventional wisdom, which itself exaggerates, and is more important than any marginal electoral impact the original incident may have had. The open-ended, unpredictable quality of contemporary campaigns poses dangers of unwanted momentum for all parties, and almost guarantees that even the most skilfully managed campaigns will encounter uncertainties and reverses.

*Partisan Bias*

The building of political momentum is the most important impact in the normal operation of the media. But a recurring concern in Australian politics has been with how proprietors' partisan views affect news judgments and perhaps the election result. Elections are in some ways poor occasions to campaign overtly or slant the news. Politicians are especially ready to protest, the electorate's partisan sensitivities are at their height, and the result is likely to be only very partially affected by news coverage. Possibly of greater political importance is the reporting between election periods, the prominence or neglect accorded to Opposition viewpoints, and the fostering of debate and controversy about Government actions.[58]

Reporting the surfeit of largely predictable criticisms and promises that comprise campaign news offers scope for political discretion both in the interpretative framework in which the contending parties' statements are put and especially in news judgments. Selection and ordering of stories are inherent in news, and always subject to some conflict: 'Every journalist bitches every day about what they didn't use'. As there is no objective measure of the importance or interest of different stories, it is an area where professional judgment mingles inextricably with personal and political influences. Beyond such inevitable differences in gauging significance, there is scope for news treatment to be affected by ulterior considerations, based on how the news will affect the supported party's prospects.

While newspaper editorials more often than not endorse one party,[59] there are great variations in how editorial support is manifested in the rest of the paper:

> 'The New York Times is perhaps the single most credible newspaper in the world,' notes New York Lieutenant Governor Mario Cuomo. 'But when they endorse you, you get one column on the editorial page. With Rupert, he turns the whole paper over to you.'[60]

When press proprietors engage in political action the delivery of appropriate news priorities is the main resource they have to offer. The action proposed in the following episode recounted by Don Dunstan is drastic, but the promise of favourable news coverage is the stock in trade for any politically ambitious proprietor:

> At this time an extraordinary thing occurred to me. I had seen a certain amount of Rupert Murdoch and Rohan Rivett (then editor of the Adelaide News). They had given me opportunities to write a provocative column . . . and in those days I got coverage in their paper in a way which was completely denied me then in the Adelaide Advertiser . . . . Rupert and Rohan asked me to go over to the News office and urged me to join Manning in the DLP, promising favourable publicity. I looked at them with bemused horror . . . . Rupert became impassive but Rohan was obviously chagrined at my lack of cooperation![61]

In terms of political direction of news, four Federal elections—1961, 1972, 1975, 1980—are particularly noteworthy. The 1961 election, which occurred against the background of the Menzies' Government's credit squeeze, produced the closest result in Australian history, a two-seat majority in the House. It was perhaps also the campaign in which media managements had the most direct influence on the parties' conduct. In particular The Sydney Morning Herald and The Daily Telegraph were more participants than observers. It was the first occasion on which the Fairfax press had editorially embraced the Labor Party. Having made such an unprecedented decision, the full resources of the organisation were mobilised in support of Labor's campaign:

> Henderson in effect became Calwell's campaign manager, providing hard-headed advice on policy, very reasonable rates for television time, and the writing services of two of John Fairfax's best men. For most of the campaign Lou Leck . . . and Maxwell Newton . . . worked in what became

known as the 'Labor Ward' on the executive floor preparing speeches and statements for Calwell.[62]

Some of them were written and set up in type before Calwell had seen them, much less spoken them.[63]

Menzies had approached the campaign rather complacently, and with the Morgan Gallup Poll failing to register the strong swing, it was left to more immediate observers to advise the Government of its peril. Alan Reid, veteran correspondent of *The Daily Telegraph*, recalled:

During the 1961 election I came back to Sydney with Menzies. Packer asked who would win? I said the ALP. Packer said how can we prevent this? I said if Menzies said he'd lift the credit squeeze in three months. He said have you told Menzies? I said no. Packer said I am giving you an instruction as your employer. He lifted the phone, spoke to Menzies and said I'm sending Alan to see you. In his next speech Menzies gave an unqualified assurance, and that became the issue for the last few days. I think that if he hadn't said that, he would have gone down.[64]

In 1972, Packer sold *The Daily Telegraph* to Murdoch, an action whose political implications Prime Minister McMahon greatly regretted:

On the night Sir Frank Packer signed the contract he asked me and my wife to go up to his home to see it, and to get an assurance from Mr Murdoch that he would treat me fairly, apart from the editorials. Of course he did not do it. He did not live up to his promise. He always let me make repair jobs, but all too frequently he told the papers what they were to write. Frank told me what was happening. I said 'Frank, I think that ends our prospects for the election. You have won two elections for the Liberals in the past, and we would have relied heavily upon you in the next election.'[65]

From a low-key beginning Murdoch's support for Labor increased as the election neared. As in other examples of proprietorial involvement, news organisations found their proprietors' suggestions irresistibly newsworthy:

By the time the campaign got under way, Murdoch was an integral part of the 'It's Time' machine .... He was in almost daily touch with [Mick] Young, [Eric] Walsh and the Whitlam office, and he attended several of Whitlam's meetings. On one occasion, Murdoch even had a hand in the issuing of a Labor Party press release. He phoned Walsh and said: 'What do you think of this idea—a press statement saying national service will end within a week of the election of a Labor Government?' Walsh thought the idea was not bad, drafted the release, and phoned the news editor of the Sydney *Mirror*, Mark Day, to give him the story. Day ... asked somewhat unenthusiastically: 'What's new about that?' Walsh replied: 'As far as you're concerned, mate, what's new is that it's Rupert's idea.'[66]

The Murdoch press and *The Age* endorsed the ALP in 1972, while most other papers remained pro-Liberal. It was, however, a period when the news tide was going against the McMahon Government, and in most papers there was sufficient autonomy for the press gallery to reflect this, although news coverage and media attitudes were far less universally pro-Labor than is often suggested.

In 1975, like 1972, news coverage of the campaign did not affect the election outcome. Even if the press had been strongly pro-Labor during the campaign, it is unlikely the ALP's 43 per cent share of the vote would have risen very much. Unlike 1972, however, there were strong complaints from political reporters that they were unable to report and analyse the campaign free from partisan editorial interference. The most blatant and sustained bias came from the Murdoch group:

> Bruce Stannard of *The Australian* was taken off the campaign. He reports that eight of his stories about Whitlam were spiked, when all the equivalent pieces he filed on Fraser's campaign were used.[67]

On several occasions, News Ltd editors squeezed an anti-Labor orientation into seemingly straightforward stories. The most blatant was the change in *The Daily Mirror*'s headline: in one edition, it read: 'Gough's Promise—Cheap Rents' and in the next: 'Gough Panics— Cheap Rents'. Similarly, *The Age* (and most other papers) on 5 December 1975 carried the headline: '20,000 fall in jobless', going on seasonally adjusted figures, while *The Australian* had: 'Unemployment up 18,368 to 4.5 per cent'.[68] Several such examples led Hayden to quip that if the Prime Minister walked across Lake Burley Griffin, *The Australian*'s headline would be 'Whitlam can't swim'.

Complaints about the other two press companies were also widespread, but the evidence is not as obvious. Edgar has suggested that the greater prominence given to economic issues rather than the constitutional issue over Whitlam's dismissal was evidence of press bias.[69] While individual decisions may be criticised, it is far from clear that all references to the Governor-General's action benefited Labor,[70] and certainly Labor would have been loath to admit all aspects of economic policy counted against them. Perhaps the most important constriction on reporting during the 1975 campaign was the lack of opportunity for analysis by the political reporters. Such inhibitions allowed Fraser's stonewalling on, for example, the precise nature of spending cuts to proceed without great political damage.[71]

The reporting of the 1980 election campaign by the Murdoch press has attracted less critical attention than 1975, but in terms of electoral impact may have been more important.[72] The result was very close (it was the only election in which a majority of the opinion polls predicted the wrong result) and only a late swing back to the Liberals seems to have saved the Government. The election was also notable as perhaps the only one where a major media company had a direct and tangible stake in the outcome: the ALP was challenging News Ltd's acquisition of Sydney's Channel Ten. As the polls showed Labor unexpectedly maintaining a lead during the campaign, the tension inside the company, according to some journalists, mounted greatly:

> People in the media like myself were under a fair amount of pressure to find some bullets. I don't look back with any great pride. It's very hard to make a judgment when you're under pressure from people you work for, but I did what was expected of me as an employee. I perhaps provided the proprietors of some papers with stories which they chose to display colourfully and with great vigour. Some shouldn't have been given anywhere near the prominence they were. I was surprised by the lack of news judgment of those involved. Also I did stories that didn't hurt the ALP which didn't get in the paper.

> It's easy for a journalist to rationalise. It becomes a matter of conscience whether you are being objective. They might have thought that I was too close to the ALP. I did a . . . campaign wrap up. It never got in . . . . There was a pattern in the stories not being used. It was much harder to get a pro-Opposition in than a pro-Government one . . . . [As the campaign was going against the Government] there was an element of hysteria crept into the organisation. It was a period when pressure was being exerted on me to produce material in certain ways. They never asked me specifically to fabricate a story, but there were arguments over news judgment.

Early in the campaign, News Ltd's news judgments were broadly in line with the Government's agenda (for example, giving less attention to the unemployment figures when released)[73] but their news priorities and interpretations became increasingly propagandistic. *The Daily Telegraph*, against its usual news priorities, led with news about falls on the stock exchange for two days in a row. 'Panic as ALP surges ahead' on October 8 was followed by 'Millions lost in new plunge/ Mums and dads hit hardest say brokers'. 'The last two weeks of the campaign saw Sydney's *Daily Telegraph* and *Daily Mirror* devote about one-eighth of their entire election coverage to the vicissitudes of the stock exchange', a much higher figure than the quality dailies.[74] Similar share market slides after the election did not occasion the same treatment. News Ltd participated wholeheartedly in the Liberals' attempt to escalate claims that Labor would introduce a wealth tax, despite denials by its leading spokesmen. 'Special powers to snoop on all' was *The Daily Mirror*'s imaginative headline.[75] Then, in the last days, it gave glowing prominence to Fraser's promise to hand back future oil revenue rises either as tax cuts or family allowances. 'Bonanza!' was the measured assessment of the Adelaide *News*.[76]

## Conclusion

There is always a tendency to stereotype the past either as a stone age (primitive and crude beyond belief) or a golden age (where all our lost ideals once thrived). This is especially true when analysing the media because most changes are relative rather than absolute, and so many other economic and political changes have occurred simultaneously. Yet not to try to sketch some of the qualitative changes in campaigning may leave us blind to important developments.

The electoral game is played more relentlessly and ruthlessly. Perhaps the change can be gauged by comparing the views of the two longest-serving Labor Treasurers, separated by 40 years, Ben Chifley and Paul Keating. Chifley urged Labor members not to lose sight of the light on the hill, while Keating has derided the politics of the 'warm inner glow'. Chifley said, 'when in doubt always make a decision on principle. Then if you lose at least you've gone down in a good cause.' Keating prefers the advice of Chifley's arch-rival Jack Lang: 'Always bet on self-interest. That way you're always sure he's trying to win.'

No-one can accuse Chifley of not following his own belief about the poll that counted being the one six months before the election. In 1949 Chifley was so unconcerned with the selling of policies that he recorded his policy speech in a studio, rather than delivering it to a public meeting; used only 36 minutes of the hour's broadcast time available to him; and while the speech was being broadcast, he was too busy cleaning up paperwork to listen. Chifley made no significant new commitments ('no glittering promises')—relying on the Government's record rather than last-minute gimmicks. Indeed he was so unconcerned with tailoring Government actions to maximise popular appeal that petrol rationing was re-introduced the day after his policy speech.[77] Chifley lost.

The impact of party campaigning and of news coverage is considered most frequently in terms of election outcomes. Partisan advantage is the immediate concern of participants, journalists, and most observers, whose main interest is, of course, who won? However, there are further questions about media and campaigning impacts, questions not just about the immediate outcome, but the larger political role of elections. Election outcomes are tangible and measurable, but considerations about qualitative changes in political processes must be more tentative. Elections are the central event of liberal democratic politics. The news media are the central arena of election campaigning. In many ways the news media have increased the accountability of politicians by subjecting them to greater scrutiny. However, the most outstanding trend over the last seven elections has been that while the problems facing governments have become more complex and intractable, the conduct of policy debate has become more simplistic, and less related to subsequent government action. Elections are at any time a very partial and imperfect means of popular control over government, but the trend in campaigning practices over the last decade and a half is to make them an even less adequate vehicle for accountability and meaningful public choice.

# 7

# Intra-Party Politics and Leadership Struggles

Politics within parties contrasts with politics between parties in the publicity interests and news coverage they generate. Australian party politics is, most fundamentally, a two-sided, zero-sum, winner-take-all game. Winning government is the central political competition for which the parties are organised. The decisive point of resolution in this competition is public support as expressed in regularly scheduled elections. Both sides have interests in:

1  the active pursuit of publicity;
2  generating a public perception of clear party differences; and
3  discrediting their opponents at every opportunity.

In contrast, intra-party politics involves conflicts among ostensible allies. They threaten the party's central purposes, and so must be controlled and subordinated. The immediate decision-making group is not the public but the party room, although in electorally pragmatic parties, internal operations must be carried through in publicly acceptable ways. Particularly in party leadership struggles, strategists are faced with a hazardous and poorly charted process with few rules of procedure. Internal party conflicts are more likely to be expressed indirectly with their aims oblique to their content, and using covert rather than overt means. The mixture of public alliance and private opposition is a minefield, fraught with potential dangers. Questions of tactics and timing—how to translate latent support into an active challenge, how to promote the struggle without producing a damaging, open schism, how to force a showdown without alienating support—are full of uncertainties.

For news reporting, intra-party politics pose distinctive problems and opportunities. Because of the importance of covert sources, and the very limited extent to which public statements illuminate what is occurring, there is more potential for 'exclusives' and penetrating analysis. On the other hand, because so much is subterranean and masked by bluff, there is a greater possibility of 'beat-ups' and of one-sided accounts which lack perspective. Determining support and momentum is difficult for both participants and outside observers.[1] Because so much is based on grapevines and covert sources there is more danger that, right or wrong, a story will be met with public denials, against which the journalist has little comeback if confidentiality is to be maintained. Moreover, because the reporting is often more substantially based than the public realises, strong party supporters in the audience commonly respond with disbelief or hostility to all but the strongest public evidence of disunity.

## Aims and Methods

This chapter focuses on leadership struggles in Australian parties, Federal and State, between 1968 and 1985.[2] Leadership challenges are not the only manifestation of internal party conflicts, but focusing upon them allows close researching and comparison of a range of cases where conflict is sharp, because personal political careers are at stake in a situation which allows little compromise, and where there is a clear showdown and outcome.

Only cases where there was an actual party room challenge by an aspirant against the leader are included. This excludes the muttering discontents, endemic in politics, which never crystallised into an active, direct challenge. Nor are we examining leadership transitions due to retirement or natural causes. Finally, and perhaps more problematically, we are not including challenges which occurred in the 'natural' period immediately following an election loss, when leadership positions normally come up for re-election.[3]

These criteria yield 23 cases which are summarised in chronological order in Table 7.1.[4] As well as the names of the main contenders and the dates at which the challenges climaxed, Table 7.1 includes whether they were in the Federal or State spheres, which party was involved, whether it was in Government or Opposition, and whether the challenge was successful or not.

After outlining some characteristics which affected news coverage of these 23 contests, the chapter examines the interaction between publicity strategies, news coverage and the development and outcomes of the struggles.

**Table 7.1    Summary of leadership challenges, 1968–85**

| Case | Opponents | Sphere | Party | Status of party | Successful outcome? | Date |
|------|-----------|--------|-------|-----------------|---------------------|------|
| 1 | Whitlam–Cairns | Fed | ALP | Oppn | No | Apr 68 |
| 2 | Bjelke-Petersen–? | Qld | NCP | Govt | No | Oct 70 |
| 3 | Gorton–McMahon | Fed | Lib | Govt | Yes | Mar 71 |
| 4 | Hall–Eastick | SA | Lib | Oppn | Yes | Mar 72 |
| 5 | Houston–Tucker | Qld | ALP | Oppn | Yes | Jly 74 |
| 6 | Snedden–Fraser | Fed | Lib | Oppn | Yes | Mar 75 |
| 7 | Lewis–Willis | NSW | Lib | Govt | Yes | Jan 76 |
| 8 | Whitlam–Hayden | Fed | ALP | Oppn | No | May 77 |
| 9 | Willis–Coleman | NSW | Lib | Oppn | Yes | Dec 77 |
| 10 | Jamieson–Davies | WA | ALP | Oppn | Yes | Feb 78 |
| 11 | Knox–Edwards | Qld | Lib | Govt | Yes | Oct 78 |
| 12 | Mason–McDonald | NSW | Lib | Oppn | Yes | May 81 |
| 13 | Hamer–Thompson | Vic | Lib | Govt | Yes | Jun 81 |
| 14 | Wilkes–Cain | Vic | ALP | Oppn | Yes | Sept 81 |
| 15 | Davies–Burke | WA | ALP | Oppn | Yes | Sept 81 |
| 16 | Lowe–Holgate | Tas | ALP | Govt | Yes | Nov 81 |
| 17 | Fraser–Peacock | Fed | Lib | Govt | No | Apr 82 |
| 18 | Casey–Wright | Qld | ALP | Oppn | Yes | Oct 82 |
| 19 | Hayden–Hawke | Fed | ALP | Oppn | Yes | Feb 83 |
| 20 | Dowd–Greiner | NSW | Lib | Oppn | Yes | Mar 83 |
| 21 | Edwards–White | Qld | Lib | Govt | Yes | Aug 83 |
| 22 | O'Connor–Hassell | WA | Lib | Oppn | Yes | Mar 84 |
| 23 | Peacock–Howard | Fed | Lib | Oppn | Yes | Sept 85 |

*Notes*
1  Occasionally a symmetrical presentation is misleading. In Case 2 there was a strong move to be rid of Mr Bjelke-Petersen, which was to be accomplished first by declaring the leadership vacant. The Premier defeated this move by the narrowest of margins, so that his potential successor did not become crystal clear, although various names were canvassed. That case is more complicated because there was action also to make Liberal Party leader Chalk leader of the Government. So the Premier's rival is only signified by a question mark.
2  In two other cases, Nos. 10 and 13, the defeats of Jamieson and Hamer, their successors were not the instigators of the challenge. Despite being allies of the vanquished incumbent, Davies and Thompson were elevated by the rebellion of others.
3  The date given is of the final showdown, resulting either in a new leader or the last party room attempt by the challenger. (In one case, No. 12 (Mason–McDonald), the former resigned in late May, and his successor was not elected until 1 June.)

## Patterns of Leadership Struggles

The initial observation from Table 7.1 is that leadership struggles have been common in recent Australian politics. Moreover, the challenges enjoyed a high rate of success—although this suggests the political numeracy of challengers rather than the inherent vulnerability of leaders, and several successful challenges were preceded by an initially unsuccessful attempt. Only two challenged leaders, the first two cases, Bjelke-Petersen and Whitlam, subsequently prospered.

Each leadership struggle is unique, but the patterns of their development and outcome are affected by answers to the four questions posed below.

## Was the Party in Government or Not?

Challenges are far more frequent in Opposition. Only 8/23 occurred when the party was in Government. Two of these involved the Queensland Liberal Party. Their limited influence as a junior coalition partner in the Government dominated by Bjelke-Petersen's National Party created dissatisfactions which were basic to understanding both challenges. Leaving aside the Queensland Liberals, challenges are more than twice as frequent in Opposition.

In Government, leadership challenges are always messy and damaging. They receive more news attention; they signal an admission of failure; they threaten to upset existing patterns of patronage. Although not necessarily the main reason for defeat, of the six Governments where a challenge occurred, only Bjelke-Petersen's won the next election (see Table 7.2).

Most usually a leadership challenge in Government is a symptom of political decay in a long-entrenched administration. In only one case

**Table 7.2  Electoral aftermath**

| Case | Opponents | Party | Result | Trend |
|------|-----------|-------|--------|-------|
| 1 | Whitlam–Cairns | Stable | Still Oppn | Large gains |
| 2 | Bjelke-Petersen–? | Stable | Still Govt | Static |
| 3 | Gorton–McMahon | Divided | Lost Govt | Losses |
| 4 | Hall–Eastick | Divided | Still Oppn | Large losses |
| 5 | Houston–Tucker | Stable | Still Oppn | Large losses |
| 6 | Snedden–Fraser | Invigorated | Won Govt | Large gains |
| 7 | Lewis–Willis | Divided | Lost Govt | Losses |
| 8 | Whitlam–Hayden | Stable | Still Oppn | Static |
| 9 | Willis–Coleman | Stable | Still Oppn | Large losses |
| 10 | Jamieson–Davies | Stable | Still Oppn | Slight gain |
| 11 | Knox–Edwards | Stable | Still Govt | Slight loss |
| 12 | Mason–McDonald | Stable | Still Oppn | Static |
| 13 | Hamer–Thompson | Stable | Lost Govt | Losses |
| 14 | Wilkes–Cain | Invigorated | Won Govt | Gains |
| 15 | Davies–Burke | Invigorated | Won Govt | Large gains |
| 16 | Lowe–Holgate | Divided | Lost Govt | Large losses |
| 17 | Fraser–Peacock | Stable | Lost Govt | Losses |
| 18 | Casey–Wright | Invigorated | Still Oppn | Gains |
| 19 | Hayden–Hawke | Invigorated | Won Govt | Gains |
| 20 | Dowd–Greiner | Invigorated | Still Oppn | Gains |
| 21 | Edwards–White | Divided | Lost Govt | Large losses |
| 22 | O'Connor–Hassell | Stable | Still Oppn | Losses |
| 23 | Peacock–Howard | Stable | Still Oppn | Gains |

(Fraser versus Peacock) was the leader who actually won Government from Opposition challenged. The others had inherited the incumbency. Sometimes a long period in Government dulls members to the ongoing demands of the external conflict, and internal struggles are waged more fiercely.[5] The longer a Government is in office, the greater is the residue of scars and liabilities, including resentments among its own members. Especially if the general debilitation is linked to electoral decline, there will be pressure to change leaders, although in practice this rarely reclaims the situation.

The falls of Premiers Lowe and Hamer exemplified the pattern. Plans for the Franklin Dam power station produced Lowe's demise. The insoluble conflicts between conservationists and developers created fertile soil for the discontents and machinations in the party which finally overthrew him. In Hamer's case, increasing pessimism over Victoria's economic future created a sense of desperation in the Government. A persistent sense of malaise manifested itself in particular issues—over shopping hours, a casino, proclamation of new economic strategies—confirming the Government and its leader in a downward spiral.

An Opposition has more incentive to change a losing pattern, and indeed about half the time a more invigorated and electorally successful Opposition resulted (Table 7.2). In the other half the party made no improvement, or even declined, the leadership instability further confirming a syndrome of ineffectual opposition. The outstanding examples have been the post–Askin New South Wales Liberal Party and the Queensland ALP.

## Was There a Clear Alternative Leader?

A successful challenge ultimately requires both sufficient discontent with the incumbent and sufficient support for a successor. There is often a fateful asymmetry in how the two develop. There are great variations in both process and outcome depending on their interaction.

The most explosive process occurs when a recognised and ambitious challenger is actively stalking the incumbent:

> There is no greater ignominy for a political leader and no force so destructive as a pretender in the ranks whose aspirations are transparent.[6]

In at least five cases (Snedden–Fraser, Wilkes–Cain, Fraser–Peacock, Hayden–Hawke, and Peacock–Howard) there was prolonged public attention, at least one preliminary challenge or rupture before the decisive showdown, and a continuing process of de-stabilisation and mounting pressures on the leader. Tensions in the party were high, and both leader and challenger knew that any false steps could be escalated to their disadvantage. This tension itself fed into the political judgments of the principal players:

> [Once Peacock contested the deputy leadership after the 1980 election] Fraser felt encircled . . . . He had to preserve not only his government, but also his grasp on the Prime Ministership.[7]
>
> With Hawke in caucus the margin for mistakes by Hayden was virtually eliminated . . . . Hayden now faced Malcolm Fraser in front of him and Bob Hawke behind him.[8]

Although in process most de-stabilising, these challenges frequently produced a sense of rejuvenation after resolution.

The worst situation for a party, both in process and outcome, occurs when the discontent with the incumbent is widespread and obvious, but there is no clearly superior alternative. Often this creates uncertain three and four way conflicts, as rival challengers jockey against each other, as well as against the leader. The damage can be prolonged, but the transition when it occurs may not generate new enthusiasm. Willis–Coleman, Mason–McDonald, Casey–Wright, and O'Connor–Hassell all largely conform to this pattern, characteristic of an Opposition unable to generate any sense that it has viable prospects.

There are many variations between these two extremes of an active pretender stalking the leader and the growth of discontent without the hope offered by a clear alternative. In some cases, although the likely line of succession was clear, the momentum of the challenge primarily stemmed from the build-up of dissatisfaction with the incumbent. There is much more variation here in process. Three involved fairly neat coups (Houston–Tucker, Lewis–Willis, and Dowd–Greiner), although in outcome only the last was advantageous for the party. The other two, Gorton–McMahon and Whitlam–Hayden, were damaging in both process and outcome.

In three cases, a long but publicly muted period of discontent climaxed quickly when a coalescence around an alternative suddenly developed. In WA discontent with the Labor Party's electoral prospects under Davies had continued for some time. Once Burke's main rival, Bryce, stepped aside, the resolution came quickly. In both cases involving the Queensland Liberals, discontent had been continuing for some years, and the mantle of leadership passed to someone after a confrontation with Premier Bjelke-Petersen. Dr Edwards opposed him over his support for the quack cancer specialist, Milan Brych, and White over the need for a Parliamentary Accounts Committee. Both became leader soon after.

In two cases, a rebellion displaced the previous leader but the beneficiaries were not the rebels, but members of the Old Guard. Both the Jamieson–Davies and Hamer–Thompson successions had the costs of upheaval without the benefits of a clearly new beginning:

> It was an act of cowardice. Having destroyed a leader they were not prepared to go the whole way . . . . The Liberals didn't strengthen themselves as a result of their change.

## Was There An Important Ideological or Factional Element?

When the leadership struggle was embroiled in a factional confrontation or in an ideological schism the showdown over leadership was not itself able to resolve the internal conflict. In five of the six cases where ideological/factional bases were important (see Table 7.3), divisions continued and electoral disaster followed. The only successful aftermath was Whitlam over Cairns, although the confrontation itself initially weakened Whitlam's standing.[9] The other five resulted in varying degrees of disaster. McMahon presided over 18 months of division before losing Government in 1972. The Queensland Labor Party, confirmed in their inward-looking factionalism and electoral ineffectiveness, had their worst result ever under Tucker in late 1974. In the final three cases, the leadership transition was the trigger for further defections, splits and electoral failure. Hall's resignation led to the formation of the Liberal Movement, first as a 'party within a party', then as a separate party. At the next election Dunstan's ALP Government further increased its majority. Holgate almost immediately lost his Parliamentary majority when Lowe and Willey went to the cross-benches, was soon forced to an election, and lost decisively. The accession of Terry White as leader of the Queensland Liberals produced a bout of brinkmanship from Premier Bjelke-Petersen. In disarray, the Liberals were excluded from Government, thence taken to an election where their poor showing allowed the Nationals to govern alone for the first time.

## Were Electoral Image and Media Appeal Considerations Central?

The dominant movement in political parties has been towards the triumph of pragmatism over factionalism, the precedence of winning office over expressing ideology. But at the same time Australian politics has moved from leadership stability to instability.[10] Most current challenges are a mixture of personal ambition and disputes over how best to prosecute the inter-party competition. The intra-party and inter-party conflicts are not independent but interdependent. Factional support is often important to the outcome, but most contemporary leadership struggles were not themselves occasioned by the wish for a factional showdown.[11] Rather, the instability evidenced by the

**Table 7.3  Bases of challenge**

| Case | Opponents | Electoral/ Image | Ideological/ Factional | Leadership qualities |
|------|-----------|------------------|------------------------|----------------------|
| 1 | Whitlam–Cairns | Irrelevant | Important | Contributing |
| 2 | Bjelke-Petersen–? | Important | Irrelevant | Important |
| 3 | Gorton–McMahon | Contributing | Important | Important |
| 4 | Hall–Eastick | Irrelevant | Important | Irrelevant |
| 5 | Houston–Tucker | Important | Important | Contributing |
| 6 | Snedden–Fraser | Important | Irrelevant | Important |
| 7 | Lewis–Willis | Contributing | Irrelevant | Important |
| 8 | Whitlam–Hayden | Important | Irrelevant | Important |
| 9 | Willis–Coleman | Important | Irrelevant | Contributing |
| 10 | Jamieson–Davies | Important | Irrelevant | Contributing |
| 11 | Knox–Edwards | Contributing | Contributing | Irrelevant |
| 12 | Mason–McDonald | Important | Irrelevant | Important |
| 13 | Hamer–Thompson | Important | Contributing | Contributing |
| 14 | Wilkes–Cain | Important | Irrelevant | Important |
| 15 | Davies–Burke | Important | Irrelevant | Contributing |
| 16 | Lowe–Holgate | Irrelevant | Important | Contributing |
| 17 | Fraser–Peacock | Contributing | Contributing | Important |
| 18 | Casey–Wright | Important | Irrelevant | Important |
| 19 | Hayden–Hawke | Important | Irrelevant | Irrelevant |
| 20 | Dowd–Greiner | Important | Irrelevant | Irrelevant |
| 21 | Edwards–White | Contributing | Important | Contributing |
| 22 | O'Connor–Hassell | Important | Irrelevant | Contributing |
| 23 | Peacock–Howard | Irrelevant | Contributing | Important |

Notes
The table's three columns each rate the importance of one basis for dissatisfaction—electoral and image factors (discontent over the party's electoral achievements or prospects, including the leader's perceived impressiveness as a public performer); ideological or factional factors (based on differences over policy stances and approaches or, what is usually closely related, on the relative power of factions or conduct of internal party relations); and leadership qualities (a less tangible set of qualities which include intelligence, decisiveness, consultation, and strategic sense). Each basis is rated as important, contributing or irrelevant. Such judgments are not foolproof, and there may be argument over borderline cases or some interpretations.

prevalence of leadership struggles is itself a product of the more pragmatic approach with ruthlessness taking precedence over loyalty and the increased emphasis on leadership in media relations and electoral success.

The primary basis of most recent leadership challenges has been concern about electoral prospects and public image. Table 7.3 shows that these were judged important in 13/23 cases and irrelevant in only three. Despite individual variations, comments about these challenges have a number of recurring themes: the predecessor rated poorly in the polls, was not popular with the press gallery, did not present well on TV, had little judgment in gaining the publicity or Parliamentary initiative, and a perception in the party that electoral victory was impossible or uncertain.

Traditionally there has been great scope for selective perception and wish fulfilment in evaluating leaders' electoral appeal. Arthur Calwell proffered the quaint judgment that the ALP would have won the 1961 election if Eddie Ward rather than Gough Whitlam had been deputy leader.[12] Although the meaning of the polls is not as straightforward as much commentary suggests—the links between leader approval and party vote are yet to be unravelled satisfactorily[13]—polling does provide a sounder basis for judgments about leaders' popularity.

Although challenges based on image and popular acceptability are typically linked with the leader's media relations, these are usually not isolated. Only occasionally (for example, perhaps Hayden and Dowd) does public image become a key factor without other abilities also being severely questioned. However, the news media are inevitably entangled in questions of public image and electoral effectiveness, and it is common for leaders challenged on this basis to feel unfair media coverage was at the heart of their problems.[14]

Sometimes the emphasis on public image misfires—especially because it is hard to predict how someone will perform under the unique demands of a leadership role. When the Federal Liberals selected Gorton and the NSW Liberals selected Lewis, the crucial factor in each case was the party's desire for a fresh face who looked good on TV. Both triumphed on the basis of support by younger backbench MPs over an Old Guard candidate who would continue the staid images of the past. Neither had had wide Ministerial experience, but in a narrow area, had impressed with a 'can-do' political style. Both quickly produced dissatisfactions about their political judgments, their tendency to 'shoot from the hip' and failure to consult colleagues or follow procedural cautions. Eventually their image appeals also seemed illusory.[15]

Such miscalculations raise the problem of the relations between the various attributes associated with successful leadership. Kemp argued after the Liberal loss in 1972 that:

> Seeing leadership in terms of 'image' misses its most important ingredient
> ... The first and most important relationship is between leader and
> followers, not between leader and the public .... The man who cannot
> unify and lead his colleagues in parliament and in the organisation cannot
> make a successful appeal to the electorate. Electoral success ... follows
> successful management of relations within one's own party first of all.[16]

But it is just as easy to reverse the claimed causal direction. Only those with the prospect of electoral success can command the authority needed for internal party management. Peter Bowers, commenting on the growth of the challenge to Whitlam's leadership in 1977, commented:

> The Government backbench openly mocks Mr Whitlam. No party, as Mr

Snedden learnt, will sit for long behind a leader who is not taken seriously by his opponents.[17]

Because of the centrality accorded leadership in many explanations of electoral success, the importance of leaders in energising and co-ordinating the party may have increased. Changes in leadership have in some instances had pervasive effects throughout the party:

> Leadership is more important than the superficial public perception of it. It's important because of its effect on the party itself. People decry leadership mania, but it's not just TV. It's party morale, getting the party moving.

## Publicity and Process

A party leadership struggle is not an institutionalised conflict. There are few rules of procedure. There is no necessity that the latent tensions and clashing ambitions will develop into a climactic showdown. Unlike inter-party conflicts, the participants have a direct personal relationship, as partners and allies as well as rivals. The mixture of intimacy and opposition is conducive to tensions, but when the interactions and relationships are distilled and exaggerated into news reports, the mixture is doubly explosive. Immediate relations are refracted through the prism of media publicity, itself often clothed in extravagant gladiatorial imagery. The battles for support, the attempts to affect the receptiveness and perceptions of their colleagues, are waged at one remove. What appears in the media, in some ways, has a larger political reality—a solidity and currency among a wide audience that the fluid group interactions do not. Indeed, publicity often has a disproportionate effect on internal dealings: it affects participants' trust of each other and their subsequent judgments and actions; it sharpens latent conflicts or crystallises developing antagonisms; it makes it harder for either contender to pull back from a confrontation without losing face.

The mix of audiences (mass public, party constituencies and immediate participants) often makes publicity strategies and effects hard to gauge. An illustration of internal signalling whose significance would have remained invisible to the public but was highly charged to the immediate participants occurred at the ALP Federal Executive in Perth in 1977. The Hawke camp wanted to communicate to the Left that through counter-lobbying they had defeated the incipient challenge to Hawke retaining the post of National President:

> Uren had tried to use psywar to frighten Hawke out of standing for the Presidency: the trick now was to frighten Uren out of attempting to execute his plan for running Young as President. Combe recalled: 'We had to

decide how to get the message through to Uren. We tried to find him and he'd gone into bloody hiding . . . . So we came up with what was a brilliant strategy: everyone would be listening to [the national ABC radio program] AM. We'd give John Highfield of AM an exclusive interview . . . I would have primed Highfield up—he'd throw in a question at the end asking 'By the way Mr Hawke, have you decided yet whether you're running for the Presidency?' And Bob would say, 'Well, John, you've caught me at a weak moment. Yes I am going to run.' It would be obvious to anyone who heard it that he had the numbers. The important people would know that Hawke was fighting back . . . . The interview took place at 1am on John Ducker's bed . . . . I remember the AM linkman saying, when the interview was over, 'that was an obviously tired and emotional Bob Hawke telling John Highfield . . .' Then we went into the executive meeting. And they were furious! . . . They'd all listened to AM and knew they were done . . . . Unanimous re-election for Hawke.[18]

Publicity is usually crucial to challengers building momentum, both in gathering support for themselves and in undermining the incumbent. Occasionally a decisive shift in support within the party has occurred without any publicly mounted campaign, and without the news media learning of the challengers' plans: When Houston was replaced in July 1974, the *Courier-Mail* headlined 'ALP Shock: New Leader'. Its only previous indication of a move was a single article four weeks earlier. Houston himself commented, 'I became aware only this morning that there was a move against me, and it came as a shock'.[19] Similarly when Willis replaced Lewis in January 1976, Kennedy described it as:

one of the niftiest political coups of the decade . . . . By Tuesday the deal was stitched as tight as a straitjacket, but, and perhaps this is the strongest indictment of all of Tom Lewis, he still knew nothing about it. The press, who inhabit Parliament House, Sydney, also seem to have been terribly slow on their feet.[20]

In neither case was the incumbent viewed as a successful leader, and there had been occasional expressions of discontent, but the change came as a surprise. Successful ambushes have the advantage of minimising disruptive publicity en route. Maintaining secrecy also prevents counter-organisation. But if exposed, the machinations will appear more sinister, and perhaps heighten the bitterness of opponents. However, it is rare for such an internal change in allegiances to have developed without the deliberate use of the media, and without the media finding out.

More typically, both the challenger's attempts at de-stabilisation and the incumbent's defence are carried on at least partially in the news. With a well-informed press gallery, even when the participants are not seeking publicity, they must have tactics for coping with the media attention they cannot avoid. News coverage has played an important part in the development of most leadership challenges, in building momentum, in triggering showdowns, and in affecting their reception. In tracing these interactions, we examine first the contrasting roles of public statements and leaks, and then the final stages—the showdown and the aftermath.

### Public Statements: Differentiation Without Disloyalty

Public statements create difficulties for rival contenders. The media are keen to pounce on apparent criticisms, elevating any qualifications into major schisms. However, a stance of unquestioning conformity and unqualified praise will not achieve the challenger's aims of de-stabilisation, and may later be embarrassing when an attack is mounted on the previously praised leader. On the other hand, public statements are a litmus test of loyalty. If the contender oversteps the bounds, recriminations will result, with party support declining rather than increasing.

The problem for intra-party contenders is to achieve the right balance between embracing and attacking their colleague/opponent, to signal differentiation without appearing disloyal. Typically the sophisticated pursuit of intra-party differences involves a minimum of direct contradiction and explicit criticism. Rather, different emphases are aired without detailing their implications, abstracted, disembodied viewpoints are criticised without their proponents being named. Positioning is achieved by 'codewords'. When Peacock stated that he had joined a Liberal Party, not a conservative party, it suggested a distinction between himself and (the unmentioned) Fraser, but without allowing any charge of disloyalty, and managing to cast his opponent as the heretic.

In short, in situations of rivalry among ostensible allies public statements resemble what Kremlinologists have termed esoteric communication:

> Soviet officials develop considerable skill in discerning the subtlest alteration in wording ... While the air may resound with echoes of the [party] line, it also carries contrapuntal themes, varying in pitch and intensity, but usually audible to the careful listener.[21]

The most constant and testing area for the rival contenders' public statements is in relation to the leadership itself. Rivals have become more adept at technically accurate professions of support which leave substantial room for manoeuvre. But at the same time, journalists have become more adept at scrutinising the loopholes in these statements. The 99 per cent of a statement which professes loyalty is not considered newsworthy, while the 1 per cent equivocation can make the headlines. There is no foolproof formula for challengers—either they leave themselves open to later charges of deception or present ones of de-stabilisation. Their dilemma is either to renounce all ambition or to be seen as disloyal. Many, such as Hawke, talked of their eventual ambition to be leader. After the 1984 election, Howard sought to avoid the whole question by saying that his record of loyalty in the Liberal Party meant that he shouldn't have to answer such questions.

The behaviour of later contenders probably owes much to the criticisms Fraser attracted in his contrasting behaviours during the overthrow of Gorton and his challenge to Snedden. In the first episode Fraser's forceful Parliamentary speech was a direct attack on Gorton, concluding:

> The Prime Minister, because of his unreasoned drive to get his own way, his obstinacy, impetuous and emotional reactions, has imposed strains upon the Liberal Party, the Government and the Public Service. I do not believe he is fit to hold the great office of Prime Minister, and I cannot serve in his Government.[22]

It was not a speech designed to enhance the prospects of the Liberal Party or to allow any later working partnership between the attacker and the attacked. Although Gorton was deposed it contributed to the odium Fraser himself earnt from the overthrow, and a reputation as a dangerous wrecker. Having learnt the dangers of open confrontation, Fraser's statements during the challenge to Snedden always professed his support for 'the elected leader of the parliamentary party'. But this formula also attracted criticism: the support always refrained from any actual praise for Snedden's performance and abilities. Fraser's public statements (and those of his supporters) always pictured him as completely without ambition, only responding to the desires of others, never initiating or acting himself. The following transaction in a TV interview captured the flavour on both sides.

> Staley:   'He said "Oh my God, don't talk to me about it. I can't bear to think of this."'
> Gorton:   'I bet he did.'[23]

Fraser's problems on this occasion stemmed from the stark contrast between the outward correctness and the background lobbying, from the disjunction between his professed lack of ambition and the determination of his followers.[24] Perhaps because the whole scenario of leadership challenges has become more familiar, or because later aspirants have been more open in their ambition, they did not attract the same hostility about hypocrisy that Fraser did in 1974–75.

Fraser's challenge also demonstrated the pitfalls for the leader under threat. Snedden's capacity for over-statement led him into the ludicrous, most notoriously in his claim, that if he asked Liberal members 'to walk through the valley of death on hot coals they'd do it'.[25] Even if he had not been engulfed in a surging challenge, it was the sort of hyperbole which both seemed hollow to the public and humiliating to colleagues. Similarly days before he fell, he was questioned about a meeting of senior Liberals, obviously called to canvass the leadership. His response was characterised by a comic unreality:

> They said they were there because of a build up of social functions and the way it happened was Bob Cotton was invited by Sir Magnus Cormack to have a meal with him on the Sunday night. Phil Lynch and Reg Withers— Reg was going to have a meal with Phil and Peter Durack was coming over for this meeting. [Vic] Garland was coming over for a couple of days for other meetings, and so they decided to put it all together. And Malcolm Fraser was driving past and he decided to drop in. They were horrified that it could be represented in the way it was represented. It was a perfectly innocent meeting.[26]

The most important question about the contenders' public statements is whether there will be an open rupture, whether the attacks make it impossible for later reconciliation without one or both looking ridiculous. When, in March 1981, Hamer and his rebellious Minister, Ian Smith, both made statements effectively calling each other liars, Hamer's attempt a few days later to paper over divisions when reinstating Smith to the Ministry made him look weak. The safest means of stressing differences is not to cast aspersions on the leader's character, or even his capacities or judgments, but perhaps on his electoral appeal. Hawke's pronouncements in 1982 that Labor could win with him as leader, but he wasn't sure it could win with Hayden as leader, may have fallen just within the bounds of party acceptability. Certainly they were more acceptable than his public outburst after feeling betrayed by Hayden at the 1979 Federal conference, when he called him a liar with a limited future.[27]

Public disunity tends to escalate, to provoke like-minded responses and set up a self-sustaining dynamic of increasing bitterness, which is hard to contain or heal. Continuing public conflict produces a gradual shifting of standards. Language used by the Queensland coalition partners in the years leading up to the final schism of 1983, was accepted there as routine, but would have caused explosions in Canberra, as it did when the Joh for Canberra move in 1986–87 produced mutual public accusations unheard on the same side in politics perhaps since the Labor split of 1955.[28]

### Leaks: De-Stabilising and Defensive

While public statements constrain allies toward correctness, covert manoeuvres allow more latitude. They allow the challenger to maintain public correctness, while constituting a form of de-stabilisation which is not easily countered. They allow guerilla warfare when the forces are not strong enough for a conventional battle. When done skilfully leaks allow a challenger to build momentum without presenting a publicly visible target for counter-attack. Leaks can raise the political temperature, keeping public attention alive, opponents uncertain:

> Hall's use of the media in the early 70s was fantastic. He was able to get his case across and argue for the Liberal movement. He would sell his story magnificently. One example out of thousands. There was a big argument about who would win the presidency of the Liberal Party. Hall said to me what would happen if I ran. I said what if I wrote that? He said I won't deny it. There was a page one story, which meant the Liberals were running scared, off balance. He kept the story going. Possibly he never intended to run. They were good stories without misinforming. He used the media extensively while the other Liberals had no idea.

Naturally, the identity and intentions behind a leaked story are often transparent to other participants. If anything, this heightens rather than lessens their impact. Chipp, for example, recalled his dismissal from the Ministry after Gorton became Prime Minister:

> Soon after Gorton was elected leader, reports started appearing in the Press that Howson and I were to be sacked. Such reports are always fairly accurate as they are motivated by the efficient leaking system undertaken by Ministers' or Prime Ministers' Press secretaries.[29]

Although there are often important uncertainties and errors when participants speculate about who had leaked what and why, in intra-party rivalries grapevines of gossip and open secrets are as common as the total concealment of the source's identity. Perhaps the most blatant example of an open secret, not public, but common knowledge among journalists and other participants, was when Andrew Peacock addressed the 1981 Annual Dinner of the Federal Press Gallery. Although journalists' accounts differed somewhat on precisely what he said, the effect was to convey the impression that he anticipated the Victorian Liberal Government would be defeated in the imminent State election, and that following the further decline this would give to Prime Minister Fraser's stocks, Peacock would launch a leadership challenge. The dinner speech could not be directly reported, but a statement to over 100 journalists hardly constitutes confidentiality.

Amid the coterie communications in the small world around Parliament, ostentatious meetings have a similar impact. A lunch between Staley and Allen Barnes at The Lobby restaurant, the day before Barnes wrote a long piece in *The Age* on Fraser's leadership plans, was a more oblique example of an open secret. Similarly, in 1969, Peter Howson wrote in his diary:

> Alan Reid tells me that Dudley Erwin is dining with Bill McMahon—an

interesting new development which will scare John Gorton when he reads it in the press.[30]

Canberra's tradition of mealtime leaks was apparently revived in October 1988, when Dawkins was seen dining with Paul Kelly, the day before a headline report in *The Australian*, saying that Dawkins had asked Hawke to decide on a timetable for his retirement.

Leaks can be defensive as well as subversive. Apart from leaks aimed at discrediting the challenger, the incumbent's main use of leaks would be to abort a gathering move against him by 'premature' publicity to it. The first publicity about Cain's imminent challenge to Wilkes in 1981 came from Socialist Left members who opposed their faction's decision to switch its support to Cain. As in that case, once challengers are fairly sure of the numbers, their interest is in secrecy, either to prevent counter-organisation or to consummate it with as little public bloodletting as possible.[31]

Often leaks are not tactically motivated, but the inevitable result of the need to gather support, to consult widely so that no-one's 'feathers are ruffled' by having been by-passed. As the net widens, leakage is more likely. In the Burke challenge, for example, it was the consultations going on at the ACTU Congress in Sydney, which alerted the *West Australian*'s industrial reporter. This inadvertent 'leak', if anything, helped Davies, giving him two weeks' warning of the coming challenge, although that was not its intention.[32]

By far the most dramatic example of an inadvertent leak was the monitoring of Victorian Opposition Leader Kennett's late night phone call to his friend Peacock, subsequently published in *The Sun News-Pictorial*. The venom and profanity directed toward Howard by Kennett was a wonderful example of the contrast between public and private in intra-party dealings. Howard subsequently dismissed Peacock to the backbench because of this incident. Howard, himself, was lucky to escape retribution for an earlier inadvertent leak also involving the Melbourne *Sun*. Following the 1984 election, *Sun* reporter Peter Rees rang Howard and sought comments about how it changed his leadership prospects. Howard misheard the caller's name, confusing Rees with Liberal MP Peter Reith. He spoke very freely about his continuing ambitions, likening the result to Snedden's narrow loss in 1974 and subsequent replacement. as leader. After the confusion over names was revealed, Rees refrained from immediate publication, but did relate the conversation after Howard became leader. Publication of this inadvertent 'leak' at the time could have severely set back Howard's leadership prospects.

Here, as elsewhere, misjudged or backfiring leaks can do the leaker great damage:

In Washington Hawke stayed with Australian journalist John Edwards, who assisted in arranging his appointments. His 'Washington scenario' [that Hayden would easily lose the 1980 election and that Hawke would take over after the debacle] was presented not just to the US Government, but to American journalists—one such meeting was conducted in the presence of two Australian journalists—and to functions he attended in New York.... Hawke was deeply embarrassed when his comments were reported in *The Sydney Morning Herald* and *The National Times* by Mike Steketee and Brian Toohey. Back in Australia he denied the stories. Edwards subsequently approached Toohey and, saying he was acting on Hawke's behalf, asked whether the journalists would be willing to retract their stories. The upshot was that Toohey wrote a more detailed version of the original story.[33]

## Flashpoints

Because leadership challenges are such an unstructured and uncertain process, publicity in the news media has often been associated with decisive escalations: the development of personal rivalries into open rupture; the translation of latent discontents into decisive disaffections, and thence into secure support for a challenger; and, finally and most problematically, the securing of a showdown, bringing the challenge into the open and resolving it without the challenger alienating support.

The process by which leaders lose the support of their colleagues is varied. But two recurring themes are the failure to perform well in the polls and the mishandling of public controversies. An unfavourable by-election result or the release of an opinion poll has sometimes triggered far-reaching re-assessments.[34] An unimpressive public performance or the mishandling of a controversy has also been the occasion for triggering further developments. To take but one example, Willis's fall from being Opposition Leader in NSW was marked firstly by an enormous gaffe. After the Granville rail disaster in January 1977, he made a statement in effect blaming the Labor Government for its occurrence. This precipitated an immediate leadership challenge, which he survived. Later in the year, the party's failure to make progress in the polls, and the leaking of an unfavourable poll by Liberal Party headquarters in June brought renewed speculation.[35] His weakened position finally resulted in a transition the following December.

In one instance it was the leader's relations with the press gallery which added considerable impetus to his colleagues' disaffection. In September 1980, before a by-election for the NSW seat of Murray, ABC reporter Peter Cavanagh reported that some senior Liberals believed (accurately as it transpired) that they would only come third, behind Labor and the Nationals. Mason, in great anger, replied, 'Anybody who knows anything...knows we won't come last'. He questioned other senior Liberals, all of whom denied making the prediction to Cavanagh. Mason then said the report was politically motivated, and said he had written to ABC General Manager, Duckmanton, although it is not clear whether he actually asked for Cavanagh to be sacked. Mason's response greatly escalated the incident. It led to 'amazing confrontations' between him and about a dozen members of the press gallery, who thought a reporter was being persecuted for accurate reporting. The sustained and unusually ferocious questioning by the journalists brought some faltering equivocations from Mason, and a week later, an ungracious apology. Several journalists thought the incident affected Mason's colleagues' estimates of his political judgment. It also highlighted the divisions and deceptions among the Liberal Party leaders.

The potential of publicity to precipitate decisive developments is best illustrated by the major episodes in the Fraser–Peacock rivalry of 1981–82. Peacock's resignation from the Fraser Ministry in April 1981 highlighted how explosive news reporting can be when internal relations are already strained. Peacock's private secretary, former MP Barry Simon, made a speech which included comments criticising the Government's handling of a recent industrial dispute. After AAP reported this, the response from other media organisations and Liberal Party figures was immediate. Fraser was determined that this breach of Cabinet solidarity must end in Simon's dismissal. Peacock thought the punishment too great, and resisted. The tension between them was compounded when a report in *The Australian* referred to Peacock's threat to resign from Cabinet before the 1980 election, unless Australia withdrew recognition from Pol Pot as the Government of Kampuchea.[36] Peacock saw the story as inaccurate in many details, and as a deliberate attempt to discredit him, and suspected the Prime Minister of planting it. Peacock demanded that Fraser issue a public denial of the story, but the denial was extremely terse and general. Peacock, who had meanwhile agreed to Simon's resignation, saw the Prime Minister's failure to issue a convincing denial as a determination to humiliate him. The following morning he resigned.[37]

In the following months:

> As the Peacock bandwagon began to roll, there was no shortage of anti-Fraser stories being fed to journalists. Coming as they did from men who knew him and worked with him, they had a ring of authenticity which was very appealing to reporters; even if few of them found their way into print, they coloured the opinions of those who heard them.[38]

The next peak of speculation about Fraser's leadership occurred in October, immediately before he was to host the Commonwealth Heads of Government Meeting. Two sets of rumours gathered astonishing momentum, each fanning the other. The first centered on Fraser's health, the second on leadership moves (including one soon denied that Howard was joining Peacock in a joint leadership ticket):

Throughout the episode news about the challengers was much more muffled. Peacock could claim that ministers were the only people talking about the leadership, and that he had confined himself to praising the Prime Minister for his efforts at CHOGM.[39]

The pre-CHOGM Peacock surge itself owed much to a misjudged attack on him by Viner, in the course of which confidential material was inadvertently leaked, much to Viner's subsequent discomfort.[40] Kelly judged that the Peacock forces indulged in 'publicity overkill' before CHOGM, and a similar error in March 1982, fanning speculation before the Victorian election which saw the Liberals lose Government after 28 years, gave Fraser an opening to bring on a leadership challenge before Peacock was close to the numbers. After the Lowe by-election and then the Victorian election:

> 'Fraser perceived that his position could only weaken unless he met the challenge head on. That Saturday I chanced my arm. [It was easy to see that Cain would win] I did a paragraph which said, 'Look out Malcolm, here comes Andrew'. It should have said 'Look out Andrew, here comes Malcolm'. He pulled on the challenge and won two to one. (Peter Bowers)

The Peacock forces had fermented so much publicity, that no-one could criticise Fraser for moving, and Peacock had gone too far not to challenge. Fraser immediately mobilised Cabinet, and defections from likely Peacock supporters, such as some Tasmanian MPs, deflated any hope Peacock had of gaining momentum.

*Showdowns*

Even after support has decisively shifted, it still may be extremely difficult to force a showdown to transfer the leadership:

> Shortly after he resigned from the Fraser ministry, Peacock was discussing the future with Bob Hawke, . . . putative challenger for the Labor leadership.
>    'How's it going, mate?' Peacock asked.
>    'All right, mate. I've got the numbers,' Hawke replied.
>    'For the leadership or for a spill?' Peacock asked.
>    'For the leadership—if there's a spill. I don't have the numbers for a spill,' said Hawke.
>    'Well then,' Peacock told him, 'if you don't have the numbers for a spill, you don't have the numbers.'[41]

Ironically, when leader, Peacock did not follow his own sage advice. The easiest path any contender was given to the leadership was when Peacock mounted a counter-productive control measure against his transparently ambitious deputy Howard. Howard had been taking a high profile with many public statements and speculation was strong. Peacock sought to force his hand, and brought on a re-ballot for deputy leader, which Howard then won. Peacock had decided, without telling his colleagues, that if this eventuated, he would resign. Howard, without having the numbers for a spill, won the leadership without the odium of 'blood on his hands'.

Peacock had also, inadvertently, eased Fraser's path to the leadership in March 1975. Snedden's stocks were low, speculation about the leadership was intense, but Fraser's constantly reiterated lack of ambition made it difficult for him to move directly. Peacock said it was totally unreal to 'ignore the leadership rumours' and 'Mr Snedden should call a meeting and ask for a vote of confidence so that speculation can be ended'.[42] 'From the day of this public statement by Snedden's closest public ally, the pressure on Snedden became irresistible.'[43] Fraser gained the party room vote he wanted, without having to alienate any support through an openly divisive action.

One of the most explosive uses of publicity brought Victorian Premier Hamer's resignation. When he left for a trip to America, first one Minister, Smith, commented to his local country paper that Liberals were 'numb with fear' at the prospect of facing an election with Hamer. In another statement he said that Hamer should nominate a retirement date. A letter from Kennett advising Hamer that he should not go was also leaked soon after he left. The immense ferment engendered by these manoeuvres resulted in Hamer's secret return and dramatic resignation. But while the rebels mounted sufficient pressure to achieve Hamer's departure they also probably ended their own chances of succeeding him, as the party voted for his loyal deputy, Thompson.

The most dramatic example of news reports being implicated in the climax of a leadership challenge was certainly the fall of Gorton. Fraser, as Defence Minister, had given background briefings criticising the Army's attitude to its civic aid program in Vietnam. General Daly and Gorton had a meeting in which reference was made to the resulting stories. Alan Ramsay of *The Australian* sought an interview with Gorton at which he put it to the Prime Minister that Daly had complained about Fraser. Gorton refused to comment, which Ramsay took as tacit confirmation that what he had been told was true, and published the story. Gorton publicly denied the published story, which led Ramsay to publish another. Speculation increased about Fraser's possible resignation, especially fanned by Packer journalists on an edition of Channel Nine's *Meet the Press* on which they were the only guests. Their unanimous view was that if Fraser did not resign, he would be politically finished. The same day Packer's *Sunday Telegraph* became the first paper to openly call for Gorton's resignation. The following day Fraser resigned, with a blistering attack on Gorton in Parliament, accusing him of disloyalty in allowing Ramsay's story to go forward. Gorton's account in Parliament of his conversation with

Ramsay was interrupted by the journalist shouting 'Liar' from the gallery. Gorton resigned after a motion of no confidence in the party room resulted in a tied vote, and several Members threatened to bring down the Government by supporting an Opposition no confidence motion.

It seems evident that Gorton was willing for Fraser to be brought into line through news stories. But equally, Fraser's own behaviour in regard to the briefings has been succinctly criticised by Edwards:

> The record of his collision with Gorton clearly establishes that Fraser, the Minister responsible for Defence . . . initiated a campaign against the Army through unattributable press leaks, assured his Prime Minister that he had not made the leaks, denied them when they were published, asked one journalist if he would deny having a briefing at all and finally misled the Prime Minister about his intentions to resign.[44]

*Reception*

The publicity needs of the participants before and after a challenge differ sharply. Afterwards, they seek to re-focus public attention, away from intra-party and on to inter-party concerns. Essentially the question is whether the coverage will be future-oriented—the success, hopes and attributes of the new leader—or backward-looking—sympathy for the deposed, and recriminations over disloyalty—a honeymoon or a post-mortem (see Table 7.4). One of the many ironies of 3 February 1983, was that thanks to Fraser calling an election the ALP immediately united behind Hawke and all public attention moved on to the election campaign. One journalist asked his editor if he should do an analysis of Hayden's fall, and was told, correctly he felt, 'no, that's yesterday's story, get on with the election'.

When does the new leader receive a honeymoon in news coverage? A sense of a new beginning is more likely when journalists and others perceive that electoral prospects are improved, and that the leader is capable of energising and unifying the party. Cain, Burke, Hawke and Howard[45] all received strong favourable publicity in the immediate aftermath of their accession. Even re-elected leaders sometimes achieve a kind of second honeymoon as did Hayden in July 1982 and Fraser in April 1982.

The opposite, a sense of futility, results when there is no sense of a new beginning. When Whitlam defeated Hayden in 1977, the first question at the subsequent press conference was when he planned to retire. Thompson's attempts to breathe new life into the Victorian Liberal Government evaporated as he failed to get more money from Canberra and then his proposal to extend shopping hours collapsed in the party room.

Table 7.4    Reception and aftermath of challenge

| Case | Opponents | Immediate reception | Loser's later relations |
|------|-----------|---------------------|-------------------------|
| 1 | Whitlam–Cairns | Doubt | Active, correct |
| 2 | Bjelke-Petersen–? | Doubt | Active, correct* |
| 3 | Gorton–McMahon | Post-mortem | Active rupture |
| 4 | Hall–Eastick | Post-mortem | Active rupture |
| 5 | Houston–Tucker | Doubt | Eclipse |
| 6 | Snedden–Fraser | Post-mortem | Eclipse |
| 7 | Lewis–Willis | Doubt | Eclipse |
| 8 | Whitlam–Hayden | Doubt | Active correct |
| 9 | Willis–Coleman | Doubt | Eclipse |
| 10 | Jamieson–Davies | Doubt | Eclipse |
| 11 | Knox–Edwards | Honeymoon | Active correct |
| 12 | Mason–McDonald | Honeymoon | Eclipse |
| 13 | Hamer–Thompson | Honeymoon | Eclipse |
| 14 | Wilkes–Cain | Honeymoon | Eclipse |
| 15 | Davies–Burke | Honeymoon | Eclipse |
| 16 | Lowe–Holgate | Doubt | Active rupture |
| 17 | Fraser–Peacock | Honeymoon | Correct |
| 18 | Casey–Wright | Honeymoon | Eclipse |
| 19 | Hayden–Hawke | Honeymoon | Active correct |
| 20 | Dowd–Greiner | Honeymoon | Active correct |
| 21 | Edwards–White | Post-mortem | Active rupture |
| 22 | O'Connor–Hassell | Doubt | Eclipse |
| 23 | Peacock–Howard | Honeymoon | Active rupture |

* Assumes challenger was Liberal leader, Sir Gordon Chalk.

## Aftermath

'Conflicts tend to interfere with each other.'[46] Intra-party conflicts are always pertinent to fortunes in the inter-party contest. The proudly anti-intellectual ALP Senator and machine man, Pat Kennelly, once said that he didn't see why universities needed whole departments of political scientists: 'There was only one rule in politics, and it could be stated in three words [although he took four] "get the bloody numbers"'. Even if life could be so neatly quantified, Kennelly's law overlooks (as did many ALP machine men in that era) the connections between getting the numbers internally and externally. Often someone popular with the public lacks numbers in the party and vice versa.

There is a conventional wisdom in Australian politics that public evidence of party disunity is always electorally punished. The very prevalence of leadership struggles is perhaps reducing their electoral damage. The time before an election when a leadership transition can occur has become ever shorter. Whitlam felt confident in early

1975 that the Liberals would not risk replacing Snedden as leader with the prospect of an early election in the air, and was soon proved wrong. The Victorian ALP replaced Wilkes with Cain only seven months before winning government. Most spectacularly, Hawke replaced Hayden the very day the 1983 election was announced.[47] In 1984, Fraser urged Howard to challenge Peacock even after the election had been announced.

The most electorally damaging aftermath follows continuing or worsening divisions in the party. It is too much to expect the vanquished to embrace their conquerors with rejoicing—Hayden's two fingered gesture during the 1983 campaign probably encapsulated the majority's feelings. But there are important differences in the loser's subsequent relations with the party, the degree of unity and consequently electoral performance. About half the defeated have gone into partial or total eclipse, while another quarter have been active but more or less publicly correct (see Table 7.4). Among these cases are several examples of a rejuvenated party following a honeymoon reception going on to greater success. In the final quarter, there has been a continuing rupture and active resistance to the new leader. Most of these involved continuing factional divisions. Some were based on personal resentments—for the injustice of having been displaced or for the methods by which the new leader won.

The most dramatic disintegration following a leadership change was the devastation of the Queensland Liberals in 1983. On 4 August, amid Parliamentary uproar, White voted with eight other Liberals and the ALP in support of a Parliamentary Accounts Committee. With Cabinet endorsement, he was then sacked from the Ministry by Edwards. The turmoil engendered in the Liberal Party saw White replace Edwards as leader five days later. There followed an extraordinary series of events in which Bjelke-Petersen out-manoeuvered and humiliated the new leadership. He was able to do so with impunity because that morning, again amid extraordinary scenes, the Liberals had supported the Premier's move to adjourn Parliament indefinitely, thereby denying themselves of any forum where his executive power might be challenged. The Premier kept White waiting an hour, refused to have him in Cabinet, then refused initially to accept the reluctant resignations forced on the other Liberal Ministers. Having routed the divided and floundering Liberals, the Premier announced the Nationals would govern alone, until an election on 22 October. While the National Party Ministers, now fully in control of government patronage, started a stream of announcements about government projects and handouts, the backlash by senior Liberals against White gathered force, offering yet further evidence of division and lack of direction. In the election, their vote dropped by 10 percentage points and they won only eight seats. The final humiliation occurred when two Liberals, Austin and Lane, joined the Government as Ministers, allowing the Nationals to govern in their own right.[48]

At Federal level, the most enduring public divisions followed Gorton's defeat. The Liberals made him Deputy Leader and Minister for Defence (replacing Fraser), from which positions his rivalry with McMahon continued. McMahon supporters blamed Gorton for Cabinet leaks. When Reid's book *The Gorton Experiment* was published in August 1971 Gorton replied in *The Sunday Australian* to what he saw as its inaccuracies. His vaguely expressed complaint about the difficulty of 'keeping anything under wraps' in his own Cabinet was considered by McMahon sufficient grounds to dismiss him. This dismissal finally turned Gorton into a folk-hero. A 'Get Gorton Back' Committee was formed. In 1972 Gorton acted 'like a Prime Minister in exile, giving speeches, opening functions, and constantly putting forward his alternative vision of what a national Liberal Party should be'. At the end of March, 'a small barrage of telegrams' went to the Liberal Party whip calling for the leadership to be discussed. McMahon 'survived, but only just'.[49] McMahon presided over perhaps the most openly divided Government in recent Australian history.

## Conclusion

Beyond all specific stances, mediating all particular policies, is the pervasiveness of leaders and leadership in the news. The emphasis on leaders as a central ingredient in political news resonates at several levels: its convenience for news gathering; its importance and centrality in reporters' direct experience of politics; audience interest in the human qualities and personal dramas of leaders; editors' and reporters' views of how politics works. The objective importance of leadership in electoral success is compounded by the widespread subjective belief in its importance, almost a self-fulfilling conventional wisdom. The very intensity of the focus on leaders endows it with electoral impact. Moreover, in a representative democracy, voters do not choose policies, but only among policy-makers. A rational choice is guided not only by stated policies but by the voter's opinion as to who will best make the decisions that arise in the ensuing term of government.

The media's importance and their concentration on the leaders have increased the emphasis on leadership which, in turn, has helped to stimulate the prevalence of challenges. As news coverage has become more penetrating, the internal affairs of both major parties are subject to more scrutiny. Indeed the prevalence of intra-party conflicts is crucial to reporters' access and to parties' attempts at news management:

Everyone in politics has enemies . . . . There are factions within parties. They tear strips off each other . . . . I was unprepared for the conflict within parties. That's one of the strengths for reporting.

As news coverage of internal struggles has improved, news man-oeuvres have become an increasingly important part of their conduct. The subsequent role of the media in those struggles is a telling de-monstration of the need to examine media effects, not only in terms of public opinion, which is not directly involved, but as a catalyst in an unfolding chain of events, as a trigger for participants, as an example of how immediate political relations are refracted through the prism of news coverage—and so, how news coverage yet again be-comes an active ingredient in the events it is reporting.

# 8

# Issue Agendas

Politics as we know it is inconceivable without the news media. They are the central forum of political communication in modern liberal democracies. Battles for favourable news coverage are a major arena in political conflicts, and the news provides a common reference point to which the different sides relate in their subsequent actions. To over-stretch a dubious metaphor, the news media are the central nervous system of the body politic. However, the media are institutionally under-equipped for this overwhelming responsibility. Their pivotal political role emerges obliquely from their own peculiar concerns. This concluding chapter is concerned with how the construction of public political agendas is shaped by the media's own orientations and vulnerabilities, and how these feed into the processes of policy-making.

## Issue Attention

Issues emerge via events. The definition of issues in news is a by-product from its primary orientation of reporting recent develop-ments. Coverage of issues depends on how their abstract principles, amorphous conflicts or continuing conditions become crystallised into newsworthy events. There is an unequal contest for news attention between the concrete and the abstract: no matter how cogent the arguments of those opposing the devotion of funds to space research, they could never command the coverage accorded to a moon landing. However the merits of republicanism may occasionally be canvassed, there is no republican equivalent of a Royal Wedding or Royal Tour.

'The press thrives on people robbing banks, not banks robbing people.'[1]

News responds primarily to two main influences: the development of politically consequential controversies and the occurrence of 'spot' news (accidents, crimes, disasters, etc.).

Whatever their commitment to diversity, no news organisation functions by promoting debate in the abstract. Their priorities are shaped by perceptions of the exercise of power, the imminence of decisive developments, the intensity of conflict and their sense of what is important to their audience. Government actions are thus a primary influence upon news. This is not to say that governments secure the coverage they want, but government activity—in public statements, in legislative and administrative action, in internal politicking—is a central focus of reporting and the central cue for evaluating significance.[2]

Issues thus emerge publicly not as autonomous topics for debate but embedded in, and secondary to, the reporting of conflicts and power plays. Donald Horne has asserted that 'avoidance of issues is institutionalised into the work patterns and norms of the press gallery'.[3] The intrinsic properties of the issue are less important in determining news coverage than the developing directions of the political conflicts and the balance of contending voices.

Publicity interests are frequently oblique to an issue's substance, with little guarantee that what gets prominence will be of most significance or that options will emerge in a manner which aids democratic choice. For the most constant contenders in controversies, political parties, public definition of an issue is a secondary battlefield in their primary conflict—the defeat of their opponents in the zero-sum party competition.[4] Both parties have often demonstrated their willingness to make policy substance secondary to their sense of political opportunities and dangers. When Sir Phillip Lynch proposed the means testing of pensions before the Lowe by-election in March 1982, the ALP attacked it.[5] When the ALP tried to move in a similar direction in late 1983, the Liberal Opposition attacked it also. On both occasions the proposal was deferred. Opposition Leader Howard changed his stance both on the introduction of an ID card and over the merger of the SBS with the ABC, when it was clear there was substantial opposition to the Hawke Government's intentions in each area. When out of power, political leaders often mount sustained attacks on the Government which are then forgotten on achieving power. Hawke for several years suggested that the Fraser Government should hold a referendum on the export of uranium, but never moved to do so himself.[6]

Positioning in political controversies sometimes involves Oppositions adopting both a sharp rhetorical difference, but also a policy whose substance is as close as feasible to the Government's, so as not to alienate support by being too extreme. Such positioning is difficult to maintain during periods of policy instability:

> One revealing sign of the extent to which the Government had changed policy was the 18 July [1982] statement by Hayden calling for a budget deficit of $1,500 million. This was below any figure Fraser ever entertained .... When the budget was brought down, he reverted to normal and proposed a moderate additional stimulus. As usual Hayden stood for a deficit of D + 1.[7]

In contrast, during the 1987 campaign, Treasurer Keating announced that the deficit would be less than the amount Howard had previously advocated,[8] leading Howard to immediately call for yet greater fiscal rectitude, a deficit always of D − 1.

In the dynamics of controversy, participants' information strategies and news practices are each responding to, and constrained by, the other:

> For the media the ideal election issue in 1945–70 was a subject which could easily reduce to simple terms; which involved principles more than complex facts, and ends more than means; which was 'fresh' and not 'stale'; which differentiated the parties with tidy polarity; and which was 'real', that is consistent with the media's view of political priorities.[9]

There is a pervasive filtering in reporting controversies towards accentuating the 'hardness' of news events; toward human interest qualities of novelty and drama; toward stressing the immediate and tangible relevance to the audience; towards moral simplicity and away from technical complexity. News formats favour policies which can be presented favourably in a few sharp sentences. The need for brevity and drama are also more suited to attack than exposition, discrediting opponents rather than arguing about competing priorities. Combined with the increased ruthlessness of political parties in targetting opponents' vulnerabilities, it is easier in political controversies for fears to be aroused than allayed.

Apart from politically consequential controversies, issues arise in news coverage through the reporting of 'spot news'. In crimes and transgressions, accidents and natural disasters, scientific discoveries and human interest stories, most coverage is self-contained with perhaps some participant briefly referring to wider implications. Sometimes, however, they are the occasion for more extensive considerations of policy responses and the adequacy of existing practices.

The capacity of a dramatic accident[10] to focus public attention and generate new momentum on an issue was perhaps best illustrated by the near-tragedy at the nuclear power station at Three Mile Island. The previously latent fears about nuclear power suddenly dominated headlines and political debate. Sharper and more sustained critical coverage of the nuclear industry followed the near-disaster than had been aroused by any of the protest activities of the anti-uranium lobbies—to the extent that President Carter complained it was the most irresponsible coverage he had seen.

A new development may draw attention to continuing conditions. After the outbreak of the Falklands war, the Western media paid far more attention to internal conditions and the military dictatorship in Argentina. Similarly the Marcos Government received more critical scrutiny in the Australian press after the 1983 assassination of Benigno Aquino and again after the politically contrived murder trial of Australian priest, Father Gore, in 1984. Crimes and transgressions sometimes generate a more embracing outrage over a situation that permits or encourages them. The political mood in the NSW ALP about the need for branch reforms in the inner city gained enormous impetus, following the brutal bashing of left-wing MP Peter Baldwin. The murders of Juanita Neilson, a campaigner against development in Kings Cross, and Donald Mackay, a campaigner against drug trafficking in the NSW town of Griffith, became symbols of deeper issues of corruption.

It is not merely the incidence of spot news events which is important. Rather, they sensitise the media more generally to the importance of an issue.[11] Judgments of newsworthiness are not always inherent in the events themselves, but as a topic becomes newsworthy the significance of relevant events is magnified. After Aboriginal suicides in police custody became an issue in 1987, acknowledged as politically explosive and a major social problem, any subsequent death became headline news, while earlier ones had largely passed with little attention. Such changes in sensitisation distort perspectives, however, if changed news priorities, rather than changes in the events reported, lead to misperceptions of prevalence and trends. The prominence given to prison escapes was greater during periods of prison reform than normally, implicitly suggesting a false perception of their causality.[12]

Because of the potential for sharp re-focusing of public attention following spot news, the policy balance often ebbs and flows with the nature and recency of major events. A terrorist attack such as the bombing at Sydney's Hilton Hotel during the Commonwealth Head of Governments Regional Conference in 1978 produces political momentum toward greater security procedures and an increase in the allocation to relevant organisations. Conversely a fiasco like that produced by the Australian Security Intelligence Service (ASIS) training exercise which terrorised guests at the Melbourne Sheraton Hotel in 1983 produces more sceptical treatment of security organisations. After Brisbane's floods in the mid-1970s there were stricter zoning laws and official attention to insurance policies. As the floods receded in memory there was more permissiveness toward building in endangered areas.[13] When little risk is apparent the dominant ethos may be against 'red tape' but after an accident of some kind there is pressure toward more stringent regulations.

## Attention Versus Action

'There is no more certain way to destroy the meaning of politics than to treat all issues as if they were free and equal.'[14] From the preceding considerations of issue attention and the dynamics of controversy, it is clear that there are great variations between issues in how and when they become newsworthy,[15] and that the amount of attention an issue receives in the news is far from synonymous with the amount of policy action in the area. Political analysis must therefore 'proceed on two levels simultaneously'.[16] Making a crude division of great or little noise and action on an issue generates four logical categories, discussed below.

### Little Noise, Little Action

The issues which fit into each of the four categories are obviously time-bound, as different issues rise and fall in the public agenda. Many examples from the first category of neglected issues ('little noise, little action') became clear only in retrospect. Before the late 1960s consumer protection, environmental issues and women's issues could all have been placed here. Many industrial health problems were also slow to gain recognition. Estimates of the appropriate amount of attention are necessarily subjective, depending on individual values and interests, but the processes shaping attention can still be traced. Neglect is likely when either:

1  no significant political group has the interest or capacity to dramatise the issues, or
2  the problem's appearance and causation are not easily perceived or formulated.

Because the news media typically reflect the various forces operating in their environment, an issue neglected by those forces typically remains neglected in the news. It is the exception rather than the rule that news acts as an 'early warning system' about looming problems. A recurring theme in criticisms of news is the lack of attention to continuing conditions which are not embodied in dramatic events. Poverty and deprivation,[17] both domestically and internationally, only sporadically and fleetingly enter the news agendas of the Western world.

Social problems that are not neatly encapsulated in normal news stories, or whose importance is not immediately apparent to organisational decision-makers, are also more prone to being neglected. Problems of relative deprivation are typically less tangible and less likely to be crystallised in discrete events than the immediate suffering through malnutrition or poor housing of absolute deprivation. A clear illustration was the early coverage of the women's movement, which was often predicated on the assumption that no real problem or grievance existed.[18] Moreover, the epitome of a non-newsworthy activity was the 'consciousness-raising' of the women's movement:

> Much of the movement's political emphasis was on 'changing peoples' heads' about such issues as women's place in the world. To say the least this is not an observable political occurrence . . . . It was relatively easy to dismiss it as 'not newsworthy' . . . . [One reporter commented] 'There were a lot of interesting things going on, but I couldn't nail things down . . . . I could see things changing, but it was hard to put my finger on it and say to the metropolitan desk, "this is what's happening".'[19]

A significant new current in society had arisen, yet it became news if at all either flippantly or in relatively 'artificial' ways, such as interviewing the first woman to enter a previously all-male domain.

## Great Noise, Great Action

The other category where there is a rough correspondence between attention and action is when there are great amounts of both. One candidate issue here is industrial relations, where there is constant evolution through a series of visible, individual disputes and developments. Public attention and controversy are not necessarily focused upon the most important changes, but at least there is continuing public scrutiny of a sort. Another is where there is close attention to policy formation, and its main dimensions are immediately apparent— budgetary policy is the obvious example.

## Little Noise, Great Action

The discrepancy, substantial action but little attention, occurs principally in areas where no-one has an interest in generating public controversy. Important policy movement with little sense of the public crystallisation of options, is also likely in areas where there is not contention between the parties and where the significance of the decision is not readily dramatised or apparent to the public. Kenneth Davidson began a consideration of the Hawke Government's policies on a satellite with the plausible general formula:

> In politics the most dangerous mixture for the public interest is a highly technical issue, an apathetic public and a few players who have a lot to gain or lose depending on which way the issue is resolved by the Government of the day.[20]

In areas where policy movement takes place within consensual parameters and where implementation is disaggregated into numerous
small decisions, marked by accommodations between executive government and pressure groups, there is little to stimulate news attention. Agricultural and industry subsidies, investment allowances, export incentives, etc. all involve substantial public spending, but are
not subjects of constant public attention.[21] A rather different example
is immigration policy which, for a generation, was officially sponsored
social change on a grand scale. The lack of public attention derived
from the bipartisan support the policy enjoyed. Perhaps, also, the
press was wary of an issue where attention seemed only to arouse
prejudice.

A major reason for the discrepancy between action and attention is
the way news gravitates towards conflict. Conflict has drama and
suspense, with a sense of fresh developments unfolding toward some
unknown resolution. Settled policies—no matter how momentous—
disappear quickly if they are not fuelled by fresh stories, while inten-
sively waged conflict—no matter how insubstantial the stakes—brings
a stream of newsworthy reactions and counter-challenges. In consequence, important developments that attract little public conflict pass
with little notice. Former Minister John Wheeldon instanced the
Whitlam Government's introduction of the Administrative Appeals
Tribunal. The Liberal Opposition, after opposing and questioning it
during the Committee stages, allowed it to pass. As a result a major
administrative departure occurred with almost no news coverage.

Because controversy prolongs coverage while areas of agreement
quickly recede, Governments find it difficult to reap sustained kudos
for their beneficence. Various tax changes by the Hawke Government
illustrated the tendency. In the May 1983 mini-Budget Treasurer Keating announced a series of measures. At first none had clear dominance
in news priorities. Within a few days coverage gravitated toward the
major controversy: the conflict over taxing superannuation lump sum
payments, which became 'the' issue, persisting in the headlines for
several weeks after all other aspects of the package had faded. Similarly in the 1985 tax changes, the abolition of 'double tax' on small
businesses disappeared from the news almost immediately, while the
complaints about eliminating entertainment expenses as tax deduc-
tions persisted for weeks. When the tax rates for upper income groups
were drastically reduced, it was the introduction of the fringe benefits
tax which stayed in the headlines as a campaign against it was waged
over a long period. In each case, measured against the substance of the
changes, attention was skewed towards costs and away from benefits.

*Great Noise, Little Action*

The final category ('great noise, little action') seems the most prolific.

It occurs in areas where there are strong stimuli to news interest, but equally strong obstacles to effective action. It occurs, firstly, where public demands and principles are clear, but their implementation is impossible or creates secondary problems. It might be universally agreed that there should be honesty in political advertising, but any attempt to enforce this principle would violate other principles regarding freedom of speech, or pose impossible problems of arbitrating honesty amid the fuzziness and hyperbole of political claims. Lower taxation is universally applauded, but creates budgetary pressures and so is talked about or promised far more than it occurs. All parties make sympathetic noises about helping small business, yet the practicalities of mounting effective, consistently implemented schemes are very difficult to conceive, so that there tends to be mainly insubstantial gestures and lip service.[22]

Secondly, much attention but little action occurs because there are newsworthy conflicts in an area, but the conflicts are such as to prevent effective action. Sometimes conflicting principles or interests made decisive or coherent action impossible. The outstanding example in Australia was economic re-structuring including tariff reform, where for decades there was endless talk about international competitiveness, efficiency, etc. but any specific proposal threatened individual companies and workers in politically risky ways.

Problems may be exaggerated as well as neglected in the news. The first main cause derives from the media's sensitivity-cum-vulnerability to major news sources, especially governments. When President Carter proclaimed Russian behaviour in Afghanistan the worst crisis since the Second World War, there was little choice for the press but to give Afghanistan front-page treatment. Governments are most likely to escalate a problem when they will enjoy consensual support for doing so, to dramatise an evil or an enemy when they know the overwhelming majority will share their views. News organisations similarly are likely to be most outraged on those issues where they know the audience will endorse their attitude. Issues with a community consensus and moral simplicity offer fertile ground for both politicians and media to affirm their virtue:

> The attitude of hostility to the lawbreaker has the unique advantage of uniting all members of the community in the emotional solidarity of aggression.[23]

In such situations there are many forces escalating and few containing the whole-hearted expression of outrage and concern. There is little political mileage to be gained, for example, by underestimating drug problems and child abuse. The horror and tragedy of particular cases are easily transformed into impressions of a prevalent epidemic.

In sum, policy action exceeds news attention in issue areas where no-one has a political interest or capacity for generating controversy, and when the movement is consonant with normal institutional operations, while news attention exceeds policy movement in issue areas where there are irreconcilable conflicts between influential groups, and policy movement is not easily institutionalised.

## Impacts on Policy-Making

### The Constraints of Disclosure

Having examined factors shaping news attention we now turn to the impacts of news on policy formation and content. The first impact is so fundamental that it is often ignored. The peculiarity of news, and its primary political significance, is that it is an institution devoted to disclosure. The most famous proclamations of this journalistic ideal were made by *The Times* in the 1850s:

> The press lives by disclosures—it is daily and forever appealing to the enlightened force of public opinion, anticipating if possible the march of events, standing upon the breach between the present and the future.
> The duty of the journalist is . . . to seek out the truth, above all things, and to present to his readers not such things as statecraft would wish them to know but the truth as near as he can attain it.[24]

Although the media's own information gathering is necessarily channelled by what other institutions and groups make available, their constant force for disclosure, and for immediate disclosure of the most recent and even impending developments, is a volatile political ingredient. The scale and centrality of the news media mean that abundantly more information is now available than in any previous era. Although it is necessarily accompanied by much misinformation, sham sensation and attempts at manipulation, 'information is the currency of democracy',[25] so that some of the conditions for informed choice and participation are more likely because of the news media.

Disclosure itself sets up tensions, irrespective of the observer's ideological stances. On some occasions, for example, religious authorities have banned distribution of the Bible.[26] Such apparently silly actions demonstrate how even the dissemination of 'ideologically correct' information threatens loss of control. It allows others to make their own decisions about proper interpretations and makes the religious authorities more accountable to Biblical precepts. Under changing circumstances, with conflicting demands, limited information, human fallibilities, and clashing ambitions, constant scrutiny even by an ideologically sympathetic observer creates tensions and problems for any authority. They are, of course, magnified when the observer is unsympathetic.

The most basic constraint which the news media place on decision-making is to guide political behaviour toward what is permissible within the public gaze. In addition to forcing disclosure where otherwise secrecy would prevail, media attention commonly forces the most publicly comprehensible and salient aspects, often the 'moral' aspects, of an issue to the fore, when political or administrative expedience might otherwise predominate. The constant possibility of publicity is a check on temptations toward egregious behaviour: '[One of our strengths is that] to an extent we keep business honest. We treat their excesses with disdain' (Business editor).

News plays an ameliorative social role here not through ideological opposition, but through highlighting individual injustices and measuring organisational performance against proclaimed ideals. The impact comes through highlighting how victims of bureaucratic anomalies or consumer rip-offs have suffered, and by highlighting problems in areas of acknowledged but unfulfilled government responsibility. Publicly ventillating these grievances often 'unclogs' institutional channels and weighs upon criteria for resource allocation and administrative priorities. Many journalists gave examples: highlighting the plight of the 'Minus Children',[27] nursing homes for elderly people, ensuring that the government enforced high rise building fire regulations are adhered to, prompting police and governments to be more vigilant in their prosecution of illegal gambling and prostitution. Acting as an institutional ombudsman, a watchdog for the public interest, was clearly central to many journalists' role conception: 'That's partly why we're here'. (Editor)

Clearly not all such impacts are an unmitigated good: public exposure may provoke defensive scapegoating and over-reaction. Moreover the media are in a luxurious position, embracing and abandoning issues as they follow the vagaries of newsworthiness. If the fear of public exposure or embarrassment causes a response in one area among those who must continue to juggle finite resources and competing priorities, this can skew bureaucratic and political priorities. However, the media's impact in monitoring institutions frequently provides a path for individual redress and enhances public accountability, acting as a check on bureaucratic or political expedience.

### Issue Priority and Definition

'Publicity enhances the salience of an issue; it imparts heat as well as light.'[28] Publicity transforms the priority accorded to an issue and so also the nature of policy-making towards it. Frequent and intense coverage of some issues and the intermittent coverage or neglect of others helps to shape policy-makers' agendas. Lord Boyle, a British Cabinet Minister in the early 1960s, put it succinctly: 'Cabinet was increasingly concerned with the agenda that the press and media were setting out as the crucial issues of the day'.[29]

The differential newsworthiness of issue areas affects their priority in policy-making. After a particularly brutal attack in Queensland in the early 1960s, shark nets were installed at all Queensland beaches.[30] In terms of resources expended on safety, this was probably not an efficient use of funds. Among causes of death, shark attack ranks low, but any particular fatality from a shark attack is so horrible and dramatic that it can provoke greater urgency than more prosaic fatalities. An example involving much greater revenue is the greater coverage (at least in Britain) given to social security abuse than tax evasion.[31] The latter is marked by technicality and lacks human interest (unless committed by a celebrity or accompanied by political conflict).

The priority among issues is a political battleground, in which the news media are inevitably implicated. News presentations involve a hierarchy of importance between stories and of information within stories. The thrust of publicity is rarely policy neutral. It tends to highlight not only a particular issue, but a particular 'face' of an issue. Some aspects or principles gain prominence to the implied subordination of others. If a problem is prominent in the news it is more likely to receive government attention; how an issue is publicised will facilitate some courses of action and inhibit, even prohibit, others. News coverage is thus implicated not only in the priority of issues, but in their definition. It affects not only the focus and speed of decision-making, but its direction. If the main emphasis in welfare news is on fraud (Golding and Middleton found fully '31% of all [welfare] stories dealt in some way . . . with social security abuse')[32] and there is little on the deprivation of welfare clients, the public ethos is not conducive to further expansion of welfare spending. To take another example:

> There tends to be a conventional wisdom in the press on any running story. [At the height of the Costigan Royal Commission revelations about tax evasion and organised crime] for example, there was little interest in civil liberties.

Not all faces of an issue are equally amenable to news coverage. The nature of news favours the highlighting of individual abuses over the consideration of relating necessary costs in achieving larger benefits, or consideration of trade-offs in the imperfections which inevitably accompany the functioning of all large institutions. It is more amenable to the pressing of a moral demand than the balancing of scarce resources. Yet for all the superficiality and one-sidedness sometimes manifested, it can be a cleansing force insisting on the primacy of moral considerations.[33]

There is also an unequal competition between present abuses and future possibilities. During the Kennedy Administration's debates over whether to continue supporting Diem, the Saigon press corps' probing reporting of the regime's counter-productive oppression strengthened the pro-coup advocates in the American Government. The nature of news did not permit the same prominence being given to fears of the instability which subsequently resulted. Equally, though, forecasting the future reflects the battle strength of present voices, and the promotion of unrealistic fears frequently dampens reform sentiments.

## Differential Visibility

Policy debate, enactment and reception are more visible in the news than policy implementation and effects. The effects of a policy are dispersed in time and space, and often hard to determine with any certainty. Implementation involves thousands of small-scale administrative actions, none of them normally observable to reporters or sufficiently dramatic to be newsworthy. It is only possible for news organisations to monitor implementation if the adverse effects are made public by complainants or by political controversy. The contrast between the public drama of enactment and the invisibility of implementation helps explains why, as Hancock noted in 1930, democracies 'having willed an end ... try to shuffle out of willing the means'.[34]

The differential visibility of various costs and benefits encourages policy makers to opt for issue resolutions where costs are dispersed and marginal rather than concentrated and intense.[35] Whether or not the Nixon Administration's policy of Vietnamisation (gradually withdrawing US troops, escalating the air war) was militarily viable, its domestic political appeal was clear. Without abandoning prosecution of the war, its visible costs in American casualties were reduced.[36] In contrast, the Fraser Government, for example, abandoned tax indexation, partly because, although it applied continuing tight disciplines on the Government, the kudos for it disappeared immediately after introduction. In managing the conundrum placed upon governments by the public's inconsistent demands for both lower taxation and more government services, the softest political option, before the floating of the Australian dollar, was not to raise taxes or reduce spending, but to let the less publicly visible Budget deficit increase:

> On the day of Labor's [1983] policy launch both the Sydney afternoon papers ran huge front page headlines about Labor's promised tax cuts. 'I can just see all those people out in the western suburbs looking at those headlines and worrying about the deficit,' one Hawke staffer remarked with glee .... It is unlikely that most voters had more than a hazy idea of what a deficit was, let alone its implications for taxation and interest rate increases.[37]

Differential visibility also explains why in some highly sensitive areas governments prefer to proceed by default rather than by decree.

A change in abortion law, for example, is a highly visible move which attracts opposition from very determined groups, but liberalising the interpretation of the existing law in individual cases is difficult for vigilantes to detect or arouse opposition against.[38] It is perhaps not surprising that in 1987 the Queensland Government was waging a high profile campaign against the moral danger posed by condom vending machines, at the same time that its Police Commissioner was telling the Fitzgerald Royal Commission that for the last decade the government's unofficial policy had been to allow prostitution to go on in a 'controlled' way.

Because news coverage dwells on conflicts, the most important determinant of the tone of publicity surrounding a policy is its reception by visible and vocal groups. The greater visibility of reception than effects encourages governments to resolve issues in a manner that accommodates conflicting parties even if, in substance, that involves less than the optimal policy.[39] Even if the government is convinced of its own rightness, there may be a stronger political interest in conciliation, to avoid a continuing parade of allegations, the creation of confusion on complex issues and the accumulation of determined enemies. Similarly, refraining from giving a benefit is less visible and damaging than a decision to remove an existing one. Removal offers a clear target, and is more likely to result in the mobilisation and resentment of those affected:

> From the time parts of the [Coombs] report [on Government expenditure] were published prematurely before the Budget, every beneficiary of the concessions, subsidies and bounties mentioned felt threatened . . . . [It] has become the classic warning to governments that the political damage done by an existing benefit removed can never be offset by a new benefit conferred.[40]

> One of Malcolm Fraser's axioms was that Government could not take benefits from people.[41]

Such inequalities of public response make the rational application of general principles politically difficult.

The differential visibility of policy formation and effects also means that political damage is more likely to accompany policy incoherence and internal division than demonstrably bad consequences. It has been argued by many defenders of the Whitlam Government (not least Whitlam himself) that in retrospect its economic record was not as bad as painted. This overlooks firstly that the electorate can of course only compare the present with the past and not the future. It also overlooks the extent to which the Whitlam Government suffered not just from the decline in objective conditions, but from the internal divisions and numerous policy somersaults that constituted its economic policy-making:

The period from June to November 1974 is probably unique in the history of decision-making in this country as the government moved from an orthodox deflationary policy . . . to an unorthodox reflationary policy . . . . These five months saw the . . . main components of advice to the government . . . all proceeding from different diagnoses of the economic problem to different solutions, operating on different value systems. The landmarks along the way were the 7 June Premiers' Conference, the 23 July mini-budget, the 17 September budget, and the 12 November mini-budget . . . . The cost was huge in blood and votes. The cabinet severed its relations with the federal treasury. Treasurer Frank Crean was subjected to a cruel political execution by the prime minister, relations between the cabinet and the caucus reached their nadir, Whitlam's prestige and control over his government was largely demolished for a period that culminated in newspaper stories that he was about to resign, and relations between senior figures in the Labor government became deeply embittered.[42]

## Reaction Versus Anticipation

Governments are confronted by many problems which do not admit of a practical or immediate solution. The most damaging issue is where there is a strong demand for impossible action. The 1980 crisis of American hostages in Iran was perhaps the most extreme and humiliating example. President Carter was faced with overwhelming pressure for action, but—given the wish for the diplomats to remain alive—total impotence.[43]

In many other areas, because news is so sensitive to Government responses, attempts at reform are more visible than the continuation of existing conditions. A Government may not suffer politically from problems it fails to acknowledge, but once recognised, it is held responsible for their solution.[44] It would seem that it is often more dangerous for governments to raise expectations that can't be fulfilled than to allow problems of low public visibility to continue unchecked. Taking decisive action tacitly means taking responsibility for happenings in that area. Governments are thus making themselves hostage to future developments over which they have little control. In some issues this sets up continuing vulnerabilities. Engaging in high profile efforts at prison reform is a high risk strategy. Future adverse developments, such as escapes, are all but inevitable, and now likely to be interpreted as failures of the new policy.[45]

Some areas are judged 'tar baby' issues, damaging everyone who becomes involved in them. Avoidance of controversy is the major political wisdom. Whitlam's decision as Opposition Leader to elevate the recognition of China and the independence of Papua New Guinea was a courageous example of placing substantive importance before political risk:

For nearly a century, China and New Guinea were linked, dimly but deeply, in the Australian consciousness: China the threat, New Guinea the bastion . . . . To place these matters [the recognition of China, the independence of Papua New Guinea] on the agenda of current political controversy involved going against some of the deepest and often the darkest instincts of Australians. This is what Whitlam decided he had to do in 1970 . . . . To keep [these] questions . . . out of the public debate was the safe course, but . . . to keep the issues on ice meant that Australia's postures would have become frozen even further.[46]

The first risk for Whitlam in both areas was some dramatic adverse development, which would put his initiatives into disrepute. Indeed Prime Minister Gorton said he would have 'blood on his hands', and large-scale violence in PNG would have rebounded on Whitlam politically.[47] Moreover both issues had an explosive symbolic dimension, evoking as they did symbolically charged questions of national identity, security and the uncertainties of change, more likely to evoke heat than light, to provoke arousal rather than provide reassurance.[48]

In conclusion, news is better at highlighting problems than canvassing solutions. In the formats of objective reporting, the debating of options emerges only obliquely, embedded in struggles for power and political advantage. News both provokes and frustrates policy action: intense publicity increases the demand for immediate action but tends to reflect existing lines of conflict, and with its attraction to controversy rather than consensus to focus upon the alleged costs of policy proposals.

Perhaps the most immediate effect of the news media on policy formation is the triumph of the short-term over the long-term, the dominance of tactics over strategy. Because there is little kudos for governments in accepting responsibility for problems which do not allow an immediate resolution, the nature of news coverage encourages *post hoc* response rather than problem anticipation. Because the news gravitates towards controversy and away from consensus, and because the politics of attack is more potent than exposition, the process mitigates against ambitious or complex reforms. The daily pressures for accountability manifested in the temporary and unpredictable excitements of news are a bias against coherence and planning, but equally a source of freshness in the political agenda and a check on the exercise of power. The cumulative impact, however, is to favour the politics of drift over mastery,[49] and of veto over initiative.

## Ideological Promiscuity and Political Volatility

News is notable among major social institutions for the lack of pressures toward consistency and continuity. The unpredictability of spot news and the sensitivity of news coverage to the claims of major sources both make it open to the emergence of a new issue. A sudden sense of urgency can be generated by a tragic event or a changing conflict among political forces.[50] The news media are perhaps hypersensitive to changes in the 'public mood', constituted by their sources' concerns, their own erratic soundings of audience interest, and their monitoring of competing organisations. When an issue gains prominence, directly concerned groups and publicity-seeking politicians are energised, further fanning the growth of political momentum. The proliferation of competing news organisations, all in search of novelty, all seeking their own 'angle' on a major story can result in a 'pack mentality' and a sudden surge of momentum:[51]

> It is a very unruly thing with no checks or balances.
>
> The Gallery are either at someone's feet or at their throat.

The sudden transition from neglect to headline news was amusingly illustrated by the rash of attention to the long neglected Cocos Islands and their ruler John Clunies-Ross in 1972. Even though Sir Paul Hasluck, when Minister for Territories in 1957, had described the Clunies-Ross kingdom as feudal,[52] the island's administration was then totally neglected in political debate and in the press until August–September 1972, when following renewed political stimulus, all Australian news organisations rediscovered the islands' newsworthiness:

> Rather in the manner of Evelyn Waugh's *Scoop*, Australia's three newspaper groups competed at great cost to reach the Cocos Islands in September 1972 after certain insubstantial but intriguing charges had been made in Federal Parliament . . . The Fairfax group chartered a Mystere jet at a cost of $13,000 . . . While waiting at Broome for permission to enter Indonesian air space, they were joined by another chartered jet-load of newspaper, television and radio people from the Melbourne Herald group. When both teams landed . . . they were met by a rightly self-satisfied journalist and photographer from News Ltd.[53]

The focus on the latest, freshest developments easily leads to an exaggerated impression of their importance, especially because news presentations have a bias against emphasising the limited significance of developments. The headline, 'Small earthquake in Chile, not many killed' captures by humorous contrast the tendency to overplay rather than underplay events. Misleading superlatives and careless comparatives abound in the news. In consequence, when viewed in the longer term, news coverage appears as a series of over-reactions, and political history becomes a chronicle of sudden lurches in partisan and personal fortunes:

> [The media tends] to magnify the short-term. When a Government is in trouble that tends to be magnified, and that tends to become reality. As Snedden started to decline [as Liberal Party leader, see Chapter 7] that was

magnified by the media, who interact with the backbench, and it became self-fulfilling.

The tendency to disproportion wedded to the weak pressures for consistency in media priorities and orientations produces a tendency for news stories to be morally simple but ideologically promiscuous. In other words, in any one situation a particular value can dominate the orientations of news reporting, but the dominating values are not consistent between stories or time periods. The processes by which this occurs were illustrated in an article about *60 Minutes* Executive Producer, Gerald Stone:

> Another rule was that *60 Minutes* dealt in specifics, not generalities.
>
> 'We never have—and never will, I hope—talk about Education in Crisis. But if we found one school that seemed to represent all that's good and bad about Australian education then we could focus on that one school.
>
> 'Don Hewitt of CBS *60 Minutes* gave us our favourite phrase. He said "A lot of people have difficulty understanding flood control but everybody can understand Noah." We look for that Noah in our work, the one issue, the one person who can seem to focus attention on it.
>
> 'Some people say, "Isn't that demeaning or superficial". I don't think so. I think it means that you're very tough about choosing what you're going to do.'[54]

The consequence of concentrating on the concrete for ideological consistency can be illustrated by two stories, both of merit in themselves, which *60 Minutes* did a couple of months apart in the early 1980s. In the first, a case of child-battering in Melbourne, which climaxed in the murder of the child, the whole orientation was on the failure of the welfare system to intervene in the family situation. The second concerned young adolescent runaways in Adelaide, who were telling welfare centres that they were afraid to go home, then staying the night there. The story resulted from the complaints of worried parents. The dominant tone was that the youngsters should be returned home, or that the parents be brought to the centre.

The strong message of the first story was the need for more state intervention in a family situation, of the second the priority of the parents' concern. In neither case were the principles of when and how the state should intervene in private family life examined. The point of moral simplicity within stories, but not necessarily with consistency between them, can be reinforced by imagining how easily *60 Minutes* could do two other stories: the first on an indignant family's complaints about harassment from an intrusive welfare bureaucracy ostensibly but wrongly concerned about a child's welfare; the second about an adolescent runaway returned home by an unthinking bureaucracy only to be beaten and mistreated by the parents. The *60 Minutes* formula not only fails to explore the general principles, but is incapable of doing so. Moreover the drama of a particular case can lead to invalid extrapolations in terms of prevalence or policy direction—despite Noah's success, building an Ark is rarely a good solution for flood control.

The tendency to exaggerate short-term trends plus the media's combination of ideological promiscuity and moral simplicity are all conducive to sharp changes in political momentum. Beyond any media impacts on policy content, their centrality doubtless contributes to greater political volatility, both in the motility of public attention and in the pressures for immediate action. It is the intensity of attention, not just its content, which feeds into the political process. The creation of bandwagons and crises changes political equations. The concentration and urgency can overcome obstacles which would operate in more pedestrian times, but the pressing deadline and the sense of threat typically also inhibit the search for and evaluation of options.

The media are one of many factors accelerating reactions in the modern polity. The new technologies in transport, communication and information processing have together increased the speed of decision-making and the short-term responsiveness of many institutions from political parties to money markets. Some journalists said that news doesn't change events but it may change their timing. But timing is almost never politically neutral. The chain of events initiated by the leaking of DLP Senator Gair's imminent Ambassadorial appointment drastically changed the immediate course of Australian politics, including the calling of the 1974 election (see Chapter 5). Similarly the manoeuvering for advantage in the timing of Prime Minister Fraser's final election was transformed by the impact of the tax evasion scandals uncovered in late 1982 by the Costigan Royal Commission. Both vividly demonstrate the interaction of timing with political outcomes.

Pressure for an immediate decision often changes its nature. Prominent and extensive reporting, an urgent tone, and the presence of journalists *en masse* waiting expectantly, all escalate the pressure for an immediate, decisive resolution. The feeling of intense surveillance produces an emotionally charged situation, which could easily alter behaviour and decisions, especially in the pressure cooker of the Federal Parliament:

> If someone is in trouble, eg the resignations of Moore and McKellar [in the 'colour TV' affair], you are all gathered around waiting for the corpse to be brought out.... Rumours were flying. It all produced a particular atmosphere. It can trigger events. Parliament House often seems to be a world in itself, all sparking off one another.

> There was that atmosphere in Brisbane [when Hayden resigned for Hawke, see Chapter 7]. It was bizarre. Everyone had to walk through the press.... Everybody was buzzing and that infects the journalists, and the politicians.

The news will never be a comprehensive or systematic or consistent searchlight on what is happening in society. This inconstancy is lamented by many, such as Walter Lippmann, who deplored how the erratic shallowness of the media interfered with more coherent approaches to government:

> The press is no substitute for institutions. It is like the beam of a search-light that moves restlessly about, bringing one episode and then another out of darkness into vision. Men cannot do the work of the world by this light alone. They cannot govern society by episodes, incidents and eruptions.[55]

On the other hand the very unpredictability adds an element of flexibility, of new opportunities for issues to emerge, of an erratic check on government programs—so that in some senses, the seeming caprice and volatility in fluctuating media attention allow more open-ness in political agendas.[56]

In terms of normal ideological categories, the inconstancy of the media produces paradoxes. There are strong strands of both conserva-tism and subversion. On the one hand, they arguably act as an agent of control and conformity. They bestow most access to the most powerful, while often denying it to dissidents. Many programs and publications are quick to seize opportunities for expressing outrage against anything beyond the accepted mainstream, in the process simplifying and distorting alternative viewpoints. On the other hand, news is a 'merchant of the novel and unexpected'.[57] The search for freshness, the ideological promiscuity which produces shifting news frames, the competitive pressures which can create sudden band-wagons, the insistence on moral standards in policy considerations and the disclosure of scandals, the adherence to professional notions of adversary and watchdog roles all lead the news (inconsistently) to 'afflict the comfortable and comfort the afflicted', to question and occasionally confront authority, to promote emerging fashions and ventilate progressive views.

Similarly news reflects and amplifies the shifting ambivalences in the community about government programs. News organisations tend to be dries in general, but wets on specifics. Their orientations display the dislike of big government and bureaucracy, but coupled with the indispensibility of every service whose removal is threatened, and indeed the ever-increasing demand for governments to assume respon-sibility for any problem that arises. Editorially, news organisations have been overwhelmingly conservative in outlook, yet the processes of disclosure highlight various problems, which cumulatively contri-bute to the expansion of the public agenda and of the demands on government. The activities of government, pressure groups and finally of news gathering all help to consolidate the trend:

'Pollution' had become a perceived problem in the media in the late 1960s and early 1970s. There was one article on pollution listed in the *Sydney Morning Herald* index of 1966, 43 in the 1970 index.[58]

Joseph Glascott . . . was appointed *Herald* environment writer in 1974.[59]

## Conclusion

The primary political significance of the news media is that they are an institution devoted to disclosure and commentary, communicating to a huge audience of mixed social classes and political persuasions, with a large degree of communicator autonomy, imposing their own priorities and conventions upon what is presented. Their presence affects the timing, the manner, and, most importantly, the extent of revelations about powerful groups. The media have achieved routine access to senior politicians, and their efforts have necessitated an elaborate machinery of information disclosure by Government. Official secrecy, the backroom operations of machine politics, the abuses of corporate power, are now all more precarious. However, although the news media live by disclosure, there are great variations in their vigilance. They are erratic in granting access to different groups and their own access to newsworthy events is equally variable.

Yet while information is pouring forth, there is an increasing sense of deception, of not knowing the real story.[60] The greater intensity of public relations politics creates a maze of rationalisations and cover stories which make it difficult to distinguish the facades from the facts. The fragmentary formats of news presentations amid conflicting claims are apparently cognitively disabling for many. There is vividness without context, information without accountability, variety without enhancing the sense of choice or control.

As the scope of media concerns has increased, public relations strategies, aimed at the most effective news presentations to a marginally attentive public, have become more simplistic and arguably bear less relation to subsequent action. As the problems with which governments must deal have become more intractable, the media's dramatic skills have progressed more than their forensic ones. The pressing economic and social problems are merely the backdrop for the panorama of passing personal dramas, the elevation and destruction of heroes, the apparently endless rhythm of raising expectations and the subsequent personalising of blame for their failure. In the process the degree of accountability and of perspective on the underlying problems are only marginally enhanced.

News is a reflective institution. It is important to grasp the balance between the news media's independence and dependence, their vulnerability as well as their limited autonomy. The media's proximity to important events is easily mistaken for power. The claims of besieged public figures and the boastings by news organisations accompanying their rare initiatives or campaigns add to an exaggerated impression of media autonomy. News is a set of routines plugged into a power structure. How well the routines enhance democratic processes depends centrally on the operation of institutions and the configurations of conflict in the media's environment. If they are all leading in one direction, the news media—especially one organisation alone—are rarely capable of effectively challenging the dominant consensus. At other times the balance of contending forces is conducive to the news media weighing the evidence from different sources, or exercising their own reportorial initiative: 'If the forces are there, then the press is like a prism. It will reflect, focus and magnify their views.'[61]

Perhaps no other social institution occasions such romantic idealising about their democratic indispensability, but simultaneously, has such an arsenal of arguments for deflating utopian hopes for its improvement. Its daily operations are bounded by organisational deadlines and production demands plus limited access to the world on which it is seeking to report. Its economic logic is governed by marketing orientations which decree that more probing and deeper reporting are rarely rewarded by larger audiences, while in terms of sensationalism and gimmicks some see an inverse relation between quality and marketing success. Its employment and managerial practices allow only the most precarious sense of any professionalism beyond technical competence and productivity. Economic trends seem to concentrate media control ever more narrowly in ever larger oligopolies while any external intervention raises the possibilities of state control. Nothing in news production or journalistic ideals offers any certain protection against either external manipulation or internal suppression.

It is silly to lay all the evils of the political system at the feet of the media, and it is futile to wish they would become less central. But concern with the news media will always be central in evaluating the quality of democratic processes. They are the pivot between the rulers and the ruled. They will continue to disappoint reformers, to be the target for many legitimate grievances, to be dominated by pedestrian mediocrity. Despite their tame connivance in the charades and feints of dominant sources, and despite the prejudices of proprietors, reporters and audiences, the news media occasionally and erratically expand the quality of social choice and enhance the accountability of the governors to the governed.

# Notes

## Introduction

1 The Calwell quote is found in Kiernan p. 92; Gorton from Freudenberg p. 162; Cairns from Barr; and Bjelke-Petersen from *Business Review Weekly* 9–1–1987, p. 61. Chipp's remark was made on the ABC's *AM* program, 9–10–1981 and quoted extensively, e.g. by Laurie Oakes *The Age* 16–10–1981. Chipp's outrage was occasioned partly by media reports of Prime Minister Fraser's illness before the CHOGM conference in Melbourne (see Chapter 7).

2 *The Age* 2–8–1982 (Greer) and 21–11–1981 (Tange).

3 This, or similar sentiment, was volunteered to me by at least a dozen journalists.

4 There are usually no costs in criticising the media. Social disagreements about politics, for example, can be neutralised by deflecting the disagreement on to an absent general target, for which neither conversationalist holds a brief. There is, of course, great scope for selective perception in the attribution of bias. As Ranald McDonald once observed, when the news confirms peoples' beliefs, they take its performance and record a zero, but when it challenges them, they see news as biased and record a minus. Because the media never scores positively, they always finish with a minus score.

5 The major works in the newsmaking tradition are Sigal, Tuchman, Roshco, Gans, Fishman, Tunstall, Golding and Elliott, Schlesinger, and Epstein.

6 'The trouble with the great man theory of history is that there is an awful lot of history and not many great men' (Golding and Elliott p. 7).

7 From Neil Simon's play *The Odd Couple*, quoted by Golding and Elliott p. 7).

8 See Epstein pp. 41ff. Journalists' emphasis on idiosyncratic and accidental factors shaping news (1) reflects their own immediate experiences, and (2) is a useful defence against conspiracy charges. It is notable that while many defences of news quality stress the contingencies of its

199

production, news presentations normally seek to conceal these (see Chapter 3).

9   Sigal p. 187.

10   On the study of media effects see McQuail (1978, 1987).

11   e.g. Tuchman p. 14. Several of the newsmaking theorists reach similar conclusions about the dominant political direction of news, in particular Schlesinger, Golding and Elliott, and Fishman.

12   In Australia, right-wing critiques of news are found regularly in *Quadrant* and the *IPA Review*.

13   Gans p. 296.

14   Cater p. 10.

15   In sum, the political effects of the news media are usually conceived too narrowly. Politicians and political activists are most concerned with immediate effects and partisan advantages, and not with how the centrality of the media affect the way in which the game is played. Most academic research has concentrated on the morass of alleged impacts on mass political attitudes. It is an enormously difficult, not to say expensive, task to trace how messages from the media interact with all the other ingredients that help form public opinion. Neither political nor academic concerns have illuminated changing political processes and so the distribution and bases of power.

16   The major manifestation of an expanded view of media effects on the audience was the work on agenda setting. See Blood's review. The seminal work was McCombs and Shaw.

17   The Lincoln and LBJ quotes are from Walker pp. 38, 57; Rousseau from Mills.

18   Geertz (1964).

19   Helpful works clarifying theoretical issues in using the concept of power are Martin, Wrong and Lukes.

20   The centrality of the media in political communication and so potentially in opinion formation raises difficult questions for democratic theory, originally posed most sharply by Walter Lippmann:

> If you had asked a pioneer democrat where the information was to come from on which the will of the people was to be based, he would have been puzzled by the question . . . . The will of the people, he almost always assumed, exists at all times [and further assumed . . .] either that truth is spontaneous, or that the means of securing truth exist.

21   Because of my other continuing research interests, a number of former foreign correspondents, especially those who have reported from Asia, were also interviewed, and some of their comments used in this study.

22   Although cooperation was excellent, there was a theme running through journalists' comments that only journalists are competent to write about news. As Golding and Elliott observe, 'not many ornithologists can achieve flight, yet we generally trust their analysis of its accomplishment by birds' (p. 7). It is a particularly paradoxical viewpoint for journalists to hold, as their work, more than most, involves describing and commenting upon others' work. Their political reporters are not expected to have been politicians, their medical reporters doctors, etc.

23  Roshco p. 3.

24  The comparative case study approach also informed a study of scandals in the news which will be published later. Although the term is the author's, the same approach has informed other studies, most notably Shibutani's classic study of rumour, where he used data about 60 rumours to illustrate and substantiate a more general theory. As with rumour, this book deals with topics which are inherently elusive and controversial. A more quantitative approach would be inappropriate because the subjects under study are too complex to allow reliable enumeration without distortion, and by condensing all data into a quantitative form, the subtleties of individual cases would be lost.

25  The content analysis results are suggestive rather than definitive because of the very limited sample on which they are based. The data and codebook have been deposited in the Social Science Data Archive from the Australian National University. The codebook can also be purchased from the Department of Government, University of Sydney.

## 1  Organisational Imperatives

1  Quoted e.g. Boorstin p. 19. Schlesinger notes, 'A BBC document, *Review of the Year 1930*, gives us a sense of the prevailing, rather genteel and amateurish approach: "When there was not sufficient news judged worthy of being broadcast, no attempt was made to fill the gap, and the announcer simply said 'there is no news tonight.'"' (p. 21).

2  'News hole' is a term taken from newspapers. They were laid out with the advertisements in place, and all the empty spaces to be filled with news was the 'news hole'. The same idea is clearly applicable to broadcasting. The primacy of deadlines was illustrated by Murdoch's grumble, when *Times* editor Harold Evans was late designing the front page after Sadat's assassination: 'No good producing the best paper in Fleet Street if you can't get it printed on time' (Leapman p. 22).

3  Tunstall pp. 7, 50–5. 'Almost all editorial expenditures are investments in the future. It's very hard on a balance sheet to say that by putting on another $50 000 or $100 000 into the investigative side ... that you're going to get a return. That's the problem really, or one of them' (Ranald McDonald, *New Journalist* 37, June 1981, p. 10).

4  Tunstall p. 1; p. 28.

5  As is well known, ownership of Australian newspapers was for a long time concentrated in three companies, and underwent radical changes from November 1986 with the disappearance of the Herald and Weekly Times group and the dominance of Murdoch's News Limited. There are several informative accounts of the ownership and nature of Australia's press companies. See especially Bowman and the forthcoming work by Paul Chadwick. Brown gives an authoritative account of the earlier ownership situation. *Communications Update* has much timely information on changes in media companies and policies. My own work on the companies and the ownership revolution can be found in Tiffen (1987, 1988).

6  From 1982 to 1988, there was also competition between morning papers in Brisbane. It began when Murdoch launched *The Daily Sun*, and ended

when that paper, now owned by its management, became an afternoon paper, after Murdoch had closed *The Telegraph*, which he had acquired with his takeover of the Herald and Weekly Times, in 1986–87.

7   Walker pp. 2, 6. See also Tunstall p. 209.

8   McQuail's content analysis for the UK Royal Commission on the press supported this (p. 21).

9   Tunstall p. 75.

10  The two main international news magazines, *Time* and *Newsweek*, both changed their Australian arrangements in the 1980s. *Newsweek* became a part of *The Bulletin* in 1984, and in 1986 *Time* began a special Australian edition, in conjunction with the Fairfax company, employing a small staff of Australian journalists.

11  *Nation Review* was formed in 1971, when Gordon Barton's *Sunday Review* merged with the small fortnightly *Nation*, founded in 1958 by Tom Fitzgerald and sustained by him and George Munster.

12  See also Gans p. 103 on US news magazines.

13  On agencies see Boyd-Barrett and Smith. Roshco cites a 1969 *Wall St Journal* estimate that agencies 'provide Americans with 75% of the state, national and international news they read in papers and listen to on radio and television' (p. 68).

14  Masterton's figures support this (p. 140).

15  eg Roshco p. 31. This view is strongly contested by Schudson.

16  'You would like to break a story but a person can't detach themselves from a major job to go and dig. We have to do it outside the main job. There is not the time to spend. That's the beauty of AAP for other journalists. It frees them to do the digging.' (AAP political reporter). In Southeast Asia I characterised the agencies as being more in the import-export than the production business (Tiffen 1978 Chapter 2).

17  One recent such poll finding appeared in *The Bulletin* (21-2-1984) showing that in late 1983 45 per cent said they relied most on TV for news, up from 31 per cent since 1975. Newspapers had declined from 37 per cent to 28 per cent over the same period. See also Western and Hughes. For a comprehensive review of Australian polls on the media, see Mayer *et al.*

18  Walker pp. 6–7 and Henningham (1988 pp. 163–5) have similar estimates.

19  See especially Schlesinger pp. 98–100. Henningham (1988, Chapter 2) gives a good summary of the TV news work day.

20  Epstein pp. 102–3.

21  Tiffen (1978) p. 94. See also Epstein pp. 136f on why TV news prefers generalists.

22  Gans p. 94.

23  On the growth of radio and TV coverage from Canberra, see Lloyd, from whose work this and some later examples come.

24  Lloyd.

25  See e.g. Horne *Years of Hope* pp. 1–2.

26  The main exception to this sense of improvement in the broadcasting media was the ABC. Indeed the improvements in the commercial channels probably deepened their sense of crisis, especially as it coincided with the prolonged funding squeeze imposed by the Fraser Government

(and with enduring industrial problems which prevented the ABC from exploiting its ENG technology). It highlighted the ABC's slowness to develop as a TV news organisation. The origins of this failure lay in the initial attitudes to the new medium. In 1951 Chairman Sir Richard Boyer wanted to have no news at all on television (Inglis p. 211), and General Manager Moses later promised a Royal Commission that responsibility for television could be simply added to the tasks of program departments without the need for substantially greater funding (p. 196). The ABC was probably the last major news organisation in the world where most reporters filed for both radio and TV. The part-time commitment to TV only ended with the introduction of *The National* in 1985. Moreover, in the two major news centres, Melbourne and Sydney, it perversely combined a mixed news service with the two media's locations separated by several kilometres and heavy traffic.

27  Janis and Mann p. 22. In terms of Janis and Mann's seven criteria for vigilant decision-making (thorough canvassing of alternatives, objectives etc.), news organisations would only consistently pass on the seventh (planning for implementation).

## 2  Gathering News

1  Gans p. 138.
2  See Gans pp. 138–44 and Tunstall p. 196.
3  'At NBC, there was at least one day's advance warning from the "news makers" on 90% of the stories used on the evening news' (Epstein p. 31).
4  Business and economic reporting are distinct: business reporting is centrally concerned with companies' activities and the investment market, while economic writers concentrate on questions of macro-economics and government policy. The two are best considered together because their histories are intertwined, and the roles sometimes overlap, with business editors, for example, writing economic analysis and economic writers discussing business activity.
5  Roshco pp. 72–74.
6  Gans p. 128.
7  Roshco p. 67.
8  Roshco p. 61.
9  Fishman pp. 51–2, 141, 143.
10  See especially Sigal's analysis of the proportions of routine channels (58 per cent) against informal (16 per cent) and enterprise channels (26 per cent) in front-page stories in the *New York Times* and the *Washington Post*. The proportions are likely to be even more pronounced in less elite newspapers and inside page stories (pp. 120–5).
11  Tunstall p. 198.
12  Clem Lloyd has written an excellent history of the Federal Parliamentary Press Gallery. Edwards offers a revealing sketch of its atmosphere and dynamics. Henderson gives a forceful critique.
13  In addition, the old Parliament House, vacated in 1988, had only two entrances and a layout which encouraged casual interaction among the occupants.
14  Rumour has strong negative connotations of unreliability. It should also be seen as a collective process of problem-solving in ambiguous situa-

tions, where the demand for information exceeds the supply. See Shibutani's pioneering work and the more recent contributions of Rosnow.

15 The unclear mixture of hierarchy and division of labour within bureaux produced several complaints from more junior members about the chief correspondent taking over stories.

16 See e.g. Roshco p. 74, Fishman p. 43.

17 See e.g. Tunstall (1976).

18 Tunstall divided source orientations into promotional, mixed and cautious/hostile (p. 162) while Gans talked of eager, agreeable and recalcitrant sources (p. 118). Tunstall further divided specialist fields into audience, advertising, revenue and mixed areas. He hypothesised: 'The greater the element of non-revenue goal, the more autonomy will the newsgatherer have in relation to his news sources; and the greater the element of revenue goal, the more will the newsgatherer be under the control of his news sources' (Tunstall p. 149; also pp. 267, 167, 93).

19 Because of the secrecy surrounding source-journalism transactions, the relative skill, integrity and charm by which journalists produce news from these relationships necessarily remains invisible to their audience (cf Tunstall pp. 151, 168, 171, 200).

20 Sigal p. 78.

21 Such 'absorption' in the ethos of their news round may even reach the heights claimed by American humourist, Russell Baker where Congressional reporters love Bourbon, tell coarse jokes and hate reform, State Department reporters act like fuddy-duddies with grave secrets to keep, and Pentagon reporters look like they've just returned from military manoeuvres (quoted, Sigal p. 48).

22 Sigal p. 49.

23 This was a common complaint of business during the 1930s, see e.g. Mayer 1964.

24 The only exception was one afternoon newspaper editor, who even then only qualified the general stance slightly.

25 Even this is changing somewhat. ABC TV news has had regular business reports, since the introduction of *The National* in 1985. Commercial TV news coverage is still sparse, but there are now regular business programs in non-prime time slots.

## 3 News Values

1 Gans p. 81.

2 Tunstall pp. 38–9.

3 Gans pp. 241–2.

4 In cultural studies from a leftist view, there is much stress on the interpretations audiences give to their entertainment, but still little on the audiences' role in the economic foundations of media institutions. Windschuttle is the only Australian left theorist to place audience concerns at the centre of his media analysis.

5 Cf also Golding and Murdoch p. 147.

6 Epstein p. 149. No Australian editor put it quite this strongly.

7 'For every one hundred copies sold most [UK] daily papers receive about four letters a year' (Tunstall 1977, p. 203).

8  Gans p. 232, and pp. 232–5.
9  Henningham 1988, pp. 182–3.
10  Schlesinger pp. 107, 108, 119, 134. See also Gans pp. 155, 230, 235–41.
11  See Murdoch's strategy with the London *Sun*, based on the presumption that the *Daily Mirror* had got above its readers (Leapman pp. 57, 77).
12  Gans p. 199, Schlesinger p. 265.
13  Quoted, Kern *et al.* p. 20; cf Walsh (1970, p. 49) on infantilism in the Australian press.
14  Australian newspaper markets are fairly stable, with monopoly and segmented, semi-monopoly situations predominating, and consumer behaviour being, anyway, slow to change. Even in the competitive British newspaper market, a survey in the 1960s found that 'newspaper reading was the most stable variable apart from sex and date of birth' (quoted, Tunstall 1968, p. 18).
15  Unlike US TV, in Australia the news announcers have typically not had a strong background in journalism. The promoters most highlighting the authority of the announcers has been Channel Nine's advertisement with a delighted chorus singing 'Brian told me. I know everything I need to know, because Brian told me so.' Nine's Sydney announcer Brian Henderson used to compere the teenage variety program *Bandstand*, while his Melbourne equivalent, Brian Naylor, compered a children's variety show, *Swallow's Juniors*. News executives defending the media against external criticism often use the example of ancient messengers who killed the messenger bearing bad news. One wonders what the ancients would have made of such irrational superstitions as surrounding the messengers with such razzamatazz.
16  Tuchman pp. 73–4. See Crouse p. 173 on how one political operative exploited competition between TV reporters from the one station at a party convention.
17  Former Sydney police rounds reporter, Paul Molloy, was one of the few to volunteer an example where he was a clear loser. After the kidnapping of a woman from Castle Cove, there was much press interest in her fate. The police arrested the kidnapper one afternoon, but until the woman was safely rescued were keeping total silence in their dealings with the media. The kidnapper finally led police to where he had left her tied up, and she arrived safely back at Chatswood police station at 1 am. Having worked on the story all day, and made strenuous efforts to find out what was happening, Molloy filed his final story at 12.30, the *Herald*'s deadline for its second edition, and went home. His story had canvassed the earlier, now superseded, question of whether there had been a ransom demand. When he picked up the papers the next morning, his heart sank as he read the *Daily Telegraph*'s headline story announcing the woman's safety. Molloy then graphically described how terrible he left, the cold reception from his superiors, and his own sense of shame, even though he had done all that he could. Molloy was at a disadvantage competing against the *Telegraph*'s Ced Culbert, who had been their police roundsman for 25 years, and had unparalleled contacts inside the NSW police force. Such a scoop could probably only happen on police rounds: firstly, it was one against one competition, whereas if one journalist in the

Canberra press gallery gets a scoop, the other hundred don't usually feel the pain of individual failure. Secondly, in few other rounds, if the latest development before deadline were missed would the consequence be two such clearly different stories appearing on the front pages of two papers. Thirdly, it is more likely on police rounds that such a dramatic development could have happened so late at night, right on the morning newspapers' final deadlines. Competition elsewhere is less cruel.

18  Tunstall p. 215.
19  See e.g. Fishman p. 7, Roshco p. 70, Tunstall pp. 158, 209, Schlesinger pp. 108, 11, and Epstein.
20  Tunstall p. 209. See also Gans p. 126.
21  Quoted, Downie p. 51. See also Sigal p. 40.
22  Sigal p. 37. Norms frequently develop to neutralise the conflicting forces towards competition and collegiality. They have been perceptively outlined by Tunstall, Tuchman and Fishman. There is wide variation in the observance of these informal norms. However, several observers have noted that journalists generally share routine information, may offer each other practical help, and swap impressions of sources and developments. At the same time, there are tacit prohibitions against being too parasitical, against contravening professional ideas of confidentiality (e.g. regarding sources, or stories currently being pursued) and that friendship should not bar one scoring an exclusive.

There are different attitudes to outsiders. For example, one industrial reporter said he wouldn't ask questions at a press conference, if it meant those who didn't normally cover the round could just use the questions as a short-cut of finding out what was going on. See also Lloyd (pp. 95–8) on 'clubbing' in the Canberra press gallery in the 1950s and 1960s.

23  It was for example, the centrepiece of *Time* magazine's famous attack on the Saigon press corps in 1963. See Halberstam (1979).
24  See e.g. Walker's discussion of perceptions of the crisis in South Korea, following the killing of President Park.
25  Sigal p. 50. See also Gans pp. 177, 180–1, Tunstall p. 216, Sigal pp. 40–1.
26  See e.g. Tiffen (1983), Knightley.
27  See Kuhn Ch X.
28  Fierce competition has always encouraged pathological rivalry between reporters, which in no way enhances news quality. Mayer (1964 pp. 14–15) offers historical examples where one paper monopolised the telegraph for hours by transmitting passages from the Bible to prevent their competitor transmitting news. While the negotiations went on during the Korean War, the three rival US news agencies engaged in reckless jeep races to gain a few seconds on their rivals (see Tiffen 1978). One Murdoch journalist once gained time over his father working for a competing organisation by deflating his tyres.
29  Sigal pp. 56, 72.
30  Crouse p. 231.
31  Sampson p. 385 says there have been several replays in Fleet Street on the theme of a new arrival going more down-market to attract larger audiences.

32  Charles Moses thought that after the broadcasting of Parliament began, the press started to report it more accurately (Inglis p. 146), while one retired correspondent also affirmed that the advent of ABC news had a salutary effect on press political reporting.

33  Tuchman p. 217. Even scientific articles are bound by such formats, Gusfield 1976.

34  Smith, A *The Politics of Information* p. 98.

35  Tuchman p. 132.

36  See e.g. Wolfe (ed.) and Scanlon (ed).

37  Gans p. 162. Occasionally there may be a conflict between story telling and seeking to reflect public attitudes. A strong strand in recent popular opinion has been a suspicion of any large increases in immigration. Yet in most specific cases of individuals being excluded, the dominant story orientation has been sympathetic to them. Similarly, the hanging of Australian drug offenders in Malaysia is not inconsistent with Australian public opinion, but the news orientation is very much on the pathos of their plight.

38  Tuchman (1972).

39  Epstein pp. 168–9. Also Sigal pp. 66, 68.

40  Gans p. 92.

41  In foreign news, it can lead to ethnocentrism (Tiffen 1978, pp. 109f).

42  Epstein p. 262. See also Gans p. 338, Schlesinger.

43  Golding and Elliott p. 143: 'Those who make the effective decisions at each stage . . . feel themselves to be more in the grip of the news than in command of it.' B. Cohen p. 132.

44  Tiffen 1978 p. 117.

45  Tunstall p. 124.

46  E.g. Gans on enduring values, Golding and Elliott.

47  E.g. Sigal p. 1, Roshco p. 4.

48  Roshco p. 4.

49  The *Bad News* study concluded, based on content alone, that because so much TV news consisted of talking heads that the conventional wisdom that TV news placed high priority on interesting film was wrong. No one who has ever been close to TV news can doubt the strong emphasis on getting interesting film whenever possible. What the study actually showed was that the value was rarely realised; cf also Altheide p. 73; cf Golding and Elliott pp. 114–15 for a different view.

50  Sigal p. 66. See also Gans p. 281.

51  See especially Baker.

52  Gans p. 283.

**4  Overt Manoeuvres**

1  Sekuless, p. 63.

2  Dale, p. 52, also p. 120.

3  For supporting observations, see Roshco p. 83, Sigal p. 127 and Margach.

4  Roshco p. 36.

5  For example, a journalist from *The Australian* interviewed me about Neville Wran's media success, and commented that it seemed that a

government practising PR couldn't lose. Despite my denial, and subsequent woolly outline of other factors at work, the story still 'quoted' me as saying a government practising PR was unbeatable.

6  A Rydges survey in 1980 found four out of five press releases sent to *The Sydney Morning Herald* end in the waste paper basket, as do one in three at the ABC, and one in two at *The Australian Financial Review* (*Media Information Australia* 17, Media briefs 17.303); cf Tunstall p. 181.

7  *The Australian Financial Review* 26–3–1982, editorial.

8  A survey of financial journalists found substantial criticisms of financial public relations officers (*Financial Review* 12–2–1987); cf Levy that journalists' private disdain in no way reduces their public conformity. Public relations manoeuvres are typically concealed in news presentations. See *Columbia Journalism Review* study (1979), Golding and Elliott, pp. 150–1, Gans p. 125.

9  Quoted, O'Reilly p. 182.

10  Gans p. 116.

11  Gans p. 119.

12  Sigal p. 70.

13  Goodin p. 33.

14  Edelman 1964 pp. 5–8.

15  Dale p. 122. See also Bruce Stannard 'Master of the New Media' *The National Times* 18–8–1979.

16  O'Hara; see also O'Reilly.

17  Dale p. 6.

18  Lunn; cf also Cater pp. 108–10.

19  Anderson p. 189.

20  See Tiffen 1985 on how Wran's six week pre-election blitz was made more effective by his relative absence from the news in the preceding period.

21  Ross Gittins 'The Storm before the Calm' *The Sydney Morning Herald* 3–6–1988.

22  Howson p. 369.

23  *The National Times* 22–12–1983.

24  *The Sydney Morning Herald* 18–5–1983.

25  Cockerill *et al.* p. 123.

26  White p. 183, Sigal p. 109.

27  Greenfield p. 34.

28  Dale pp. 89, 120.

29  *The Australian Financial Review* 26–5–1978. It is potentially dangerous for leaders if journalists are assigned to cover an event and they have no clear news to deliver. Wran, for example, always made sure that at every party conference, there was some 'hard news', a definite government action, to announce. Otherwise media attention might wander onto unfavourable aspects, such as internal brawls. Cf also one frustrated US journalist's observation that Nixon was one of the best students of news formats of any politician (Crouse p. 269).

30  Cf also President Johnson's pledge to withdraw all US troops from Vietnam within six months of an agreement being reached. The pledge originated in his desire for something 'short and snappy' that 'would get the headlines' (Sigal p. 183).

31  See especially Peter Hastings, *The Sydney Morning Herald* 2-5-1987.
32  cf Dale p. 61.
33  Chipp p. 110.
34  Cockerill *et al.* p. 195, also p. 192. On the ability to simulate spontaneity, see e.g. White p. 404, Lloyd p. 35.
35  See e.g. *The National Times* 19-1-1980.
36  Although note 'The Officious Bystander's' advice on how to win a court appearance, *The Bulletin* 28-7-1981.
37  Marian McDonald *The Sydney Morning Herald* 30-5-1981.
38  See e.g. Tiffen 1985, Hersch pp. 495, 544.
39  Boorstin p. 21.
40  Quoted, *New Journalist* 3, August 1972. In this context, someone once defined bribery to me as offering journalists anything which cannot be consumed on the spot. Humbert Wolf's famous rhyme also comes to mind:

> You cannot hope to bribe or twist
> (Thank God) the British journalist,
> But seeing what the man will do
> Unbribed, there's no occasion to.

41  Dale p. 121.
42  Calwell pp. 88, 91-2. Calwell probably wins a close contest as the most constant hater of the media among Australian politicians. As well as thinking his refusal to shake hands worthy of recall in his memoirs, see Mayer 1964 p. 76, Souter p. 251, Freudenberg p. 185 for other examples.
43  See Lloyd p. 61, McNicholl.
44  See e.g. *New Journalist* 11, November 1973, Dale p. 3, O'Reilly p. 212.
45  Kelly 1976 p. 152.
46  Quoted, Goodin p. 41.
47  Summers 1983 p. 128, cf D'Alpuget p. 144 on Hawke's sensitivity to being called a liar.
48  *The Sydney Morning Herald* 12-10-1982.
49  Reid 1971 pp. 17, 22.
50  Cockerill *et al.* p. 167 noted how during the Falklands war, Prime Minister Thatcher's 'desire for favourable publicity clashed with the military need for operational secrecy and was aggravated by the media's hunger for instant information'.
51  In 1960, Kennedy claimed to a friend that campaigning was more exhausting for Nixon than for him, because he knew who he was, but Nixon did not know who he was and at each performance had to decide which Nixon he was at that moment, which was very exhausting (Halberstam 1974 p. 114).
52  The press are accustomed to criticising such increases. Stewart Cockburn offered one example against himself: as press secretary to Menzies he had gone to the US in 1952 and saw 'wire recorders' being used at press conferences. When he introduced such taping in Australia, the journalists cried big brother. The verbatim transcript allowed them to compare what was said with what appeared. 'After a while some of the lazier journalists used to rely on our transcript because they had poor shorthand.' Yet when the Dunstan Government introduced a media monitoring unit,

Cockburn, as a columnist for *The Advertiser* denounced it, although in retrospect thinks it was all fairly harmless.

53 See Sigal p. 54. Walsh in 1970 pondered whether the lucrative conditions given to press secretaries would mean the best journalistic talent would be managing the news rather than collecting it, 'the latest episode of Gresham's Law' (p. 52). See also Rothmyer on the lavish funding of the New Right groups in the US, and Mannheim and Albritton on the tendency for national governments to hire consultants to improve their country's news coverage in the US, with favourable results.

54 *The Age* (and most papers) 9–4–1981. See also Russell Schneider *The Australian* 4–4–1981.

55 Lorenzo Boccabella, *The Age* 13–5–1981.

56 *The Age* 29–10–1982, *The National Times* 31–10–1982.

57 *The National Times* 12–4–1981, 11–4–1982.

58 See Paul Kelly *The Australian* 22–9–1988 and Errol Simper *The Australian* 26–11–1988.

59 *New Journalist* 31, November 1978, 'Queensland's Department of Truth' described how ABC TV news used film of Minister Hinze's visit to the Aurukun Aboriginal settlement provided by the Queensland Government, and suggests the film contradicted their reporter's descriptions.

60 Quoted from Nixon's *Six Crises* by Hersch p. 500. See also McGinness and Crouse.

61 Cockburn and Steketee p. 162. Many ALP leaders, including Dunstan and Wran, were attracted to the potential of broadcasting because of what they saw as the anti-Labor bias of the press.

62 Jenni Hewett 'Ambushed in the Gutter' *The Sydney Morning Herald* 24–5–1982.

63 Parliamentary Question Time has shown a similar trend. The term 'Dorothy Dixer' was coined in the 1960s for questions by Government backbenchers which had been planted by Ministers. The term has almost died out, mainly because the practice is now so prevalent any question by a Government backbencher can be assumed to be arranged. On the press relations of Australian Prime Ministers, see especially Lloyd. On the decline in US Presidential press conferences, see Roshco pp. 81–2.

64 See e.g. Edelman 1964 pp. 76–81; 1971, p. 38. See also Kelly 1984 p. 356.

65 Roughly paraphrased, based on author's note made afterwards. On divisive issues, such as race relations, leaders, by omission and 'codeword' formulations, may hope to signal their sympathies, but without losing too much support from the other side. They are of course especially sensitive to their fragile formulas being punctured. Sigal cites one example: 'At a Presidential press conference in 1969, . . . in response to the President's statement that he favoured neither instant segregation nor instant integration, Loory asked whether the years 1954 through 1968 could be termed "instant". The result was that Loory began losing access to the news. He was dumped from the Air Force One press pool.'

66 Howson p. 513.

67 Morgan p. 42.

68 Quoted, Goodin p. 45.

69   Seymour-Ure 1980 p. 254.
70   White p. 286.

5   **Covert Manoeuvres**
1   Summers 1982 p. 161.
2   Or even 'I give guidance, you leak' (Seymour-Ure 1977, p. 127). Simi-larly both Premier Askin and the few journalists to whom he gave regular access coyly denied that leaking was involved (O'Reilly pp. 213–14).
3   Kelly 1976 p. 282–3.
4   The secrecy involved in leaking encourages the idea that it is a sinister action. For example, a long-running dispute in Australian cricket stem-med from a leak during the bodyline era in 1932–33. The Australian captain, Woodful, was forced to retire hurt when a ball struck him above the heart. The English manager came to offer condolences. Woodful's reply 'There are two teams out there. One is playing cricket, the other isn't' has passed into cricket history. Yet contention remains over who leaked Woodful's private comment. It is part of a feud between Australia's greatest cricketer, Bradman, and one of his team-mates, later one of Australia's best-known cricket writers, Fingleton. Fingleton says Bradman leaked it. Bradman says Fingleton leaked it. The dispute has been revived periodically, most recently between surro-gates for the principals, following publication of a biography of Brad-man (see e.g. *The Australian* 3–9–1983, *The Age* 23–8–1983), Even though the effect was to place on the public record words that came to encapsulate the evils of bodyline, the premise of the feud is that the act of leaking was odious.
5   Such grapevines, indispensible to political reporting, vary enormously in their reliability. A survey of stock market rumours by *The Australian Financial Review* between July and December 1985 found that of 150 takeover rumours only eight had come true (24–12–1985).
6   On the definition of briefings, see e.g. Sigal p. 144, Weller and Grattan pp. 162–3.
7   It is almost axiomatic, for example, that as soon as the judiciary is involved in conflict, leaks follow. Following the Governor-General's dismissal of the Whitlam Government in 1975, Chief Justice Sir Garfield Barwick's letter supporting the action was published. Justice Lionel Murphy ensured it was not the only High Court view in the public domain: 'At his home in Canberra that night, Lionel was sitting in the lounge room in a singlet. He gave me a scathing letter he had written to Barwick criticising the Chief Justice's actions, and a copy of Barwick's reply' (Richard Ackland *The National Times on Sunday* 2–11–1986). Similarly, it is unlikely that the NSW Crown Prosecutors were too upset when their internal protests over their workload leaked (*The Sydney Morning Herald* 29–7–1987).
8   Max Bourke, *Rupert* April 1977.
9   In support of this view, we may briefly compare the two published diaries of Australian Cabinet Ministers, Casey and Howson. Casey's covers his period as Foreign Minister, from 1951 to 1960, while

Howson's runs from near the end of the Menzies era until the Liberals' defeat in 1972. Although differences in editing priorities are partly responsible, the media figure much more prominently in Howson's account, especially his preoccupation with leaks. It is notable how little media intrusions upset Casey's political regimen, or by his account affected the making of foreign policy, and there are few, if any, references to leaks.

10  The first such major leaks occurred in November 1985, two months after Howard's accession to the leadership, with documents on tax policy leaking and then after a leak on industrial relations policy, the new leadership forced Peacock supporter, Burr, to resign as chairman of the committee. (See Michelle Grattan *The Age* 16-11-1985.) In March 1986, the single most embarrassing leak occurred, when Minister for Employment and Industrial Relations Willis read out in Parliament a document for marketing the party's industrial relations policy, which included a list of businessmen and media commentators who would be favourable and others who would need to be neutralised (all papers 21-3-1986). In May, a series of Liberal Party draft documents was leaked to Labor, and exploited less for their content than for the great opportunities for one-upmanship and gloating over Opposition Leader Howard's lack of authority in his own party which the leaks presented (most papers 22, 23-5-1986). Finally, the morning that Howard was to deliver his reply to the Budget, Liberal Party research showing his low popularity was leaked to *The Australian Financial Review*.

11  Kelly 1984 pp. 253-4. Their strained relations were again evident during the 1987 election campaign, when Stone attacked Fraser's handling of the 1982 Budget. Fraser said the only reason Stone's remarks as a former public servant did not breach the Crimes Act is that they were inaccurate (*The Sydney Morning Herald* 11-6-1987).

12  Kelly 1976 pp. 188-9.

13  Howson 23-4-64, p. 89. Among the numerous references to leaks in the diaries, the most remarkable is the following: 'Bill [McMahon] also told me of a talk he had had with the Governor-General [Casey] concerning his own position, in which it had also been made clear by the Governor-General that McMahon's relationship with [journalist Maxwell] Newton should cease in the interests of national security' (18-12-67, p. 366). This suggests not only an extraordinarily wide definition of national security, but also an amazingly broad conception of the vice regal role.

14  Reid 1971 p. 236. The incident turned into a major political liability for the Government. Ironically, Newton is the only political journalist I know who has publicly confessed to paying sources for leaks: 'During this time I had various officials in the government working for me. They used to give me copies of documents and I paid them. I had a sort of milkrun. I'd go round on Saturday morning and poke cheques underneath their doormats and pick up envelopes' (quoted Packer p. 119). The potential for such payments is greater where early access to information has commercial value—cf 'ABS leaks: like a sieve, or just the market's imagination?' *The Sydney Morning Herald* 1-5-1987.

15  George pp. 28, 173.

16  Cf Halperin pp. 194–5.
17  This, for example, was Hawke's complaint to his Cabinet during a surge in leaking in early 1985: 'The Government's "good news" job scheme for the young, announced by Mr Hawke on Wednesday for the Victorian election, had all but disappeared under the negative news of what might happen' in projected budget cuts and means testing some benefits (*The Age* 1–2–1985).
18  Oakes and Solomon 1973 p. 82.
19  E.g. Kelly 1976 pp. 72–5. Cf Seymour-Ure 1974 on how a leak transformed Macmillan's hoped for image of rejuvenation through several Ministerial changes instead into the 'night of the long knives'.
20  See e.g. Freudenberg pp. 263–4, Oakes and Solomon 1974.
21  Freudenberg pp. 290–1.
22  The immediate story is best told in Oakes and Solomon 1974 pp. 3–34. The consequences were many-sided, some impossible to fathom: did the early election, as some have claimed, allow Labor to win a second term, which it would have failed to do at any later date? Did the breaking of convention with the Senate blocking Supply ease the way for this to be repeated in 1975? Did the expedience in the move destroy Whitlam's reputation for sincerity and 'his appeal as a rare repository of political morality?' (Walsh 1979 p. 75), even aiding the return of the Socialist Left to influence in the Victorian ALP? (ibid.).
23  See e.g. Tiffen 1978 Chapter 7.
24  Oakes and Solomon 1974 p. 5.
25  St John has an account of the episode.
26  There are great individual differences in journalists' skill at handling confidential information: '(State political journalist X) was a neanderthal. He was so bad. I had a leak from Treasury. I gave it to him. It was a major page one story. I got him over and said here are the budget documents. He said I must show them to the editor. I said the markings on the documents could reveal the source. He photocopied the documents and rang the Treasury Department. It led to a witch hunt in Treasury. Three people were interviewed: one was the source, but another got the blame. We had two years putting up with this (expletive deleted)' (Opposition press secretary).
27  Kelly 1984 p. 253.
28  All three analyses of leaks by Canberra participants have included some reference to compulsive leakers. In an early discussion, George Baker in 1957 in *Quadrant* divided leakers into three types: the person who leaks for indirect reward, the one who leaks 'as in duty bound', to advance a principle and the involuntary leaker who apparently cannot help himself (Quoted, Lloyd). In the mid-1970s, former Snedden staff member Geoff Allen had five types of leakers, including the compulsive talker (see Weller and Grattan p. 161), while in the 1980s Anne Summers also talked of politicians who couldn't help themselves in giving leaks.
29  Howson 24–2–70, p. 601.
30  See e.g. Tiffen 1978.
31  E.g. *The Sydney Morning Herald* 2–12–1986.
32  The discussion seeks to illuminate political strategies. In doing so, it

makes no judgments about personal motivations—the relative degree of conscience or expedience, public principle or self-interest, which guided the leaker. Journalists are more concerned with news values than moral values: 'Most leaks are for base motives, but that doesn't lessen the value of the stuff'.

33 Even the source may not know. When Chipp resigned from the Liberal Party, he showed his resignation speech to Michelle Grattan before delivering it: 'I have since wondered why I did this' (Chipp p. 180).

34 *The Sydney Morning Herald* 16–7–1981. The leak produced an enormous outpouring of indignation at what many conservative commentators interpreted as the sabotaging of the Fraser Government, all premised on the assumption that the leaker was a politically opposed public servant. None was more colourful than Max Harris, who began: 'There's a sweet and sickening stench of moral gangrene in the Canberra air ... The general theorem [of the ordinary thinking citizenry] is that we are observing a squalid situation ...' *The Australian* 20–9–1980. They are negated, or need to be redirected, if the leak turned out to reflect Ministerial manipulation rather than bureaucratic sabotage.

35 Summers 1981; Cockerill *et al.* p. 136, Seymour-Ure 1974, p. 256 and Dale *passim* have similar examples.

36 *The Sydney Morning Herald* 11, 12, 14, 18–4–1986.

37 Hawker *et al.* p. 260.

38 Howson 21–8–72, p. 899. Howson complains on several other occasions of Coombs leaking to pressure the Government toward action, e.g. p. 765.

For a parallel example in international affairs, cf Sigal pp. 164–5, Tunstall p. 199 on a background briefing by US Secretary of State Dulles to pressure the British Cabinet to decide that it would support the US in intervening in Indochina at the height of the 1954 crisis.

39 Evans pp. 381–2.

40 Kelly 1976 p. 61.

41 Schlesinger, quoted Sigal, Halperin pp. 192–4.

42 Halperin p. 194

43 Kelly 1976, pp. 213–14.

44 Glezer p. 105. Journalists' typical response when caught up in such policy moves is that they don't calculate the effects in deciding what to publish. They do it as a good story, that the public's right to know is paramount over any particular effects, etc. This is not always true. Glezer gives the example of one journalist, informed about the Whitlam Government's impending tariff cut in 1973, who refrained from publishing the leak because he did not want to endanger the move.

45 Kate Legge 'Uranium: PM wants park mined' *The National Times on Sunday* 14–9–1986, and references in the week following, e.g. *The Australian Financial Review* 17–9–1986, *The Sydney Morning Herald*, 18, 19–9–1986. Hawke reportedly angered by what he saw as misrepresentation of his intentions called the Fairfax press Labor's 'natural enemy' (*AFR* 17–9–86).

46 See e.g. 'Leak "torpedoed" talks on ships: Lange' *The Age* 12–3–1985. The same week saw concern in the Australian Government about its

attitude to the ANZUS crisis, as conveyed in some leaked stories to *The Australian*. The Prime Minister issued a written and strongly worded denial of the stories (*The Age* 8–3–1985). Cf also 'Many leaks relating to Russia's capabilities occurred during the SALT negotiations' (Halperin p. 184). Before a crucial arms summit in Geneva in late 1985, a memo from Defence Secretary Weinberger to Reagan urging him not to compromise on SALT II was spectacularly leaked. The leak was blasted by National Security adviser McFarlane in a background briefing as sabotage, which later he sought to back away from, all blowing the incident up into a bigger furore. See 'Anatomy of a Leak' in *Deadline: The Press and the Arms Race* March 1986.

47  See Rowlings' interesting account of the episode.
48  Kelly 1984, p. 23.
49  Kelly p. 263.
50  Howson 12–2–68, p. 393. Fraser prevailed. Both Howson and Chipp were soon after dropped in Gorton's first Ministry.
51  Chipp p. 176.
52  See e.g. Summers 1983, p. 30; Kelly 1984, p. 152. On the determination of one ALP Executive member to ensure that blame for the party's disastrous showing in the 1975 Bass by-election became public, see Kelly 1976, p. 201–2.
53  See e.g. the leaking of Erwin's desire to be Ambassador to Washington soon after his falling out with Prime Minister Gorton (Reid 1971).
54  *The Laurie Oakes Report* 14 August 1978. Later a story in *The Bulletin* dated 16 August gave a very anti-Fraser version of a meeting of Ministers on 8 August about earlier events in the episode leading to Withers' dismissal: 'It led to speculation among some Ministers that someone was "out to get" the Prime Minister by leaking the report.... The *Bulletin* story, which Mr Fraser could not categorically dismiss and refused for days to elaborate on, produced a major crisis for the Prime Minister.' After stormy scenes in Parliament, Fraser at last responded, first with a briefing to journalists travelling with him to Tasmania (Michelle Grattan 'Anatomy of a Political Leak' *The Age* 28–8–1978). August 1978 was a high point of leaks also because that year's Budget was more thoroughly leaked, to the Opposition and thence to some reporters, than any other except Laurie Oakes' report of the 1980 Budget. See Alan Ramsey *Time* 25–8–1986.
55  Summers 1983, p. 84.
56  Amanda Buckley 'Dirty tricks claim rocks Joh's NT Nationals' *The Australian Financial Review* 6–3–1987.
57  Chipp p. 60; cf Weller and Grattan p. 160 on the same technique for Ministers to distance themselves from their Departments. Sometimes the stakes can be serious: Defence Secretary McNamara raised the possibility of using nuclear weapons in Vietnam in a background briefing, apparently a warning to China, but then sought to reassure the American public by publicly denouncing the subsequent press speculation. See Sigal p. 80.
58  A particularly vivid instance was offered when British Minister Pym made a speech about economic prospects at variance with the

Government's view: 'Mrs Thatcher publicly defended Mr Pym calling his "an excellent speech". But...her press secretary was, almost simultaneously,...saying the exact opposite in her name' (Cockerill *et al.* p.136).

59 Peter Bowers *The Sydney Morning Herald* 24–5–1986; see also 31–5–1986 and Michelle Grattan *The Age* 26–5–1986. Cockerill *et al.* record two instances where the British national press reported on the basis of Lobby briefings that a Prime Minister had severely chastised an erring Minister (Wilson reprimanding Callaghan in 1969, Thatcher, Pym in 1982) but where it later emerged that the actual encounter hardly measured up to the reports of it (pp. 124, 137–8). In a rather different manoeuvre they report how Prime Ministerial office briefings about dissent in Cabinet over the Budget were used to force public conformity (pp. 136–7).

60 Clancy *The National Times* 12–7–1985.

61 Vinson p. 158. The stories were prominently displayed by prison officers attacking Vinson's reform policies.

62 Chipp p. 134.

63 Chipp p. 127. When it seemed as if Kissinger might lose his position after the 1972 Presidential election, an article by James Reston observed that Kissinger would then be free to 'write the whole story of the Paris talks and why they broke down, and this would probably be highly embarrassing to Mr Nixon'. 'The President of the United States was being warned and not subtly' (Hersch pp. 630–1, cf also p. 400 and p. 475).

64 See e.g. White p. 378 on 'post-primary briefings' in America. According to Dale, Australian practice is rather cruder. Parties simply change the results of their polls somewhat when leaking them to the press.

65 Mayer 1975, p. 37 notes how Treasury briefings influenced press coverage against the Vernon Report on Australian economic policy in the 1960s.

66 Hersch, for example, notes that the American press relied almost totally on Kissinger for its interpretation of the Paris Peace Accords of 1973. His briefings were a substitute for their reading: 'The agreement simply overwhelmed the press' (Hersch p. 634).

67 *The Age* 2–4–1982.

68 Oakes 1976, p. 148.

69 Kelly 1976, pp. 242–3.

70 Kelly 1984 p. 275. 'Such behaviour generated a pervasive cynicism, not just between the press and the Prime Minister, but between Fraser and many of his colleagues. Yet Fraser regularly became impatient and angry when the public and the press failed to take him at his word' (p. 276). Further pointed references on the same theme are on p. 278 and p. 300.

71 *The Age* 5–1–1980.

72 Ross Gittins 'The Sigh of Relief Syndrome' *The Sydney Morning Herald* 26–1–1980.
See e.g. Gittins' article revealing a Department of Main Roads document calling for huge increases in road funding. The document became public simultaneously with an attack by the Minister Brereton attacking

the financial burden it would lead to, at least neutralising the impact if the document had been released uncontested (*The Sydney Morning Herald* 11-6-1984). A neat British example was offered by Cockerill *et al.* (p. 127).

74 *The Sydney Morning Herald* 30-3-1962. Similarly Kern *et al.* (p. 48) note that when Kennedy changed policy during the Laotian crisis of the early 1960s: 'In such a delicate situation, it is thus not surprising that the President and his advisers approached the press primarily through the background briefing.... The President was able to switch policies after (earlier) trumpeting the communist threat with very little criticism.'

75 The first press account which traced such speculation to the Prime Minister's office appeared in an editorial in *The Australian Financial Review* as early as 25-7-1977, which also commented on leaks by the same source regarding Justice Fox's allegedly changing attitudes on uranium export. See also Lombard p. 110. For similar examples, see Cockerill *et al.* pp. 206-7 on Mrs Thatcher and the 1983 election and Dale p. 133 on the 1978 NSW election.

76 See Hawker *et al.* pp. 269-70 on the 1974 Budget.

77 Earlier, in February, March and June, there had been considerable leaking over the shape of the 1986 Budget. The leaks—both times the 'left' blamed the 'right' and vice versa—reflected the battle that year as the Treasurer sought to impose on the 'spending' departments a more pessimistic view of Australia's economic prospects. The most important reporter during these leaks was Mike Steketee: *The Sydney Morning Herald* 21-2-1986, 4, 5, 6, 7, 11-3-1986, 20-6-1986.

78 See Weller and Grattan p. 160 for one example; cf also Summers 1981 who judged that some Ministers seek immunity from criticism by making themselves indispensible sources to major correspondents. By the same logic, the withholding of leaks or granting them to a journalist's competitors can be a form of punishment. In 1973, the *New Journalist* claimed 'The right-wing Fairfax group is currently the object of a news-leak boycott by the [Whitlam] Government' (Vol 9, July 1973). The claim is implausible if only because such coordination was palpably lacking from all that Government's other public relations activities. For an example of a reporter retaliating because Senator Joseph McCarthy gave a leak to a competitor, see Bayley pp. 156-7.

79 Richard Ackland *The National Times on Sunday* 2-11-1986.

80 *The Australian* 30-8-1986.

81 Freudenberg p. 214. After Whitlam's 1971 visit to China as Opposition Leader, some Liberals, especially Wentworth and Fraser, attacked him for abandoning a friend. 'Publicly, Whitlam kept steadfastly silent' so as not to endanger his private entreaties to the Chinese Government.

82 It should not be thought that Mrs Thatcher was an innocent abroad in such covert manoeuvres. In the 1987 CHOGM conference, for example, 'Mr Hawke backed up the complaints of African leaders and accused the British Prime Minister of "leaking misinformation" to British journalists to discredit sanctions against South Africa and conducting a "despicable campaign" against Canada's Prime Minister, Mr Mulroney' (*The Sydney Morning Herald* 19-10-1987).

83 See Walsh 1979, pp. 115-16, 136.

84 The term 'Mullinsgate' imports the American habit, post-Watergate, of adding 'gate' to names to signify a scandal, producing such epithets as Koreagate and Iran–Contragate. This trend reached its apotheosis in 1987 when the scandals surrounding evangelist, Jim Bakker, were christened 'Pearlygate', and the acceptance from a corporation of a free security system around his home by Lieutenant-Colonel Oliver North became 'Gategate'.

85 The best references on the episode come from *The Sydney Morning Herald*, 19–30 November 1979, especially several indignant analyses by Peter Bowers, the original recipient of the leak. *The Australian* had some analysis, but generally seemed less concerned that it had been duped.

86 For two examples of attempted fabrications, and for occasions where the conventions of confidentiality were strained by sources promoting misleading information, see Tiffen (1989).

87 Marr p. 291.

88 See Marr p. 292.

89 Lloyd p. 215. *New Journalist* reported that after John Morgan became editor of *The Sun News Pictorial* in 1976, he decreed that the paper use only on the record information.

90 The most famous case in Australia is Detective-Sergeant Phillip Arantz, former head of the NSW Police Force's Computer Bureau. In 1971, he revealed that the actual crime rate was up to 70 per cent higher than official statistics, that clean-up rates were much lower, and that there was deliberate falsification of figures condoned by Police Commissioner Allan and Premier Askin. After admitting to the leak, Arantz was vilified by the Premier, forced to undergo a psychiatric examination, and fired from the police force without compensation. His act of conscience, designed to serve the larger good of the police force and the public, resulted in his career being ruined. See Hickie, Whitton and Pullan for accounts of the episode.

91 E.g. on Mick Young's introduction of briefings after ALP Executive meetings, see Oakes and Solomon 1973 p. 20.

92 Summers p. 163. The vignette suggests one reason why 'open government' policies rarely result in more favourable news coverage. It also lends credence to one American politician's complaint that reporters 'were so busy trying to find out what was going to happen that they did not provide a decent account of what had happened' (Cater p. 112).

93 Nixon realised that in news accounts of Kissinger's secret Vietnam peace negotiations in Paris, the 'cops and robbers' aspect would overshadow the substantive content of the negotiations (Hersch p. 483). The exploiters, however, shared the same susceptibility: '[Laird] had deduced a vital truth about Nixon and Kissinger: They paid far more attention to information that seemed to be secret, or came from a clandestine source' (ibid., p. 208). Perhaps it is also why 'In the shadowy regions between diplomacy and defence, the British secret organizations have long generated a fascination out of all proportion to their numbers' (Sampson p. 240).

Sources sometimes seek to enhance the importance of the information they are offering by stressing its confidentiality. Alan Reid suggested that a politician would tell him something on background and then he would see the same politician saying the same thing on TV. Ironically, the same thing happened to me with Reid. He told me on background of an incident involving him, Menzies and Frank Packer during the 1961 election (see Chapter 6). Later on the TV program, *Sunday*, he repeated publicly what he had only told me on background.

94 Freudenberg pp. 331, 338.
95 Bowman concluded: 'It is difficult to resist the conclusion that we have on this occasion been witness to a scrap not so much between a politician and a journalist as between two politicians of different persuasions' (p. 35).
96 Cf e.g. Vinson pp. 157–8. Also 'the price of such systematic access to Kissinger was deference, and it was a price willingly paid by the journalists, who were unable to meet regularly or casually with Haldemann, Ehrlichman, or other top aides' (Hersch p. 204).

'Kissinger, as usual, found it easy to overwhelm the White House press corps, which continued to rely almost totally on his version of events' (Hersch p. 578).
97 (The Lobby) was happily reproducing a highly partial account of the government's foreign policy that came directly from Lobby briefings by the Prime Minister, Neville Chamberlain. The Foreign Secretary, Lord Halifax, not only had no idea the briefings were going on, but, as his diaries were to reveal, profoundly disagreed with their contents (Cockerill *et al.* p. 37). Thatcher leaked no income tax rises, but did not mention the large increase in indirect tax that were included (ibid., pp. 138–9).
98 Summers p. 161. For overseas examples of how politicians are aware of and use the system see Cockerill *et al.* pp. 124, 127, Hersch p. 203. Examples of officials lying, usually for short-term needs include, e.g., Hersch pp. 499–500, Cater p. 139, Cockerill *et al.* p. 124.
99 Ibid.
100 John Whale, quoted Seymour-Ure 1977, p. 120.
101 Seymour-Ure 1977, p. 120.
102 Cf Pullan pp. 26–28 on how the barristers' code of anonymity forced Staples and Graham to publish a book about the prison bashings at Bathurst anonymously, which meant it had less credibility and weight. Cf also Hersch pp. 182–3 on leaks published by Jack Anderson, accurate but not followed up by any other news organisations.
103 'Instead [of appearing as it was one Admiral repeating long-held but not widely shared views] the sudden publication of the unattributed stories in many of the major newspapers [about the inevitability of war in Asia] made it look as if all Washington had arrived simultaneously at the prediction of war' (Cater p. 140).
104 William White, quoted Cater pp. 139–40.
105 Summers 1981, p. 160.

## 6 Inter-Party Politics

1 'The very existence of a national campaign was conditional upon the presence of the media: they were no mere eavesdroppers of an independent

argument but participants—whether or not they were partisan. Their general effect was to help define an evolving campaign pattern ... relating the parties to each other in a dialogue which otherwise would not exist.... The national campaign is formed by a continuous interaction between the behaviour of party leaders and managers and that of the mass media' (Seymour-Ure 1974, pp. 233, 205). Most academic studies of elections devote a single chapter to the media. Such compartmentalisation makes it difficult to capture the interplay between the media and other factors, which is central to understanding the campaigns and to charting changes in electioneering.

2   Australia is not strictly a two-party system. Minor parties often win representation in the Senate, and the existence of the Country-cum-National Party is often a complicating factor, especially at State level. However, since World War II, the contest over who forms the national government has been essentially two sided: Labor versus non-Labor.

3   See e.g. Walsh 1979, pp. 89, 93; cf Butler p. 20 a decade earlier. On the relation of UK politics to the wider society, cf Sampson p. 32. On the comparatively weak and further weakening links between social structure and party support, see Aitkin 1983, p. 19.

4   Such judgments will vary with the observer, but e.g. 'The truth about the 1983 campaign is that beneath the contrasting images both Fraser and Hawke were offering very similar policies' (Kelly 1984, p. 412).

5   Cf also White p. 327 on Reagan's 1980 ascription of American ills to the Democrats.

6   Kelly 1976, p. 282.

7   There are very few examples in the contemporary era where one party has refrained from scoring political points for the social good. In late 1974, following the collapses of Mainline and Cambridge Credit, the Liberal Opposition showed restraint in doing nothing to aggravate any fears about the liquidity of finance companies (Ormonde p. 183). Chipp has testified that when he became Minister for Customs in the McMahon Government:

> [Whitlam] came to me early in that portfolio and gave me an undertaking on behalf of the Opposition that they would never oppose any censorship reforms I introduced, or try to embarrass me over them. He kept his word (p. 156).

It is hard to imagine such promises in the 1980s. Before Opposition Leader Howard's escalation of the issue in 1988, issues regarding racial prejudice toward Asian immigrants, with some notable past exceptions, may have been another area of mutual restraint.

8   Kelly 1984, pp. 422–3. Horne, writing after the 1980 election, commented: 'Labor is a party ... built around programmes. The Liberals are, fundamentally, a party of winners. There is much toughness and cynicism in Labor's internal factional battles but when it comes to approaching power in Australia, Labor—at least in national politics—does not act with the ruthlessness and cunning one might expect from people who enter hostile territory' (1981, p. 95). If there was once a difference between the parties in these regards, it certainly disappeared during the 1980s.

9  Crouse gives a very readable account of herd journalism during the 1972 US Presidential campaign. The recollection of Melbourne *Herald* correspondent Harold Cox provides a contrast: 'The 1934 election was my first. At most, five newspapermen followed Lyons around. Joe was a great old tippler. He would make a speech, finish by 9 pm, and after we'd done the copy by 10, he would call us in for a drink. You couldn't get away till 1 or 2 am.'

10  See Beed for a capsule history of political polling in Australia.

11  Mike Steketee, *The Sydney Morning Herald* 10–7–1987. For some US examples, see White pp. 32, 192.

12  E.g. Freudenberg p. 61.

13  See e.g. Oakes and Solomon 1973, pp. 262–3, 268; MacCallum p. 42.

14  Oakes and Solomon 1973, pp. 239, 268–9, 'The most charitable explanation anyone is prepared to accept is that McMahon fell momentarily out of his tree, and forgot that all the things he had been saying in private were not exactly on the public record' (MacCallum *Mungo on the Zoo Plane* p. 48). Cf also Walsh 1976, p. 99.

15  See e.g. Freudenberg pp. 271, 300; MacCallum pp. 89. 98–9; Kelly p. 42 and especially Oakes and Solomon 1973, *passim*

16  Summers 1983, p. 162.

17  Summers 1983, pp. 162–5; Kelly 1984, p. 409.

18  Fraser's gaffe sprang from his well-established practice of conveying the disastrous nature of Labor economic policies in simple imagery. In 1975, he likened the national economy to a family that was over-spending. 'In 1980 the Liberals had simplified the less complicated issue of a capital gains tax by the brilliant device of using photographs of suburban homes, implying that Labor planned to tax ordinary homes. By saying Labor would rob your savings from the banks, Fraser was trying to repeat this strategy: he needed a simple but graphic concept to represent a complicated issue.' Summers 1983, p. 152.

19  ANOP's post-election survey for the ALP found the worst feature of the Liberals' campaign was the mudslinging (27 per cent), (Kelly 1984, p. 408).

20  The contributions of National Party leader Sinclair deserve special recognition here:

> If it wasn't for the promotion of homosexuality as a norm by Labor, I am quite confident that the deaths of these three poor babies would not have occurred (discussing the deaths of three babies from AIDS in 1984).
>
> While you cannot suggest that the Anita Cobby murder was a direct result of the attitudes of [the Hawke] Government, there is no doubt the general neglect was a contribution towards the attitude of those who murdered the Cobby lass.
>
> To have Bob Hawke pretending that he is suddenly going to have a new care and concern for the Australian family is like Charles Manson saying he is going to care for Sharon Tate. (Quoted by George Negus, *The Bulletin* 7–7–1987).

21  Summers 1983, p. 138.

22  The ALP's other 'leak' in 1980 was the allegation that internal Defence Department documents showed a study canvassing the re-introduction of conscription, which, whatever the basis, never eventuated. Labor's

pollster had in March 'recommended an organised rumor campaign' (Goot 1983, p. 160).

23  See Tiffen 1983, p. 42 for further discussion.

24  Summers 1983, p. 162; see also p. 161 and Haupt and Grattan p. 104. The Liberals attempted to leak the ALP accord with the unions during the campaign, seeking to dilute its impact as is usual in inter-party covert manoeuvres. The attempt backfired, because the last three pages were missing, allowing Hawke a counter-attack for misrepresentation (Summers p. 146; Haupt & Grattan p. 102).

Probably the most damaging leak by an opposition against a government came just before the last week of the 1976 NSW campaign when Wran's Labor Opposition obtained the confidential transcript of the February 1976 Premiers' Conference. This allowed Wran to mount an attack that Premier Willis, by agreeing with Fraser's 'New Federalism' policies, would be mounting double taxation (Dale p. 105).

25  Summers 1981, p. 162.

26  Harrison pp. 74–5. See Seymour-Ure (1974) for figures in the 1966 and 1970 elections.

27  O'Grady. One advantage for leaders is that unless there is overt rebellion during the campaign, news attention to intra-party conflicts is greatly reduced. This arguably helped Howard in 1987 for example when divisions in both Coalition parties had been considerably aired up to the campaign, but it almost disappeared after Sir Joh Bjelke-Petersen's early withdrawal. On the other hand, it makes it almost impossible to 'hide' an unpopular leader. In 1977, the ALP felt frustrated in its attempts to project Hayden, whom the polls found to have more economic credibility, but the TV crews and news focused almost entirely on Whitlam (Lloyd 1980, p. 263).

28  In many news organisations the use of polls has become worse rather than better, especially in regard to sampling. Broadcasting organisations indulge in phone-in polls, at best only an indicator of actively aroused opinion, while popular papers run local surveys with small samples, and give their readers no data about sampling error or demographic representativeness. There were some improvements by the quality press in 1987, notably the use by *The Sydney Morning Herald* of Ernest Chaples and by *The Times on Sunday* of Murray Goot to do comparative analyses of the polls. See especially Goot's article comparing the accuracy of different pollsters in elections from 1972 to 1987 (*The Times on Sunday* 19–7–1987).

29  Not, it should be stressed, that the framing of policy speeches was ever an occasion for extensive party consultation. The Liberals have always given their leaders sole prerogative in such things, and the ALP history is not markedly different in practice. Evatt's disastrous promise to abolish the means test in the 1954 campaign was made with almost no consultation, and his dramatic offer in the 1958 campaign to resign if the DLP would re-join the fold was made without the knowledge, even of deputy leader Calwell. (See Calwell). 'The centre-piece of Calwell's 1961 campaign, a proposal to stimulate the economy with a 100 million pound deficit, was inspired by the management of *The Sydney Morning Herald*' (Freudenberg p. 228). The most sustained party participation in framing

the themes and directions of the policy speech was under Whitlam in 1969 and 1972 (ibid., p. 226).

30  These quotes are both from the ALP's pollster Rod Cameron, quoted in *The Sydney Morning Herald* 11–7–1987 and Kelly 1984, p. 86. Liberal pollsters have offered similar diagnoses, see especially Mills, Chapter 2. Moreover it is plausible that such images are becoming more ingrained in the key operators' approach to politics. Reviewing the 1980 election, Horne wrote (accurately), 'The key ... was that Labor was still scared of the Australian voters.' (1981, p. 29). By 1987 that was probably no longer true. While the overwhelming empirical trend is for swinging voters to be less informed and interested, the association is not invariant. In 1972, for example, Kemp found no significant relationship between interest in the campaign and tendency to swing (Kemp 1973, p. 286).

31  Summers p. 108.

32  Freudenberg p. 160. For the role of TV in its first election, see Rawson, also Inglis p. 214.

33  For example, after his fairly successful use of TV in 1975, 1977 and 1980, in 1983 Fraser's scheduling and arrangements brought many complaints from TV reporters.

34  Geoff Kitney, *The Times on Sunday* 28–6–1987. There may be a slight curve back to more relaxed campaigning. One veteran journalist recalled that 'in Menzies' day electioneering meant that you stopped under a tree for lunch between Sydney and Bathurst. Now every hour is programmed.' For the next two decades it became more frenetic and mobile. Now perhaps with TV the main priority the campaign is becoming less a test of endurance.

35  Harrison p. 77.

36  Kelly 1976, pp. 306–7, 308; cf also: 'candidates say less and less because the chance remark, the meandering thought, the snap-back answers, are apt to explode' (White p. 394).

37  Kelly 1984, p. 402.

38  Kelly 1984, pp. 74, 146.

39  The attack, which many considered cost the Labor Party the extremely close election, caused much bitterness in Labor ranks. Senator Gareth Evans wrote: 'Even by Fraser's own standards, the wealth tax ads ... reached a new low in gutter-crawling.... Obviously something is going to have to be done to ensure some kind of basic decency in political advertising' (*Media Information Australia*, 20.10). Paul Keating drew a rather different conclusion: 'What Labor needs is a couple of vicious and utterly cynical ad. men to do to the Liberals what they do to us' (Goot 1983 p. 200). It would seem the Keating view prevailed.

40  Hayden, quoted by Weller 1983, p. 270.

41  Kelly 1984, p. 396. 'Tax scare campaigns are now becoming characteristic of Australian elections' (Horne 1981 p. 105). As well as Fraser's wealth tax scare in 1980, Horne cites Wran's attacks on 'double taxation' plans during the 1976 NSW election. Similarly, in 1987, according to Michelle Grattan, Hawke descended to the big lie, when he asserted the Liberals would have an 11 per cent consumption tax (*The Age* 9–7–1987).

42  The parallels between the parties are never complete, firstly, because

when one is enjoying success, the other is trying to recover from failure, and so the patterns of possibilities and vulnerabilities are affected by incumbency and the developing political mood; and secondly, because although the common pressures of the party contest transform both, they are still approaching the contest from either right or left of centre.

43   Gittins launched a strong critique of Howard's loss of economic credibility (*The Sydney Morning Herald* 13–7–1987). Max Walsh's attack on the consequences of tax cuts for the wealthy on balance of payments was greatly resented by the Liberals. See Henderson's critique of the Rat Pack.

The last explicit trade-off offered by a political leader was Whitlam's politically improbable appeal to forgo tax cuts in favour of cutting payroll tax, an appeal to the altruism of the employed to give up tax cuts to help cut unemployment which failed. (See e.g. D'Alpuget pp. 332–3, Lloyd 1980, p. 240–3.)

44   Stokes.

45   Horne 1981, p. 56.

46   Kelly 1984, p. 331.

47   *Laurie Oakes Report* 14–2–79:

> [Mr Fraser] claims now that he never promised during the election campaign that interest rates would fall by 2% but merely said there could be reductions of up to that amount .... However, the truth ... is that Mr Fraser and other senior Ministers did make definite statements about interest rate reductions. On 2 December 1977, for example, Mr Fraser referred to a 2% drop in interest rates over the ensuing year and added: "It is a target that can be and will be achieved." And on 25 November the Deputy Prime Minister, Mr Anthony, made his extensively reported statement that interest rates would come down at least two percentage points in the next 12 months or he would eat his hat (p. 2).

48   Michelle Grattan *The Age* 9–7–1987.

49   Freudenberg p. 296.

50   MacCallum p. 86. For other examples see e.g. Walsh p. 75, Kelly 1976, p. 60.

51   One should distinguish different types of broken promises. When in 1949 Menzies promised to put value back in the pound and then presided over record inflation, there is no doubt that if he had the capacity he would have preferred to have lower inflation (although the promise to deliver was recklessly and beneficially optimistic). Conversely when in 1961, he denounced Calwell's proposal to stimulate economic recovery with a 100 million pound deficit as wildly inflationary, and then himself budgeted for a deficit of 118 million (Reid 1971 p. 22), it was a deliberate act.

52   Freudenberg p. 257. The political advantages for Whitlam of stressing the mandate included an assertion of legitimacy over the Senate (elected in 1967 and 1970), and of asserting Parliamentary authority over other party structures (ibid., p. 243).

53   See e.g. Kelly 1976, pp. 324–5, Chipp pp. 134–5, Walsh 1979, pp. 114–15.

54   Given the tendency of oppositions to exaggerate rather than minimise the ills of the government they are displacing, such explanations should be viewed as inherently implausible. There may be occasional episodes like

the blow-out of the Fraser Government's 1982 Budget to over $9 billion, which are generally a shock to the incoming government, but more common would be Kennedy's observation after becoming President, that his biggest surprise was discovering everything was as bad as we said it was during the campaign. See Peter Bowers' list of the Hawke Government's 31 broken promises *The Sydney Morning Herald* 29–6–1987, 3–7–1987).

55 'Throughout 1966, the polls showed support for Labor at 40 per cent. So it turned out. There is no reason to believe that the campaign itself improved or worsened Labor's position' (Freudenberg p. 85).

56 See *The Bulletin* 23–6–1987, 14–7–1987. Sampling variations account for an unknown amount in these fluctuations. Aitkin (1983) argues that electoral volatility has not increased, citing, for example, figures indicating that strength of party identification was about the same in 1979 as it was in 1967 and 1969 (p. 15), although another table shows that the number professing to have voted for different parties in different Federal elections rose from 28 per cent in 1967 to 39 per cent in 1979 (p. 17).

57 Seymour-Ure, 1968.

58 For an interesting content analysis of amounts of attention to Government and Opposition during two three year periods of Liberal and Labor, see Henningham.

59 With one exception, no TV station has editorialised in support of one party. The exception was in 1972, when Sir Frank Packer's Channel Nines in Sydney and Melbourne, had an editorial supporting the McMahon Liberal Government, describing Whitlam's policies as the marijuana dreams of a utopian Disneyland (Oakes and Solomon pp. 284–7, also Mayer 1973).

60 Quoted by Stephens in an account of Murdoch's *New York Post*'s wholehearted support for Reagan in 1980, which included such exclusive headlines as 'REAGAN: I'LL SAVE THE MIDDLE CLASS', 'ISRAEL FEARS CARTER VICTORY', and 'KHOMEINI PULLS THE STRINGS'—and then, in smaller type, 'CARTER BACK ON CAMPAIGN TRAIL'. This intriguing pairing of thoughts covered two-thirds of the front page on the day before the election (pp. 44–5).

61 Dunstan p. 61.

62 Souter p. 380.

63 Freudenberg p. 16. If Newton's account is to be believed, Henderson was not immune to the vanities such influence offered: 'If I told Arthur Calwell to stand on his head in the corner, he'd st-a-a-a-nd on his head in the corner' (Packer p. 110, cf also p. 114).

64 This quote is an amalgam of what Reid said to me in interview (on background) and of what he then also said on Channel Nine's *Sunday* program, 28–11–1982. The only discrepancy between the two is that in interview he said the advice was to end the credit squeeze, and on TV to restore full employment.

65 Cited, *Media Information Australia* 24, Media Brief 270. Presumably the two elections which McMahon felt Packer won for the Liberals were 1961 and possibly 1963, when *The Daily Telegraph*'s picture of Calwell and Whitlam standing outside, waiting for the ALP Federal Executive to

make a decision on US bases, produced enormous controversy over the external control of the Parliamentary Labor Party, that its policies were decided in Menzies' famous phrase by 36 faceless men.

66  Oakes and Solomon 1973, pp. 275, 278. According to Freudenberg, Murdoch also suggested that Whitlam appoint Dr Coombs as an adviser and that Australia have a new national anthem, but that promising tax deductibility for housing interest rates was not Murdoch's idea although he did 'guarantee publicity for such a proposal' (p. 236).

67  *New Journalist* 21, December 1975, p. 3.

68  *New Journalist* 21 has many examples.

69  Edgar.

70  '"Whitlam must have done something wrong for Kerr to sack him"'— it's a phrase you hear with monotonous regularity outside Canberra. And it suggests, along with the Morgan poll, that perhaps Whitlam is on the wrong track going on, and on, about the injustice of his dismissal. Perhaps it would be more sensible to let that issue simmer along by itself, and take Fraser on over the issue Fraser chose himself—the economy' (MacCullum p. 138). Cf also Kelly 1976, p. 308 that the Liberals were delighted that Labor kept promoting the constitutional issue because they were convinced it was a mistaken strategy.

Beyond questions of immediate impact is an unresolved methodological problem concerning to what extent the parties' nomination of issues should be the criterion for news coverage: in 1972 Prime Minister McMahon said that foreign affairs and defence were the main issues in the election. Does that mean that half the issue coverage in the election should have concentrated on them? One must also be aware of the difference between parties' professed focus and their actual behaviour. Bell *et al.* cite the ALP's formal nomination of unemployment as an issue in 1980 as evidence for its improper neglect in the news, but do not mention that under advice from their pollster, the ALP in fact de-emphasised the issue in the campaign.

71  'The radicalness of Fraser's program received almost no media attention, simply because he refused to be drawn on it' (Kelly 1976, p. 308). After the election, managing director of David Syme, Ranald McDonald, also commented on the media's failure to properly scrutinise Liberal policies.

72  In the previous year, the South Australian 1979 election became the only occasion on which there has been any official arbitration on election bias. The Press Council found that *The News* had treated the ALP unfairly on several counts. See e.g. Badcock and *Labor Forum* 2 (2) March 1980, for the ALP's submission to the Press Council. News Ltd withdrew from the Council soon afterwards, only to rejoin after its takeover of *The Herald and Weekly Times* in 1987. In the 1983, 1984 and 1987 elections the Murdoch papers generally had the same news priorities as the rest of the press.

73  Goot 1983, p. 154.

74  Goot 1983, p. 166–7.

75  Goot 1983, p. 167–9.

76  Goot 1983, p. 170. Note also the contrasting treatment of violent incidents in Fraser's and Hayden's campaigns. Incidents of violence by

Liberal supporters were mentioned on the front page of four papers, but the News group did not mention them anywhere (pp. 171–2).

77  See e.g. Daly pp. 76–81; *The Sydney Morning Herald* 15–11–1949.

## 7  Intra-Party Politics

1  Perhaps the most spectacular example comes in the two biographies of Peacock. Carey and McCrae suggest that if Peacock had followed a plan he could have become Prime Minister in April 1981 (p. 23), while according to Schneider 'many backbenchers and some ministers . . . believed at the time that if Peacock had put his cards on the table . . . then he could have been within a few weeks sitting in the Prime Minister's chair. Peacock chose not to do so . . . Deep down he knew he was not ready' (pp. 6–7). No evidence can definitively resolve such claims. That Peacock lost to Fraser a year later by a two to one margin suggests either that they were wrong or that in the intervening year he mounted a very badly judged campaign.

2  Leadership changes and tensions are continuing apace in Australian politics: MacKinnon replaced Hassell in the WA Liberal Party; Kennett has survived four leadership contests as Leader of the Victorian Liberal Opposition; Burke paved the way for his chosen successor, Dowding, to become head of WA Inc in a skilfully managed exit. In contrast, the exit of Sir Joh Bjelke-Petersen, screaming and kicking to the end and beyond, was a healthy reminder that all attempts to discern patterns in politics will sometimes be overpowered by the uniqueness of events. The two other political parties in Queensland also changed leaders.

3  The most interesting case so excluded is Wran's displacement of Hills as leader of the NSW Labor Party following the 1973 election. *The Sydney Morning Herald*'s headline after the July 1987 election: 'Now the brawls begin' captures the way in which intra-party strife immediately following an election has become the norm in Australian politics.

4  Three marginal cases were not included. When the fortunes of the South Australian Liberals were at their nadir, a swell of discontent against leader Eastick collapsed into a unanimous vote of confidence in the party room (Jaensch and Bullock). Tasmanian Labor Premier Reece was forced to stand down by the State party conference adopting a resolution that all members should retire after the age of 65 (Lowe p. 51). Tasmanian Liberal Opposition Leader Pearsall resigned for personal reasons in somewhat mysterious circumstances (Lowe p. 157). The remarkable ructions which have occurred over the years in the ruling Northern Territory Country-Liberal Party have also been excluded. It would take years of anthropological study to deal adequately with them.

5  The most spectacular example of an internal split and leadership challenge in an entrenched government was the break-up of the Queensland ALP Government in 1957, going from an era of almost constant incumbency to one where they have never since regained office. Queensland was the last state to be suffering from the Split's legacies of internecine vindictiveness, the interlocking of Parliamentary and machine struggles, and the resultant electoral ineffectiveness and mediocrity in the party (see Murphy pp. 68–73).

6  Kelly 1976, p. 98.
7  Summers 1983, p. 51.
8  Kelly 1984, p. 108, cf also Summers 1983, pp. 28, 32.
9  Whitlam precipitated the challenge by resigning and seeking re-election following a rebuff from the National Executive. His margin of victory was unexpectedly narrow. Only Freudenberg defends Whitlam's move: 'It has been put down as Whitlam's greatest failure and worst mistake before 1972. In fact, it succeeded in all its essential aims . . . . It was an essential part of [Labor's] recovery' (p. 129). However, he also concedes that Gorton 'might still be Prime Minister of Australia if he had held an election in 1968' (p. 139).
10  From 1917 to January 1966, conservative governments ruled for 38 years, and for all but Fadden's 40 days, they had only four Prime Ministers: Hughes (6 years), Bruce (6), Lyons (8), and Menzies (17). More surprising was the leadership stability of the ALP. The six leaders before Whitlam either retired voluntarily or died in office—Charlton (retired 1928), Scullin (retired due to ill health, 1935), Curtin (died 1945), Chifley (died 1951), Evatt (retired to become Chief Justice of NSW, 1960), Calwell (retired, aged 70, 1966). All had lost at least one election, some several, yet remained leader. Electoral ineffectiveness and failure were not considered sufficient grounds for change.
11  Factionalism often bears an oblique relation to leadership manoeuvres—such as the conflict between McEwen and McMahon and its relationship to Gorton's leadership. In some cases, e.g. the ALP left and the Liberal dries, the faction had no plausible candidate of its own, but wooing its members was sometimes important in establishing majority support.
12  Calwell. In 1961, Whitlam campaigned mainly in Queensland where the ALP secured its greatest swing, winning eight seats. There is still scope for divergent perceptions about individuals' influences. Compare D'Alpuget's evaluation of Hawke's role in the 1974 election (pp. 322–5) with MacCallum (p. 70) and Oakes and Solomon (1974).
13  Leaders of the Opposition commonly have relatively low approval ratings before being elected—perhaps partly because a central part of their public role consists of criticising and complaining. Many electorally successful leaders—Whitlam, Wran, Fraser, Thatcher—had relatively low ratings when first elected.
14  For example, former press secretary for Wilkes, Noel Turnbull, criticised the Victorian media and in particular their agenda-setter, *The Age*, for giving only grudging coverage to Wilkes (*The National Times* 11–10–1981).
15  For an account of Lewis's political relations, see O'Reilly Chapter 6.
16  Kemp 1973b, p. 50.
17  Quoted Kelly 1984, p. 28.
18  D'Alpuget pp. 322–3.
19  *Courier-Mail* 3–7–1974, also 5–6–1974; the following day the paper highlighted its earlier article as a sign of its prescience. More telling, however, is the vacuum in the intervening month.
20  Quoted, Mackerras 1977.
21  Sigal p. 188.

22 Quoted, e.g. Killen p. 171. Peacock deliberately used some of the same phrases when resigning from Fraser's Cabinet.

23 Kelly 1976, p. 57.

24 See e.g. Kelly 1976, p. 109.

25 Kelly 1976, p. 45.

26 Quoted, MacCallum pp. 166–7.

27 D'Alpuget pp. 374–7, Kelly 1984, p. 83.

28 Public statements have a marked effect when they crystallise grapevine rumblings, and bring into open something media know is real, offering a tangible news peg on which to hang a report of the underlying reality.

29 See also Chipp's description of 'the worst kick in the guts I had ever experienced' (Chipp pp. 87–8).

30 Howson 17–12–69, p. 587.

31 Cf Summers 1983, pp. 35–6, Kelly 1984, pp. 343–5 on stories in *The Australian Financial Review* around Christmas 1982 about Button and leadership moves against Hayden. When Hawke had moved in the July 1982 challenge, active use was made of the media to de-stabilise Hayden, but the essence of the summer moves was a successful secrecy, broken only by Greg Hywood's stories at Christmas.

32 My understanding of the internal politics of the major parties in WA during this period was helped considerably by a mimeoed article by Norm Taylor, and by Patrick O'Brien's paper to the 1982 Australasian Political Science Association conference, as well as by interviews.

33 Kelly 1984, p. 117–18.

34 In 1982, 'the fortnightly poll published in *The Bulletin* began to cast a curious spell on the Caucus. Miniscule fluctuations had a ludicrously dramatic impact as Caucus shifted from despondency to delight' (Kelly 1984, p. 187).

35 *Australian Journal of Politics and History* December 1977, pp. 421–2.

36 Accounts of the Pol Pot incident in Kelly, Summers, Schneider and Carey and McRae contain significant discrepancies from each other. Fraser's determination that Simon be dismissed perhaps also owed something to news manoeuvres:

> From the start of his employment by Peacock Simon ran a highly political operation. Journalists were briefed and information was fed out about Peacock's view on Cabinet items; activity such as this was anathema to the Fraser Government . . . . Ministers felt Peacock was defying Cabinet solidarity through press briefings given by his office; Lynch and Viner were particularly upset. (Kelly 1984, pp. 132–3.)

37 The incident is related in greatest detail in Carey and McRae pp. 7–41, with other accounts in Summers and Schneider. Kelly 1984, p. 136 details the intense briefings and media appearances Fraser and Peacock mounted after the resignation.

38 Summers 1983, p. 130.

39 Seymour-Ure 1983, p. 8.

40 Kelly 1984, pp. 160, 164.

41 Schneider 1981, p. 135.

42 Quoted, e.g. Killen p. 233. Killen is critical of Peacock's role, as is Chipp. Kelly thought it 'the most perplexing feature' of the episode (1976

p. 119). By 1984 he concluded Peacock's judgment (aiming to stop Fraser) was badly astray (pp. 124–5). Carey and McRae give an account favourable to Peacock (pp. 115–18).

43 Freudenberg p. 313 Dramatic contrary public statements by a prominent ally precipitate a crisis of authority for leaders. See e.g. Seymour-Ure's (1974) account of 'Enoch Powell's Earthquake'.

44 Edwards. Apart from putting the public spotlight on the extent of background briefings being conducted by ministers, Gorton's downfall has special interest for media analysts because of the role widely ascribed to the Packer press in his downfall. See 'Mr Y' in *Australian Quarterly* and Fairfax's reply. Even one of the leading party movers against Gorton was unsure about how extensive Packer's role was:

> It is interesting that back in the diary in December I see a reference to a talk with Alan Reid in which he forecast that there could be a change of Prime Minister in March. One wonders now to what extent people like McMahon and Packer had been planning this move three months ago, waiting only until McEwen had retired from Parliament. I feel that they had been planning, knowing that some crisis would develop, and knowing that there were people in the party room who would be prepared to act along similar lines. It will be interesting if in the history books we can see the full planning that led up to the March crisis. (Howson, 1 April 1971, p. 712)

45 Howard's immediate reception was very positive. Peacock's resignation after failing to force Howard out of the deputy leadership had allowed him to become leader with little 'blood on his hands'. In the ensuing weeks it became clear that he had little prospect of uniting the party.

46 Schattschneider p. 67.

47 'Melbourne provided a prototype for the Hawke strategy [against Hayden]. In an operation of surgical precision the Victorian ALP had removed its leader Frank Wilkes in favour of John Cain quite close to the state election and had then won a smashing victory. The moral drawn was that Canberra should act accordingly. The Victorian experience showed that any time before the election was soon enough' (Kelly 1984, p. 186). The Victorian challenge also stimulated the WA rebels to move, replacing Davies with Burke.

48 See Miller and Koch.

49 Quotes are from Aitkin's editorial overview, Howson p. 809. Many accounts of these events are available, e.g. Oakes and Solomon, Freudenberg, Howson. See Butler p. 61 on Gorton's dismissal. A systematic study of press coverage is in Western and Hughes.

## 8 Issue Agendas

1 Entmann and Paletz p. 132.

2 Cf Golding and Middleton p. 121; see p. 114 on the importance of Government in the amount, timing and direction of social policy news.

3 Horne 1981, p. 69. In support of Horne, note Kelly's conclusion that 'The 1974–83 period, which saw the collapse of Whitlam and the dominance of Fraser, is more likely to be remembered for the destructive energy and Shakespearian drama of its power struggles than for the creative output and policy advances of its Governments. The decade became an orgy of

spectator satisfaction . . . The irony . . . [is] there was such political excess for so little genuine policy gain' (1984, p. 424). This may well be true, but Kelly gives insufficient attention to policy concerns for it to be evident from his book.

4   The same point can be made about pressure groups, whose primary purpose often involves the winning of material benefits from government, the likelihood of which is often in inverse proportion to their amount of public noise. Cf Schattschneider's shrewd comments on the 'socialisation or privatisation' of conflicts (pp. 2–7).

5   Kelly 1984, pp. 162–3.

6   See also White p. 14 on Reagan and the Panama Canal controversy before and after being elected and Dale p. 22: 'Like all politicians in Opposition, Wran knew he could get media support for freer and more open libel laws'. But he never moved for them in Government.

7   Kelly 1984, p. 260.

8   The deficit announcement was carried in most papers, 6–7–1987.

9   Seymour-Ure 1974, p. 223.

10  Cf Molotch and Lester p. 258.

11  S. Cohen used the term 'sensitisation' in his study of news coverage of Mods and Rockers, while Fishman (1978) argued cogently for the importance of themes in news judgments. See Tuchman p. 152 on editors' changing responsiveness to feminist themes. See also Golding and Middleton p. 114 on the importance of the larger political agenda in shaping judgments: 'Alongside [the immediate peaks and troughs of activity], however, is a longer wave cycle in which journalists generally sense that certain issues are in the foreground'.

12  Vinson. Epstein (1975) cited a similar example from the US, news coverage of early morning traffic accidents after the introduction of daylight saving in the early 1970s, suggesting a link, but failing to note that there had been no change in the rate of such accidents (Chapter 1).

13  See e.g. Lunn.

14  Schattschneider p. 72.

15  Most academic analysis concentrates on news coverage of a single issue. Their standard form is to criticise the news as biased or inadequate. They vary greatly in quality and value, but have in common that there is little or no comparison with coverage of other issues, and so the factors influencing the chosen issue's coverage are not specified. On the other hand, public policy scholars have generally not allowed their orderly analyses to be disturbed by the unruly and erratic entry of news.

16  Edelman 1964, p. 12; Cf also pp. 5, 149.

17  Neglect of deprived groups is one of the best documented tendencies in news coverage: e.g. in the US, 'during the long period from 1892 to the Supreme Court's school desegregation case of 1954 . . . less than 1% of the total news space was normally devoted to blacks' (Walker p. 10; Cf also Roshco p. 99).

18  See e.g. Tuchman p. 137. The point about relative deprivation could perhaps be extended to what Hirsch calls 'positional goods', access to which is dependent on distribution, e.g. harbour views, and which cannot be ameliorated through general economic growth.

19  Tuchman p. 139, 148.
20  *The Age* 17–11–1983.
21  Such developments roughly correspond to what Lowi calls distributive issues and Wilson calls interest group politics.
22  Wildavsky has plausibly suggested that policy decisions are more effective when changing the allocation of resources than when seeking to change the behaviour of large groups of people (p. 23).
23  G.H. Mead, quoted Vinson p. 149.
24  See e.g. Walker.
25  Ralph Nader, quoted Spigelman.
26  Pullan pp. 12, 62.
27  The most successful example of sustained investigations initiated by a news organisation changing public priorities toward an issue was *The Age*'s work on 'The Minus Children', describing the conditions in the children's cottages at Kew, Melbourne. Over several years, *The Age* did hundreds of articles and Victorian Government decisions and public appeals resulted in a great increase in the resources devoted to the children's care.
28  Sigal p. 185.
29  Quoted, Seymour-Ure 1974, p. 36.
30  Lunn 1980.
31  Golding and Middleton pp. 98–9.
32  Golding and Middleton p. 10, also pp. 68, 116–17, 122–8.
33  Walker p. 10.
34  Quoted, Sandercock p. 219. Cf also Edelman 1964 pp. 25, 39.
35  The terms are Wilson's.
36  The consequences for news reporting have been discussed by Knightley and Tiffen (1983).
37  Summers 1983, p. 160.
38  Clear decisions can be targetted more easily. Consider how the 1973 tariff cut became a scapegoat during the Whitlam Government's later economic troubles (e.g. Freudenberg p. 283).
39  In some conflicts managing appearances to accommodate the concerns and pride of the different parties is the most important part of the resolution. See e.g. Sigal p. 169 on the Skybolt affair. For a good example of re-casting a conflict see French Prime Minister Debre's handling of state subsidies and regulation of church schools through his aptly named 'de-politisation' policy (See Smith p. 170).
40  Freudenberg p. 281.
41  Kelly 1984, p. 445.
42  Kelly 1976, p. 59. Whitlam has outlined several reasons why reform governments face publicity difficulties (Oakes 1976, p. 24). Beyond these, complaints about lack of consultation created many internal conflicts during his government (see e.g. Dunstan p. 225, D'Alpuget and Walter). Internal conflicts and inconsistencies also provide a partial answer to Horne's complaint about news treatment of the Whitlam Goverment:

>    The Whitlam government will be treated by historians as one of the great

governments in Australian history. Yet, from day to day the media increasingly presented it as a government of crooks and clowns . . . . Why didn't [their] achievements come through more strongly in the media? (Horne 1976, pp. 68–9).

For reasons of both audience interest and organisational convenience and safety, the Western news media have traditionally focused more on means than ends in politics, on procedure more than policy substance, which is reported chiefly as it impinges on procedures by generating conflict. See e.g. Gerbner 1961.

43   See also Kern *et al.* on Kennedy's handling of the 'crisis' following the building of the Berlin Wall, where there was a strong demand for action, but no feasible response short of risking all-out war.

44   Compare how Carter suffered from his elevation of energy issues (apart from war, 'the greatest challenge our country will face'), from his inability to impose his energy package to the Great Gas Panic of 1979 (White pp. 261–4) while under Reagan energy issues almost disappeared from the political agenda.

45   Vinson pp. 127–8.

46   Freudenberg p. 189.

47   Freudenberg p. 197. Instead:

> The Mataungan meeting was to have a curious aftermath. By a strange twist it was to play a part in Gorton's fall. His ill-advised and opportunistic reaction against Whitlam led to a series of misjudgements culminating in his authorization for the use of the Army to control disturbances on the Gazelle. This was one of the grievances which Fraser harboured until he was ready to strike in March 1971. (Freudenberg p. 197)

48   On the importance of symbolic politics, see Edelman, and on the closely related nature of status politics, see Gusfield.

49   Lippman 1961 originally 1914.

50   Cf Roshco p. 63.

51   The build-up of political momentum on an issue should not be equated with editorial sympathy: public exposure, even through critical coverage, may fan a movement's growth. News coverage of terrorism and riots is hardly positive, yet some critics claim that it fans their growth and adds to their impact. While critical editorial attitudes or unsympathetic news coverage are important, the ventilation of an issue or a movement will alert other potential activists and push the group's issues to the fore.

52   Carey and McRae p. 94.

53   Souter p. 643.

54   *The Sydney Morning Herald, The Guide*, 27–2–1983.

55   *Public Opinion*, cited Roshco p. 121.

56   On the other hand, there is often a marked lack of correlation between when the peak of news attention to an issue occurs and the optimum time for social choices. East Timor only became a subject of intense controversy in Australia after its fate had been sealed. There is a recurring scenario with environmentally sensitive development projects, where the critical reaction takes time to become organised and gain support, while governments and corporations claim that the controversy has developed

too late to reverse the due processes and decisions already made. Perhaps the most perverse example was the Hawke Government's attempts to introduce an ID card. This was the excuse for the 1987 double dissolution election, but then neither side mentioned the issue much during the campaign. After the election, supposedly called to decide its fate, the controversy developed a sudden new intensity. Finally the issue was disposed of when the Opposition discovered its administrative implementation required Senate approval, which it was in a position to block. Hardly an edifying example of democratic decision-making.

57   Roshco's phrase. Cf also Smith, A. 1978, pp. 96–7.
58   Horne 1980, p. 77.
59   Souter p. 471. Although policy directions change, it seems fairly rare for issue concerns to disappear. Downs has outlined an issue attention cycle, including gradual decline of public interest and post-problem stage. Environmental issues were his only candidate to decline.
60   Smith, A 1978, p. 85.
61   Kern *et al.* p. 195.

# Interviewees

Matt Abraham, Ben Ainsworth, Peter Allen, Chris Anderson, John Arthur, Tony Baker, Simon Balderstone, Geoff Barker, Ted Barker, David Barnett, Peter Barnett, Ron Barry, Russell Barton, Bob Baudino, Brett Bayly, Ken Begg, Rob Bennetts, Warwick Beutler, Geoff Bird, Verge Blunden, Lorenzo Boccabello, Ron Boland, Bob Bottom, Peter Bowers, Colin Brammall, Sir Theodore Bray, David Broadbent, Terry Brown, Wally Brown, Joe Buchanan, Creighton Burns, Allen Callaghan, Richard Carleton, Shaun Carney, Bob Carr, Barrie Cassidy, Peter Cavanagh, Peter Cave, Rob Chalmers, Frank Chamberlain, Colin Chapman, Peter Charlton, Philip Chubb, Andrew Clark, Milton Cockburn, Stewart Cockburn, Tom Connors, Peter Costigan, Warwick Costin, Brian Coulter, E.H. (Harold) Cox, Frank Cranston, Brian Dale, Gay Davidson, Ken Davidson, John Davies, Ian Davis, Adrian Deamer, Quentin Dempster, Graeme Dobell, Rod Donnelly, Bob Duffield, Warren Duncan, John Dux, Paul Ellercamp, David English, John Feary, Paul Fenn, Tom Fitzgerald, Cameron Forbes, Ron Ford, Bryan Frith, Steve Gibbes, Michael Gill, Trevor Gilmour, Ross Gittins, Bill Goff, Harry Gordon, Robert Gottliebsen, Greg Grainger, Michelle Grattan, Michael Grealy, Fraser Guild, Peter Hanrahan, John Hartigan, Greg Hartung, Peter Harvey, Peter Hastings, Max Hawkins, Trevor Hawkins, Geoff Heriot, Bruce Hewitt, Jenni Hewitt, John Higgins, Brian Hill, Ben Hills, Pat Hinton, Les Hoffman, Derry Hogue, Simon Holberton, Michael Holmes, John Hurst, Greg Hywood, Frank Jackson, Bruce Jones, David Jones, Rex Jory, Wio Joustra, Bruce Juddery, Paul Kelly, Alex Kennedy, Geoff Kitney, Phillip Knightley, Michael Lawson, Clem Lloyd, John Lombard, David Love, Hugh Lunn, Jack Lunn, Mungo MacCallum. Paddy McGuiness, John McIlwraith, Paul McKeough, Toni McRae, Des McWilliam, Jerry Maher, Peter Maher, Ian Matthews, Robert Milliken, John Mills, Stephen Mills, Paul Molloy, Peter Morley, Paul Mullins, Brian Mulvey, Les Murphy, Ed Nash, Simon Nasht, Grant Nihill, Gerard Noonan, Laurie Oakes, Helen O'Flynn, John O'Hara, John O'Loan, Gary O'Neil, Patrick O'Neil, David O'Reilly, Neil O'Reilly, Dan O'Sullivan, Geoff Paddick, Colin Paterson, Neville Petersen, Mark

Plunkett, Bill Pinwill, Yvonne Preston, Ken Randall, Mike Rann, Peter Rapp, Peter Rees, Alan Reid, Don Riddell, Denis Ringrose, Martin Riordan Brian Robins, Peter Robinson, Grant Rowlands, John Rudd, Bill Rust, Russell Schneider, John Schofield, Gary Scully, Colin Segelow, Stuart Simson, Don Smith, George Smith, Vincent Smith, Deborah Snow, David Solomon, Geoff Sorby, John Sorell, Gavin Souter, Terry Spence, Doug Steele, Mike Steketee, Peter Stephens, Max Suich, Anne Summers, Trevor Sykes, Jack Taylor, Mike Taylor, Norm Taylor, Tony Grant Taylor, Peter Terry, Alan Thornhill, Brian Toohey, Murray Trembath, Noel Turnbull, John Wallace, Eric Walsh, Max Walsh, Peter Ward, Denis Warner, Tony Warton, Richard Watson, Dan Webb, Tony Wells, Mark Westfield, John Wheeldon, Barry Wheeler, Osmar White, Evan Whitton, Bob Willoughby, Brian Wills-Johnstone, David Wilson, Nigel Wilson, Renton Winders, Rod Wise, Ian Wisken, David Withington, Peter Wombwell, Ralph Wragg, Peter Wylie, Peter Young.

# References

Aitkin, D. (1983) 'The Changing Australian Electorate' in Penniman, Howard (ed.) *Australia at the Polls: the National Elections of 1980 and 1983* (Sydney, George Allen and Unwin)

Altheide, David L. (1976) *Creating Reality: How TV News Distorts Events* (Beverly Hills, Sage Publications)

Anderson, Patrick (1968) *The President's Men* (New York, Doubleday)

Badcock, B. (1982) 'Was the South Australian Labor Party Struck Down by a Bus?' *Politics* 17, 1.

Baker, Ian (1980) 'The Gatekeeper Chain: a two-step analysis of how journalists acquire and apply organizational news priorities' in Edgar, Patricia (ed.) *The News in Focus* (Melbourne, Macmillan)

Barnouw, E. (1975) *Tube of Plenty* (New York, Oxford University Press)

Barr, T. (1977) *Reflections of Reality: the Media in Australia* (Adelaide, Rigby)

Bayley, Edwin R. (1981) *Joe McCarthy and the Press* (Madison, University of Wisconsin Press)

Beed, Terence W. (1975) 'Opinion Polling and the Elections' in Penniman, Howard (ed.) *Australia at the Polls: the National Elections of 1975* (Washington DC, American Enterprise Institute for Public Policy Research)

Bell, Philip, Boehringer, Kathe and Crofts, Stephen (1982) *Programmed Politics: a Study of Australian Television* (Sydney, Sable)

Blood, Warwick (1982) 'Agenda setting: a review of the theory' *Media Information Australia* 26, pp. 3–12.

Blumler, Jay G (1969) 'Producers' Attitudes towards Television Coverage of an Election Campaign: A Case Study' in Halmos, Paul (ed) *The Sociology of Mass Media Communicators* (The Sociological Review Monograph No 13, University of Keele, 1969)

Boorstin, Daniel (1963) *The Image: a Guide to Pseudo-Events in America* (London, Penguin)

Bowman, David (1984) 'The Secret Leakers' *Australian Society* May 1.

—— (1988) *The Captive Press* (Ringwood, Vic, Penguin)

Boyd-Barrett, Oliver (1980) *The International News Agencies* (London, Constable)

Brown, Allan (1986) *Commercial Media in Australia* (St Lucia, University of Queensland Press)

Butler, D. (1973) *The Canberra Model: Essays on Australian Government* (London, Macmillan)

Calwell, A. A. (1972) *Be Just and Fear Not* (Hawthorn, Vic., Lloyd O'Neil)

Carey, Jim and McCrae, Toni (1982) *Peacock MP* (Adelaide, Rigby)

Cater, Douglass (1959) *The Fourth Branch of Government* (Boston, Houghton Mifflin Co.)

Chipp, Don and Larkin, John (1978) *Don Chipp: the Third Man* (Adelaide, Rigby)

Cockerell, Michael, Hennessy, Peter and Walker, David (1984) *Sources Close to the Prime Minister: Inside the Hidden World of the News Manipulators* (London, Macmillan)

Cohen, Bernard (1963) *The Press and Foreign Policy* (Princeton, NJ, Princeton University Press)

Cohen, S. (1972) *Folk Devils and Moral Panics* (London, MacGibbon and Kee)

*Columbia Journalism Review* (1979) 'It's in the *Journal*. But this is news?'

Crouse, Timothy (1973) *The Boys on the Bus* (New York, Random House)

Curran, James *et al.* (eds) (1977) *Mass Communication and Society* (London, Edward Arnold and the Open University)

D'Alpuget, Blanche (1982) *Robert J. Hawke: a Biography* (East Melbourne, Schwartz)

Dale, Brian (1985) *Ascent to Power: Wran and the Media* (Sydney, Allen and Unwin)

Daly, Fred (1977) *From Curtin to Kerr* (Melbourne, Sun Books)

Downie, Leonard, Jr (1976) *The New Muckrakers* (Washington, DC, New Republic Book Co)

Downs, Anthony (1972) 'Up and Down with ecology—the 'Issue-Attention Cycle' *The Public Interest* No 28, p. 38–50.

Dunstan, Don (1981) *Felicia: The Political Memoirs of Don Dunstan* (Melbourne, Macmillan)

Edelman, Murray (1964) *The Symbolic Uses of Politics* (Urbana, University of Chicago Press)

—— (1971) *Politics as Symbolic Action* (Chicago, Markham Publishing)

Edgar, Patricia (1979) *The Politics of the Press* (South Melbourne, Sun Books)

Edwards, John (1977) *Life Wasn't Meant To Be Easy: a Political Profile of Malcolm Fraser* (Sydney, Mayhem)

—— (1981) 'Political Reporters: An Isolated Community' in Windschuttle, Keith and Elizabeth (eds) *Fixing the News: Critical Perspectives on the Australian Media* (Ringwood, Penguin Australia)

Epstein, Edward Jay (1973) *News from Nowhere* (New York, Random House)

—— (1975) *Between Fact and Fiction: the Problem of Journalism* (New York, Random House)

Evans, Harold (1983) *Good Times, Bad Times* (London, Weidenfeld and Nicholson)

Fairfax, Warwick (1971) 'Letter to the Editor' *The Australian Quarterly* 43, 3, September.

Fishman, Mark (1978) 'Crime Waves as Ideology' *Social Problems*, 25, pp. 531–43.

—— (1980) *Manufacturing the News* (Austin, University of Texas Press)

Freudenberg, G. (1977) *A Certain Grandeur: Gough Whitlam in Politics* (South Melbourne, Sun Books)

Gans, Herbert (1979) *Deciding What's News* (New York, Pantheon Books)

Geertz, Clifford (1964) 'Ideology as a Cultural System' in Apter, David (ed.) *Ideology and Discontent* (London, Free Press of Glencoe)

George, Margaret (1980) *Australia and the Indonesian Revolution* (Melbourne, Melbourne University Press)

Glasgow Media Group (1976) *Bad News* (London, Routledge and Kegan Paul)

Glezer, Leon (1982) *Tariff Politics: Australian Policy-making 1960–1980* (Melbourne, Melbourne University Press)

Goldenberg, Edie (1975) *Making the Papers* (London, Lexington Books)

Golding, Peter and Elliott, Philip (1979) *Making the News* (London, Longman)

Golding, Peter and Middleton, Sue (1982) *Images of Welfare: Press and Public Attitudes to Poverty* (Oxford, Martin Robertson)

Goodin, Robert E. (1980) *Manipulatory Politics* (New Haven, Yale University Press)

Goot, M. (1983) 'The Media and the Campaign' in Penniman, Howard (ed.) *Australia at the Polls: the National Elections of 1980 and 1983* (Sydney, George Allen and Unwin)

Greenfield, Jeff (1980) 'A Charm Book for Candidates' *Columbia Journalism Review*, July.

Gusfield, Josem (1963) *Symbolic Crusade: Status Politics and the American Temperance Movement* (Urbana, University of Illinois Press)

—— (1976) 'The Literary Rhetoric of Science: Comedy and Pathos in Drinking Driver Research' *American Sociological Review* 41, pp. 16–34.

Halberstam, David (1974) 'Press and Prejudice: How Our Last Three Presidents Got the Newsmen They Deserved.' *Esquire* April.

—— (1979) *The Powers That Be* (New York, Dell Publishing)

Halperin, Morton (1974) *Bureaucratic Politics and Foreign Policy* (Washington, DC, Brookings Institution)

Harrison, Martin (1982) 'Television news coverage of the 1979 General Election' in Robert M. Worcester and Martin Harrop (eds) *Political Communications: The General Election Campaign of 1979* (London, George Allen and Unwin)

Haupt, Robert with Grattan, Michelle (1983) *31 Days to Power: Hawke's Victory* (Sydney, George Allen and Unwin)

Hawker, Geoffrey, Smith, R.F.I. and Weller, Patrick (1979) *Politics and Policy in Australia* (St Lucia, University of Queensland Press)

Henderson, Gerard (1987) 'The Rat Pack' *IPA Review* 41, 2, pp. 6–13.

Henningham, J. P. (1980) 'Anti-Government Stories in Two Australian Newspapers, 1972–1978' *Politics* 15, pp. 89–94.

—— (1988) *Looking at Television News* (Melbourne, Longman Cheshire)

Hersch, Seymour (1983) *The Price of Power: Kissinger in the Nixon White House* (New York, Summit Books)

Hickie, David (1985) *The Prince and the Premier* (Sydney, Angus and Robertson)

Hirsch, Fred (1977) *Social Limits to Growth* (London, Routledge and Kegan Paul)

Horne, Donald (1976) *Death of the Lucky Country* (Ringwood, Vic., Penguin)
—— (1980) *Time of Hope: Australia 1966–72* (Sydney, Angus and Robertson)
—— (1981) *Winner Take All?* (Ringwood, Vic., Penguin)

Howson, Peter (1984) *The Howson Diaries: The Life of Politics*, edited by Don Aitkin (Ringwood, Vic, The Viking Press)

Inglis, Ken (1982) *This is the ABC* (Melbourne, Melbourne University Press)

Jaensch, Dean and Bullock, Joan (1978) *Liberals in Limbo: Non-Labor Politics in South Australia 1970–1978* (Melbourne, Drummond)

Janis, Irving L. and Mann, Leon (1977) *Decision Making: a Psychological Analysis of Conflict, Choice, and Commitment* (New York, Glencoe Free Press)

Kelly, Paul (1976) *The Unmaking of Gough* (Sydney, Angus and Robertson)
—— (1984) *The Hawke Ascendancy: a Definitive Account of Its Origins and Climax 1975–1983* (Sydney, Angus and Robertson)

Kemp, David (1973a) 'Swingers and Stayers: the Australian Swinging Voter, 1961–72' in Mayer, Henry (ed.) *Labor to Power: Australia's 1972 Election* (Sydney, Angus and Robertson)
—— (1973b) 'A Leader and a Philosophy' in Mayer, Henry (ed.) *Labor to Power: Australia's 1972 Election* (Sydney, Angus and Robertson)

Kern, Montague, Levering, Patricia W. and Levering, Ralph B. (1983) *The Kennedy Crises: the Press, the Presidency, and Foreign Policy* (Chapel Hill, The University of North Carolina Press)

Kiernan, Colm (1978) *Calwell: a Personal and Political Biography* (Melbourne, Nelson)

Killen, Sir James (1985) *Killen: Inside Australian Politics* (Sydney, Methuen)

Knightley, Phillip (1978) *The First Casualty. From the Crimea to Vietnam: The War Correspondent as Hero, Propagandist, and Myth Maker* (London, Quartet Books)

Kuhn, T. S. (1970) *The Structure of Scientific Revolutions* (Chicago, University of Chicago Press)

Leapman, Michael (1983) *Barefaced Cheek: the Apotheosis of Rupert Murdoch* (London, Hodder and Stoughton)

Levy, Mark R. (1981) 'Disdaining the News' *Journal of Communication*, 31, 3, pp. 24–31.

Lippman, Walter (1961a) *Drift and Mastery: an Attempt to Diagnose the Current Unrest* (Englewood Cliffs, NJ, Prentice Hall)(Originally published 1914)
—— (1961b) *Public Opinion* (London, Allen and Unwin, originally published 1920)

Lloyd, C. J. (1979a) 'The Development and Organization of the Federal Parliamentary Press Gallery, 1901–1978' (MA thesis, Department of Political Science, Australian National University)
—— (1979b) 'A Lean Campaign for the Media' in Penniman, Howard (ed.) *The Australian National Elections of 1977* (Washington DC, American Enterprise Institute and Australian National University Press)
—— (1988) *Parliament and the Press: the Federal Parliamentary Press Gallery 1901–88* (Melbourne, Melbourne University Press)

Lombard, John (1980) 'Federal Parliament/Press Gallery Relations' in Turbayne, David (ed.) *The Media and Politics in Australia* (Public Policy Monograph, Department of Political Science, University of Tasmania)

Lowe, Doug (1984) *The Price of Power: the Politics Behind the Tasmanian Dams Case* (South Melbourne, Macmillan)

Lowi, Theodore J. (1964) 'American Business, Public Policy, Case Studies and Political Theory' *World Politics* 16 pp. 677–715.

Lukes, Steven (1974) *Power: a Radical View* (London, Macmillan)

Lunn, Hugh (1978) *Joh* (South Melbourne, Sun Books)

—— (1980) *Behind the Banana Curtain* (St Lucia, University of Queensland Press)

MacCallum, Mungo (1979) *Mungo on the Zoo Plane* (St Lucia, University of Queensland Press)

McCombs, Maxwell E. (1981) 'The Agenda-Setting Approach' in Nimmo, Dan D. and Sanders, Keith R. (eds) *Handbook of Political Communication* (Beverly Hills, Sage)

McCombs, Maxwell E. and Shaw, D. L. (1972) 'The Agenda-Setting Function of the Mass Media' *Public Opinion Quarterly*, 36, Summer, pp. 176–87.

McGinness, Joe (1970) *The Selling of the President, 1968* (Middlesex, Penguin)

Mackerras, Malcolm (1977) 'New South Wales 1976' *Politics XII, 1, May, pp.* 158–62.

McNicoll, David (1979) *Luck's A Fortune* (Melbourne, Sun Books)

McQuail, Denis (1977) *Analysis of Newspaper Content* Royal Commission on the Press, Research Series 4, HMSO, London.

—— (1987) *Mass Communication Theory: an Introduction* (Second edition) (London, Sage Publications)

—— (1977) 'The Influence and Effects of the Mass Media' in Curran, James *et al.* (eds) *Mass Communication and Society* (London, Edward Arnold)

Manheim, Jarol and Albritton, Robert (1984) 'Changing National Images: International Public Relations and Media Agenda Setting' *American Political Science Review* 78, 3, September.

Margach, James (1979) *The Abuse of Power: the War Between Downing Street and the Media from Lloyd George to James Callaghan* (London, W.H. Allen and Co)

Marr, David (1984) *The Ivanov Trail* (Melbourne, Thomas Nelson)

Martin, Roderick (1977) *The Sociology of Power* (London, Routledge and Kegan Paul)

Masterton, Murray (1983) *But You'll Never Be Bored: the five Ws of Australia's Journalists* (Adelaide, South Australian College of Advanced Education)

Mayer, H. (1964) *The Press in Australia* (Melbourne, Lansdowne Press)

—— (1973) 'Two Editorials and a Modest Gift: Sir Frank Packer and the Election' in Mayer, H. (ed.) *Labor to Power: Australia's 1972 Election* (Sydney, Angus and Robertson)

—— (1975) 'The Press and Public Service' *Newsletter of the RAIPA ACT Group* 11, 4.

Mayer, H., Garde, P. and Gibbens, S. (1983) *The Media: Questions and Answers* (Sydney, George Allen and Unwin)

Millar, T. B. (ed.) (1972) *Australian Foreign Minister: the Diaries of R.G. Casey 1951–1960* (London, Collins)

Miller, Ian and Koch, Tony (1983) *Joh's KO* (Brisbane, Boolarong)

Mills, C., Wright (1956) *The Power Elite* (New York, Oxford University Press)

Mills, Stephen (1986) *The New Machine Men: Polls and Persuasion in Australian Politics* (Ringwood, Vic., Penguin)

Molotch, Harvey and Lester, Marilyn (1974) 'News as Purposive Behavior: on the Strategic Use of Routine Events, Accidents and Scandals' *American Sociological Review* 39, pp. 101–12.

Morgan, Patrick (1974) 'Having It Both Ways: Opinion Formers and the Federal Elections' *Quadrant* August.

O'Grady, Michael (1979) 'The Party Leaders: Hamer and Wilkes' in Hay, Peter, Ward, Ian and Warhurst, John *Anatomy of an Election* (Melbourne, Hill of Content)

O'Hara, John (1968) 'The Challenge—Day by Day' *Fourth Journalism Summer School*, February.

O'Reilly, David The Work of the Press Gallery Journalist and the Ministerial Press Secretary in New South Wales: 1965–83 (MA thesis, Department of Government, University of Sydney, 1983)

Oakes, Laurie and Solomon, David (1973) *The Making of an Australian Prime Minister* (Melbourne, Cheshire)

—— and —— (1974) *Grab for Power: Election 74* (Melbourne, Cheshire)

Ormonde, Paul (1981) *A Foolish, Passionate Man: a Biography of Jim Cairns* (Ringwood, Vic., Penguin)

Packer, Clyde (1984) *No Return Ticket* (Sydney, Angus and Robertson)

Paletz, David L. and Entman, Robert M. (1981) *Media Power Politics* (New York, The Free Press)

Pullan, Robert (1984) *Guilty Secrets: Free Speech in Australia* (Sydney, Methuen)

Rawson, Don (1961) *Australia Votes: The 1958 Federal Election* (Melbourne, Melbourne University Press)

Reid, Alan (1971) *The Gorton Experiment* (Sydney, Shakespeare Head Press)

Roshco, Bernard (1975) *Newsmaking* (Chicago, University of Chicago Press)

Rosnow, Ralph L. (1988) 'Rumor as Communication: A Contextualist Approach' *Journal of Communication* 38, 1, pp. 12–28.

Rothmyer, Karen (1981) 'Citizen Scaife' *Columbia Journalism Review* July/August pp. 41–50.

Rowlings, Bill (1988) 'Time Out: Clocking the Media on Timed Local Telephone Calls' *Media Information Australia* 49, August, pp. 7–12.

Sampson, Anthony (1982) *The Changing Anatomy of Britain* (London, Hodder and Stoughton)

Sandercock, Leonie (1977) *Cities for Sale: Property, Politics and Urban Planning in Australia* (Melbourne, Melbourne University Press)

Scanlon, Paul (1977) (ed.) *Reporting: the Rolling Stone Style* (New York, Anchor Press)

Schattschneider, E. E. (1960) *The Semi-Sovereign People* (New York, Holt, Rinehart and Winston)

Schlesinger, Philip (1978) *Putting 'Reality' Together: BBC News* (London, Constable)

Schneider, Russell (1981) *The Colt from Kooyong. Andrew Peacock: A Political Biography* (Sydney, Angus and Robertson)

Schudson, Michael (1978) *Discovering the News: A Social History of American Newspapers* (New York, Basic Books)

Sekuless, Peter (1984) *The Lobbyists* (Sydney, George Allen and Unwin)

Seymour-Ure, Colin (1968) *The Press, Politics and the Public* (London, Methuen)

—— (1974) *The Political Impact of Mass Media* (London, Constable)

—— (1977) 'Parliament and Government' Report to the McGregor Royal Commission on the Press (London, HMSO)

—— (1980) 'Presidential Power, Press Secretaries and Communication' *Political Studies* XXVIII, 2, pp. 253–270.

—— (1982) 'Rumour and Politics' *Politics* 17, 2, pp. 1–9.

Shibutani, Tamotsu (1966) *Improvised News: a Sociological Study of Rumour* (Indianapolis: Bobbs Merrill)

Sigal, L. (1973) *Reporters and Officials: the Organization and Politics of News-making* (Lexington, Mass., Heath)

Smith, Anthony (1978) *The Politics of Information: Problems of Policy in Modern Media* (London, Macmillan)

—— (1980) *The Geo-Politics of Information: How Western Culture Dominates the World* (London, Faber and Faber)

Smith, T. Alexander (1975) *The Comparative Policy Process* (Santa Barbara, Clio Books)

Souter, Gavin (1981) *Company of Heralds* (Melbourne, Melbourne University Press)

Spigelman, J. (1972) *Secrecy: Political Censorship in Australia* (Sydney, Angus and Robertson)

St John, Edward (1969) *A Time to Speak* (Melbourne, Sun Books)

Steketee, Mike and Cockburn, Milton (1986) *Wran: an Unauthorised Biography* (Sydney, Allen and Unwin)

Stephens, Mitchell (1982) 'Clout: Murdoch's Political *Post*' *Columbia Journalism Review*, July–August.

Stokes, Donald (1966) 'Spatial Models of Party Competition' in Campbell, A et al., *Elections and the Political Order* (New York, John Wiley)

Summers, Anne (1981) 'The Role and Ethics of Leaks' *Australian Quarterly*, 53, 2, Winter.

—— (1983) *Gamble for Power. How Bob Hawke Beat Malcolm Fraser: the 1983 Federal Election* (Melbourne, Nelson)

Tiffen, Rodney (1978) *The News from Southeast Asia: the Sociology of News-making* (Singapore, Institute of Southeast Asian Studies)

—— (1983a) 'News Coverage of Vietnam' in King, Peter (ed.) *Australia's Vietnam* (Sydney, Allen and Unwin)

—— (1983b) 'Media-centric Electioneering' in Smith, Ted J III, Osborne, Graeme and Penman, Robyn (eds) *Communication and Government: Issues, Policies and Trends* (Canberra, Canberra CAE)

—— (1985) 'The Dynamics of Dominance: Wran and the Media, 1981' in Chaples, Ernie, Nelson, Helen and Turner, Ken *The Wran Model: Electoral Politics in New South Wales 1981 and 1984* (Melbourne, Oxford University Press)

—— (1987) 'Quality and Bias in the Australian Press: News Limited, Fairfax and the Herald and Weekly Times' *The Australian Quarterly* 59, 3 and 4.

—— (1988) 'The Revolution in Australian Media Ownership 1986–87'

*Working Papers in Australian Studies* No 36, Sir Robert Menzies Centre for Australian Studies, University of London.

—— (1989) 'Confidential Sources in the News—Conventions and Contortions' *Australian Journalism Review* 10, 1.

Tuchman, Gaye (1972) 'Objectivity as Strategic Ritual: an Examination of Newsmen's Notions of Objectivity' *American Journal of Sociology* 77, January pp. 660–79.

—— (1978) *Making News: a Study in the Construction of Reality* (New York, Free Press)

Tunstall, Jeremy (1971) *Journalists at Work* (London, Constable)

—— (1976) 'The Communicators—a Study in Contrast' *Journalism Studies Review* 1, 1, June, (University College, Cardiff)

—— (1977) 'Letters to the Editor' Report to the McGregor Royal Commission on the Press (London, HMSO)

Vinson, Tony (1982) *Wilful Obstruction: the Frustration of Prison Reform* (Sydney, Methuen)

Walker, Martin (1982) *Powers of the Press: the World's Great Newspapers* (London, Quartet Books)

Walsh, Max (1970) 'The Social Responsibility of the Press' *Sixth Summer School of Journalism*, pp. 42–52.

—— (1976) 'Bias in News Reporting' in Major, G. (ed.) *Mass Media in Australia* (Sydney, Hodder and Stoughton)

Walsh, Max (1979) *Poor Little Rich Country* (Ringwood, Vic., Penguin)

Walter, James (1980) *The Leader: a Political Biography of Gough Whitlam* (St Lucia, University of Queensland Press)

—— (1986) *The Ministers' Minders: Personal Advisers in National Government* (Melbourne, Oxford University Press)

Weller, P. (1983) 'The Anatomy of a Grievous Miscalculation: 3 February 1983' in Penniman, Howard R. (ed.) *Australia at the Polls: the National Elections of 1980 and 1983* (Sydney, George Allen and Unwin)

Weller, Patrick and Grattan, Michelle (1981) *Can Ministers Cope? Australian Federal Ministers at Work* (Richmond, Vic., Hutchinson)

Western, John and Hughes, Colin A. (1983) *The Mass Media in Australia* (2nd edition) (St Lucia, University of Queensland Press)

White, Theodore (1982) *America in Search of Itself: the Making of the President 1956–1980* (New York, Warner Books)

Whitton, Evan (1988) *Can of Worms II. A Citizen's Reference Book to Crime and the Administration of Justice* (Sydney, the Fairfax Library)

Wildavsky, Aaron (1979) *Speaking Truth to Power: the Art and Craft of Policy Analysis* (Boston, Little, Brown and Company)

Wilson, James Q. (1980) (ed.) *The Politics of Regulation* (New York, Basic Books)

Windschuttle, K. (1984) *The Media: a New Analysis of the Press, Television, Radio and Advertising in Australia* (Melbourne, Penguin Books)

Wolfe, Tom and Johnson, E. W. (1975) (eds) *The New Journalism* (London, Picador)

Wrong, Denis H. (1979) *Power: its Forms, Bases and Uses* (Oxford, Basil Blackwell)

'Y, Mr' (1971) 'A Packer Plot?' *The Australian Quarterly* 42, 2, June.

# Appendix

## Australian Media Ownership

Australian media ownership has changed dramatically in recent years. The following tables give a guide to the metropolitan newspapers and television stations and their present and former owners.

**Table 1  Metropolitan and national daily newspapers**

|  |  |  | Owner Nov 1986 | Owner Mar 1989 | Circulation 1987 ('000) |
|---|---|---|---|---|---|
| The Sun News Pictorial | Melb | AM | HWT | Murdoch | 559 |
| The Herald | Melb | PM | HWT | Murdoch | 213 |
| The Age | Melb | AM | Fairfax | Fairfax | 235 |
| Sydney Morning Herald | Syd | AM | Fairfax | Fairfax | 259 |
| Daily Telegraph | Syd | AM | Murdoch | Murdoch | 275 |
| Daily Mirror | Syd | PM | Murdoch | Murdoch | 284 |
| The Sun | Syd | PM | Fairfax | (Ceased)* | 232 |
| The Courier-Mail | Bris | AM | HWT | Murdoch | 214 |
| The Telegraph | Bris | PM | HWT | (Ceased)** | 113 |
| The Daily Sun | Bris | PM | Murdoch | Own management | 126 |
| The Advertiser | Adel | AM | HWT | Murdoch | 216 |
| The News | Adel | PM | Murdoch | Own management | 156 |
| The West Australian | Perth | AM | HWT | Bond | 238 |
| Daily News | Perth | PM | HWT | United Media | 91 |
| The Mercury | Hob | AM | HWT | Murdoch | 54 |
| The Canberra Times | Can | AM | Fairfax | Packer | 43 |
| The Australian | Natl | AM | Murdoch | Murdoch | 139 |
| Aust Financial Review | Natl | AM | Fairfax | Fairfax | 78 |

*Notes*
HWT means Herald and Weekly Times, the company purchased by Murdoch in the summer of 1986–87.
\*    The Fairfax papers *The Sun* and *The Times on Sunday* ceased publication in March 1988.
\*\*  *The Telegraph*, bought by Murdoch from the Herald and Weekly Times, closed in March 1988. The Brisbane morning paper *The Sun*, begun by Murdoch in 1982, sold by him to Northern Star/WCC in early 1987, and later sold to a group based on the paper's management, immediately switched to being an evening paper.

245

Some papers went through more than one ownership change in the period: the *Financial Review* was sold to Holmes à Court but reverted to Fairfax some months later before the final sale was to be consummated, as did *The Times on Sunday*, which was closed soon after. *The West Australian* went first to Holmes à Court, but after his sale of Bell Resources went to the Bond group. *The News*, like *The Sun*, went first from Murdoch to Northern Star, and thence to a local company based on the paper's management.

**Table 2   Metropolitan TV stations**

|  |  | *Owner* | *Intermediate* | *Owner* |
|---|---|---|---|---|
|  |  | *Nov 1986* |  | *Mar 1989* |
| HSV7 | Melb | HWT | Fairfax | Skase |
| GTV9 | Melb | Packer |  | Bond |
| ATV10 | Melb | Murdoch |  | WCC |
| ATN7 | Syd | Fairfax |  | Skase |
| TCN9 | Syd | Packer |  | Bond |
| TEN10 | Syd | Murdoch |  | WCC |
| BTQ7 | Bris | Fairfax |  | Skase |
| QTQ9 | Bris | Bond |  | Bond |
| TVQ0 | Bris | Skase |  | Darling Downs |
| ADS7 | Adel | HWT | Stokes | WCC |
| NWS9 | Adel | Lamb |  | Lamb |
| SAS10 | Adel | HàCourt |  | Skase |
| TVW7 | Perth | HàCourt |  | Skase |
| WCW10 | Perth | Stokes |  | WCC |
| STW9 | Perth | Bond |  | Sunraysia |
| TVT6 | Hobart | ENT |  | ENT |
| CTC7 | Canb | Stokes |  | WCC |

*Note*
After the change from the two station rule to one preventing cross-media ownership in the same market, but up to 60% reach of the total Australian market, three companies Christopher Skase's Quintex, Bond Media, and Frank Lowi's Westfield Capital Corporation (WCC) have become supreme in most capital cities.

# Index